GOING HOME

The return of children separated from their families

Roger Bullock

Michael Little

Spencer Millham

Dartington Social Research Unit

Dartmouth

Published by
Dartmouth Publishing Company Limited,
Gower House, Croft Road, Aldershot,
Hants. GU11 3HR, England

and

Dartmouth Publishing Company,
Old Post Road, Brookfield, Vermont 05036,
USA

A CIP catalogue record for this book is available from the British Library and the US Library of Congress

ISBN 1 85521 329 X

Cover photograph by Barbara Laws
Typeset by Michael Kelly

Printed and Bound in Great Britain by
Athenaeum Press Ltd, Newcastle upon Tyne.

Contents

List of tables

List of figures

Acknowledgements

This study was completed with the help of several local authorities and voluntary organisations and we are extremely grateful to staff who helped us. We are especially indebted to the children and families who participated in the research. They welcomed us into their homes in difficult circumstances and it is only through their perseverance in answering our tedious questions that we were able to learn so much about the return process.

The research was funded by the Department of Health and we would like to thank the former Chief Scientist, Professor Francis O'Grady, the Director of Research and Development, Professor Michael Peckham, the Community Services Division and the Social Services Inspectorate. We are particularly grateful to Rupert Hughes, Herbert Laming, Tom Luce, John Parker, Wendy Rose and Sir William Utting. We have also benefited greatly from the research liaison undertaken by Carolyn Davies.

We also wish to thank colleagues at the University of Bristol who have advised and commented on our work. Particular thanks go to Elaine Farmer, Dave Gordon, Roy Parker, Phyllida Parsloe and Harriet Ward. We have also been much helped by Sally Hinchcliffe, Barbara Kahan and Kathleen Kufeldt who read earlier drafts of this report and by Caroline Hobson, Yitzhak Kashti and Bernard Saxton who contributed to our discussions.

Finally, we would like to thank The Elmgrant Trust for helping fund the dissemination of the research and our colleagues at the Research Unit, particularly Hedy Cleaver, Jean Packman and Lumsden Walker who criticised our work in such a constructive manner, and Brenda Bullock, Pam Freeman, Carol Hammond, Stuart Harragan, Kenneth Hosie, Michael Kelly, Irené Kragt, Kevin Mount and Oliver Noakes who all helped in various ways. We are deeply grateful to them all.

Erratum

In certain Tables symbols have printed as numerals. In each case, a number 4 indicates a positive answer ($\checkmark$) and 8 a negative answer ($\times$). Such mistakes occur on Pages 87, 217, 219, 221, 225 and 226.

On Page 53, a similar error is accurately explained by the key.

1. Introduction

Since the Second World War, one of the most cogent issues to preoccupy those concerned with the care of children has been the effects of separation and the best ways in which to manage involuntary rifts between parents and children. In several previous studies, we and others have charted the effects of separation on children and the difficulties parents and wider family have in maintaining contact, particularly when the absence is long and stressful. Yet, despite this knowledge, there has been relatively little interest in return which, after all, is the corollary of separation. As is so often the case with social systems, it seems that more emphasis has been given to issues surrounding entry rather than exit.

Nonetheless, despite the paucity of research interest in return, getting children back home has long been an integral part of child-care. Fifty years ago, the evacuation of children from cities vulnerable to attack during the Second World War aroused great anxiety among those affected because the maintenance of links between families and absent loved-ones was very difficult. Telephones were few, letters often went astray and reciprocal visits were almost impossible. Separation was also difficult to manage at an administrative level. Many of those who were subsequently to take key roles in the children's departments of local authorities, created in 1948 as a consequence of the Curtis Report (Home Office, 1946), began their child-care careers coping with the tearful, brown-labelled exodus of city children who arrived in the shire counties, Welsh valleys and sleepy West Country. These experts, along with a posse of wireless gurus whose broadcast chats enlivened many a damp evening in the Anderson shelter, all shared the pervading gloom that children evacuated to the countryside would soon lose touch with home and become rootless. Return, of course, would also be difficult. Winnicott, Priestley and the Brains' Trust joined with Lord Haw-Haw in a chorus of doom.

But, like the maelstrom from which the children were rescued, so the consequences of evacuation proved to be different from those first feared. Even coming back was easily achieved by the majority. In fact, little evidence was produced about the difficulties experienced by the waifs torn from city mothers and much of the widespread unease generated by separation sprang from the difficult and well publicised behaviour of a few children entering Winnicott's clinic. Indeed, it was emphasised that some children had the time of their lives and were much better cared for. Neither was there a catalogue of abuse and neglect inflicted by their frequently grudging hosts.

While documentation was sparse, it seems likely in the light of evidence described in the following pages that children were more distressed than was earlier thought. It is possible that the pains of leaving home were reduced because both separation and return for children were group experiences, undertaken with school friends, supervised and organised by teachers who themselves were keenly sharing the pains of upheaval; a point emphasised by other dislocations which have been better documented. The Jewish experience at the 'return' to Israel of children surviving the holocaust suggests that the pains of separation and loss were reduced because it was a group experience and a shared ideology gave it purpose and direction. Yitzhak Kashti, a survivor of the holocaust, described to us how,

> 'Normality was confirmed by the group, particularly for young children, in that they found it difficult to envisage any alternative and were swallowed up by the daily demands of coping. I cannot remember being acutely distressed at being separated, I was just numb and busy keeping afloat.'

These may be among the reasons why the return of evacuated children caused fewer administrative problems than expected and why the apprehension that many children would find themselves abandoned or the victims of dual loyalties did not materialise. Thus, the problems of separation remained seared into the administrative memory, mainly because it was very difficult to organise, while return, which was, after all, going back to normal, caused little lasting concern (Titmuss, 1976). Separation also touched a sad chord in group consciousness, amply orchestrated by Vera Lynn, Gracie Fields and other hardy annuals, while the difficulties of return did not. Coming home was obviously a rapturous experience, the stuff of which made many good 'B' movies. The fact that return contained many private griefs had to wait for returning servicemen, prisoners of war and residual evacuees to highlight the issues (Johnson, 1968).

Interest in the return of children from long separations and the problems faced by families on reunion are of a much more recent genesis. Concern has been awakened by a variety of pressures. First, there has been increasing exploration of the outcomes of care interventions and profound questions have been raised concerning the State's ability to parent. Particularly influential in raising the issue of return has been the stress on the need for hard criteria to evaluate the success or otherwise of various aspects of child welfare. Sadly, numerous studies of children in state care revealed the drift and insecurity many experience while away from home. In addition, there has been a growing awareness that the majority of children and adolescents return home after separation in spite of lengthy absences and cogent reasons for the initial rift. Whether professionals like it or not, good substitute care is difficult to provide and most children's families shoulder the burden of support for their offspring when our interventions falter. Therefore, return should be a crucial issue in child-care.

A second reason for the increased interest in return has been an awareness that not only do children eventually go home but that both children and families find return stressful. For example, Pill (1979) highlights how difficult children coming home from hospital are likely to be.

> Return is likely to be stressful for the whole family not only for the returning child and the degree of upset is not necessarily related to the length of time spent away.

Winnicott (1984) also warned mothers in a broadcast talk in 1945 that returning evacuees would not be easy to manage.

> What I want to say now is that when children come home they are not necessarily going to fall into and fit nicely into the holes that they made when they went away, for the simple reason that the hole has disappeared. Mother and child will have become able to manage without each other and when they meet they will have to start from scratch to get to know each other. This process must take time and time must be allowed. It's no use mother rushing up to the child and throwing her arms around his neck without looking to see whether he is going to be able to respond sincerely.

And, in a subsequent talk he emphasised,

> their return means that your life will be richer, but less your own. There will be few immediate rewards. At times, you will wish all of them back again in billets. Indeed, some children will have been so hurt by evacuation that it is beyond the power of parents to manage them;

not a welcome prospect for mothers also waiting for husbands to return.

The stress that return places on children and families has once more become of interest to social workers because much work demonstrates not only that return is difficult but that the problems generated by reunion can also be sufficient to cause breakdown and re-entry to care. Little's study of *Young Men in Prison* (1990) also highlights that the dilemma of return is not confined to children; a young man comments,

> 'banged up in here is bad enough but going home isn't likely to be a bed of roses either.'

A third explanation for an increased concern about the return of children in care has been the gathering emphasis on the need for family participation in the care process and on the continuity of care essential for satisfactory child development. This means that return as well as separation have to be managed and going home no longer represents the close of the care episode. Indeed, the multi-disciplinary teams now obligatory in the approach to child abuse and delinquency mean that we cannot forget that the difficulties families face are usually complex and of long standing. Problems may be inter-generational and have long careers of their own in which the children's difficulties play but a small part. Thus, return and separation are again being viewed as part of a process in which roles, territory and family relationships are continuously under negotiation.

These theoretical and practical concerns should excite more than academic curiosity. Research findings now consistently stress the complicated careers of children in care and the adverse consequences of many apparently benign interventions. However, in contrast to other groups of separated children, such as those in hospital or boarding schools, the returns of children in care are difficult to predict. Frequently, the child's natural family will have dissolved and reconstituted during the child's absence and, as a consequence, key family members will be scattered across different households, the membership of which is fluid and volatile. In addition to these changes in children's families, geographical movement is common while the child is away. When these probabilities are linked to the changes of placement and care providers experienced by many children while in care and the movement of social workers, the complexity surrounding the child's return home becomes apparent.

Return for many a child in care is more than just fitting back into a niche previously left; it is re-negotiating a set of roles, adapting to new faces, fashioning a social network and mastering unfamiliar school and community territories. All of these occur in a context where family structures and memberships will have changed and where the links between children and families may also have become tenuous. Thus, return home is by no means the end of a child's care episode; indeed, as we shall see, re-admission to substitute care after return is not uncommon.

Nonetheless, for most children, the swift, enduring rehabilitation to their family is an obligation on social services. The successful management of a child's return home and his or her subsequent adjustment to family, neighbourhood and school should, therefore, be among the indicators of a satisfactory social services' intervention and the willingness or ability of the family to change. Unfortunately not only is there a dearth of information both in terms of established concepts and research explanation but there are also few practical guide-lines for social workers faced with the management of a child's reunion with his or her family.

It was against this background that we saw the need to scrutinise the cluster of decisions surrounding a child's return home from care and to suggest ways in which reunion might be effectively managed. Our aim has been to gather insights into the social work process and to develop an understanding of the adaptations of individual family members during the return period. We have sought to develop clear guide-lines which can be used by social workers faced with return decisions and have taken considerable care in defining when a reunion can be said to be successful. How, then, have we approached our scrutiny of return?

Fashioning a research design

Return as a process

Our study *Lost in Care* focused on the child-care process, exploring the decisions made by social workers about children over time. Since the completion of this work, two other child-care studies have confirmed the benefits of this perspective and the importance of return as a research issue. Rowe, Hundleby and Garnett's (1989) study of child-care placement patterns and outcomes, for example, indicates that the large majority of children discharged from care go home. However, as Farmer and Parker (1991) have shown, the outcomes of return are not always satisfactory, either in terms of endurance or of meeting the child's needs.

The social work profession has long been anxious for more information on and guides to good practice in returning children to home. However, child-care practitioners also thought that it would be helpful in viewing children's return to weigh the implications of particular factors, such as family reconstitution or elements of 'risk', in the social work management of individual cases.

Thus, a broad view of return was encouraged. For example, could return be viewed as the state re-investing or sharing parenting duties with the child's natural family? As we shall see later, it is noticeable that whereas the divesting of parental power on a child's entry to care is marked by elaborate symbols and rituals, the re-investment of parental power appears to have fewer rites of passage, legal safeguards or accountability. Indeed, if parents were able to give up parenting responsibilities as easily as the State, they would probably be viewed as deficient. On the other hand, as Farmer and Parker (1991) point out, few parents of children in care would qualify as suitable foster parents, although many have their children 'home on trial'.

We chose, therefore, to focus on a wide range of children in care, including voluntary receptions and children admitted to care in emergencies. These children also experience reunion and the length of separation they endure is not necessarily related to their legal status. Scrutiny has also fallen upon *oscillators* or 'yo-yo' children as they were previously known, that is children who frequently move in and out of care. However, we would stress that return should not be equated with the legal process of leaving care nor necessarily be viewed as a successful resolution to a child's difficulties. Return home should be perceived as a placement, which like others, has positive and negative aspects and should be viewed in the context of children's longer term care 'careers'. Indeed, a child may experience a number of reunions and have to manage return to a wider variety of situations, of which the family is only one.

Children's care careers

Several of our previous studies have highlighted the difficulties experienced by children and adolescents in making transitions. Many of these moves involve not only changes of role and status but also geographical separation and subsequent return home. These issues were explored in our follow-up studies of young offenders, those leaving residential care and children moving from school to employment. It was found that at each transition, the options open to children were often limited by what had gone before. These inter-connections were best understood by using the concept of a 'care career' as this incorporated a developmental perspective on children's experiences.

Naturally, the ways that different children and parents cope with return will vary but it seems from these previous studies that leaving any care situation that is alternative to their home will engender difficulty, even for those children whose separation has been short. Children's subsequent care careers can also be complex. We will note later that many older adolescents leaving care to live in the community stay intermittently with relatives.

It is noticeable that existing theoretical perspectives on children's care careers concern individual children's experiences. Yet, we know that many children return home from care accompanied by siblings and have to re-negotiate entry into households radically changed in membership and location. Thus, the theoretical perspectives guiding this study have had to accommodate this dynamic situation for, as Wedge and Mantle (1991) have shown, it commonly influences the success of the returns of children in care to their families.

Definitions of return

Although going home after an absence in care may appear straightforward, return is a concept requiring considerable clarification. For example, at what point does frequent access between parents, family and child become return? When does lengthy absence from the home, as is common amongst adolescents, cease to be family membership? At what point do children cease to view their households as 'home'? What level of structural change in the natural family renders the transition not a 'return' but a move to a completely new ambience? Is the family to which the child returns a site or a set of relationships? It has been necessary in this study to clarify these issues, particularly as answers to these questions will differ according to the age, gender, social class, ethnicity and culture of participants.

In view of these difficulties in defining return, we decided that the research should be concerned with all children in care who go *home* to *live*. By *home* we refer to the house of a parent or other relative but not necessarily the parent or other relative from whom the child was separated. By going home to *live,* we are thinking of children who go home for an extended stay. As such, our focus does not include children returning for weekend leaves or for preparatory visits prior to eventual reunion, although these restorations have been scrutinised as possible indicators of a successful return.

Outcomes

A further concern has been the development of appropriate outcome measures, the complexities of which have been recently explored for child-care by Parker and colleagues (1991). Clearly, any child-care outcome emanates from the outcomes of earlier interventions. Hence, an understanding of a child's return to home and family is incomplete without a consideration of the reasons behind the initial separation.

As a consequence, we have looked at features of the return itself, such as whether it endures and what it provides for the child; we have considered participants' perceptions of return, such as whether the families' and children's expectations are met, agreements upheld and stresses mitigated; and, finally, we have looked at the consequences of the child's return for social services and other agencies, such as whether the child re-enters care, what problems arise and how effectively agencies co-operate in their resolution.

Because of the complexity of child-care cases, as the following pages reveal, the returns experienced by children can seldom be viewed as entirely successful or as catastrophic. As in most human relationships, credits have to be weighed against debits.

Aims of the research

It was against this background that we designed a study with the following aims:

i) To clarify the concept of return through an exploration of relevant literature.

ii) To chart the processes and return avenues experienced by all children in care.

iii) From this data to identify groups of children particularly vulnerable to return difficulties, such as re-abuse, placement breakdown, behaviour problems and family rejection.

iv) To scrutinise the return experiences of these children, concentrating particularly on different household situations to which children return and different styles and levels of social work support.

v) To highlight factors significantly associated with successful returns.

As we also wished the study to inform social work practice, we sought:

vi) To inform social workers about the most effective ways of preparing and managing children's returns.

As the following pages reveal, we set about addressing the issue of return by mounting several complementary studies. Initially, we looked at reunion in child-care law. Secondly, we explored the way in which return has been dealt with in research studies, not only in child-care but also in other contexts.

We then set about designing a methodology which would tell us more about the general patterns of return as experienced by children in care and reveal something of the problems faced by individual families welcoming home a son or daughter from a substitute care placement. We have, therefore, completed an extensive study involving 875 children in care who return in a range of circumstances. In addition, we have scrutinised in detail the progress of 24 families and their 31 children who were selected by social services as highly likely return candidates. We monitored the progress of these 31 children over 18 months to discover the trials and tribulations of the return process.

Having set the scene, we begin our description of the findings of the study with a look at return as it has been addressed in child-care policy and law.

Summary points

1. The impact of the Second World War on the relationship between the state and the family was considerable. Since that time, the rights of parents and children have been increasingly recognised and the need for parents to remain in contact and to share in the welfare and happiness of their separated children has been clearly demonstrated.

2. As most children return home after separation it would seem wise to know more about reunion and to manage the reconciliation sufficiently well to minimise subsequent breakdown and repeated severance of family bonds.

3. We need to know how many children and adolescents go home, in what ways groups of young people differ and the reunion problems each group presents. How long do they remain away in care and in what ways do aspects of separation affect the likelihood and success of reunion?

4. There has been an increase in interest in the outcomes of welfare interventions, particularly in the success or failure of social work to solve the problems of separated children and their families.

5. This investigation of children and families experiencing reunion has two strategies: a) An extensive scrutiny of a wide variety of children and adolescents as they return home. We look at 875 cases, the majority of whom go home with varying degrees of alacrity and success. b) An intensive look at the experiences of 31 children from 24 families likely to experience reunion.

2. Return in child-care policy and law

Since the Second World War, there has been a shift in child-care policy from child rescue and the exclusion of the natural family towards encouraging parental participation in the care task, in 'shared care'. There has been growing recognition of the heterogeneity of family and children's needs and the strategies necessary to meet them. Here we explore the implications of the 1989 *Children Act* for returning children and what the legislation says about reunion.

The last decade has seen considerable changes in the situation of parents and separated children. For example, with regard to the education of children with special needs, the recommendations of the Warnock and Fish reports have led to greater provision being made for these children within the ordinary day school. The growth of residential schools serving the difficult or less able child has been checked. In addition to expanding provision for children, greater powers have been granted to parents.

Similarly, for those children in care of social services, not only has separation been discouraged but, as we shall shortly note, the 1989 *Children Act* has given parents considerable power *vis-à-vis* social services and enjoins co-operation from all parties. Particularly welcome is the emphasis given to parental participation in the rearing of their children even if they are unable or reluctant to provide nurture themselves. Far from being excluded from the care of separated children, parents are now expected to take a key role.

Unfortunately, resistance to change among professionals in bureaucratic organisations is well documented and it remains to be seen how effective these new legal arrangements prove to be. Already several studies have demonstrated that improvements in social work practice are difficult to engineer. The reluctance of social workers to share with parents the care of their separated children has a healthy pedigree and a philosophy of child rescue may still influence policy and practice unnecessarily.

Certainly the rights of parents who, for a variety of reasons, failed or were unable to look after their children did not haunt the conscience of those who administered the Poor Laws and it is not difficult to understand why. Today it is fashionable to criticise 19th century welfare approaches to children at risk but any guided holiday tour of downtown Cairo or

Mexico City would encourage us to entertain more charitable attitudes towards the efforts of Lord Shaftesbury, Dr. Barnardo, Thomas Coram and others. The sprawling inner cities of the Third World today mirror the problems of Victorian England. Even the gaunt walls and closed gates of the industrial and reformatory schools might excite a more sympathetic understanding, springing, as they did, from a context where anarchy seemed constantly to threaten and half the population was under twenty-five years of age.

The numbers of children living in desperate circumstances were very considerable and through vagrancy, disease and prostitution, the 'street Arabs' represented an omnipresent threat to the respectable; and, quite as potent, a constant reproach to the religious. Certainly the doors of the workhouse were unwelcoming but destitute children represented an almost overwhelming burden. As Parker (1990) points out, for more than a century, one-third of those receiving indoor relief were children and, if separation from impoverished parents gave these waifs access to better conditions, allowed them to be educated and receive vocational skills, then isolation from families and neighbourhood seemed a small price to pay.

There were also other constraints on the Poor Law besides discouraging the poor able-bodied and their children from seeking relief. As today, economy suggested that the fewer children and families for whom the state assumed responsibility, the lower would be the cost. Frequently severance from children occurred as a by-product of efforts to get parents back to work and off relief. There was universal concern at the cycle of 'deprivation' and of pauperisation; that poverty and dependence in one generation were highly likely to lead to poverty and dependence in the next. If poor children could be rescued swiftly and early enough and placed far from contaminating influences, among which natural families and inner city neighbourhoods were deemed as particularly potent, then cyclical misery could be broken; particularly when youthful independence, resilience and orthodoxy were cemented and strengthened by strong religious faith.

In practice, however, not all child-care organisations worked with such vigour to separate and rescue the luckless, impoverished and delinquent children of the 19th Century. In Aberdeen, for instance, Sheriff Watson and Alexander Thomson established the Industrial Feeding Schools and proudly stated that the family is the place prepared and ordained by God for the training and upbringing of children, and this is an ordinance which men can never infringe with impunity.

(Smeaton, 1869)

Moreover, despite the enduring concern of the voluntary organisations, highly influenced by the severance lobby, that training would be rendered ineffective when parents reclaimed their children at 16, many separated children did, in fact, go home. Ward (1990) found that over a quarter (27%) of children coming under the aegis of the Waifs and Strays Society between 1887 and 1894 were reunited with parents or other relatives.

But it was not surprising in such a welfare climate that the return of children after a long separation was not a practice priority. Those children who did return went home more by default than through active encouragement. Indeed, when parents requested the return of older children who had been long separated in care, particularly when their offspring's earnings might cancel out the insupportable burden that they had previously posed, official eyes usually viewed parental desire for reunion as evidence of cupidity. While the late 19th and early 20th century legislators repeatedly anguished over curtailing the common law rights of fathers in relation to the custody of their children and legitimatising the State's power to intervene, there was in the legislation almost no mention of return. Not until 1948, when a duty was placed on local authorities to ensure that children and parents were reunited as soon as possible, if appropriate, did the law face up to the problems of access and reunion.

During the Second World War a marked shift in policy can be detected, although practice, in some areas, had already outstripped policy. The prevailing ideology in the 1940s and 1950s was to increase the role of public services in the care of children, to extend foster care and to get separated children back home as quickly as possible.

There were several reasons for these policy changes. As we have seen, the evacuation of children from the inner cities exposed to an ignorant public the deprivations and needs of the poor. In addition, many residential institutions for children and young people were taken over by the military and were never subsequently re-opened. Most evacuees were successfully placed in private family homes, that is fostered by default, and at the end of the war, much to everyone's surprise, all but a very few children were reclaimed by their parents so contradicting popular and professional expectations cited by Parker (1990) that a quarter of a million children would be left abandoned. Such parental devotion, in spite of the many difficulties facing inner-city families as the war ended, challenged assumptions about fecklessness and indifference among poor parents.

Furthermore, the increased scrutiny of child-care provision revealed low standards in much of child-care and in residential institutions in particular. These deficiencies were highlighted in the Curtis Report of 1946. There were other problems after the war, the high costs of capital renewal and a strict quota on building materials deterred welfare agencies from renewing or expanding institutional provision. The changing employment patterns among women also added to the difficulties of providing substitute care. Finally, of course, the growing acceptance of psychological theories which stressed the damage wrought by separation also led to a re-assessment of the importance of family and the wisdom of maintaining bonds with parents.

All of these trends were reflected and implemented in the new legal and administrative framework brought about by the 1948 *Children Act* and the local authority children's departments which were created as a result.

Nevertheless the vigorous pursuit of the swift rehabilitation of separated children has been tempered by two factors. First, there has been an increasing concern with prevention rather than treatment. Indeed in the last 15 years, the number of children in care has fallen across the country as a result of deliberate policies; one criterion against which a successful child-care service is measured has become the low numbers in care at any one time. The 25% drop between 1983 and 1988 has no historical precedent. Alongside this, child protection has been a growing issue throughout the 1980s and has highlighted the damage done by keeping children in, or returning them to, dangerous situations. This tension and the need to balance services are accepted as intrinsic features of child welfare and have modified extreme commitments to prevention and return. Thus, we now entertain a far more sober view of children's situations.

There is also a growing awareness of the heterogeneity of children's needs and the range of provision required to meet them. Rather than pretend that vulnerable children need never enter care, we have turned our attention to improving their experiences while there. The perception of prevention as being merely one child-care approach and not the only valid policy should modify the negative view of care as something harmful and worthless, a view which has been particularly influential in recent years.

The 1989 *Children Act,* has reduced these difficulties by establishing a range of services for children and families, some of which may involve the child's living away from home. The aim has been to reduce the stigma of welfare interventions, to provide services which encompass the family's involvement and to achieve re-unification as smoothly and speedily as possible, should it be in the best interests of the child.

Return in child-care law

The return of separated children is rarely mentioned in child-care law. Indeed, compared with the elaborate procedures surrounding the removal of a child from his or her parents and the precise delineations of those attendant duties to be assumed by others, the arrangements for a child's leaving care and returning home seem almost cavalier. The tendency we have noted earlier for welfare systems to be more concerned with how children get into systems than how they get out is confirmed. In the Curtis report of 1946, return is not even discussed.

However, while the word 'return' did not appear in the legislation that followed, there was an explicit statement in the 1948 Act that children in care voluntarily should not remain there longer than is absolutely necessary for their welfare.

> Nothing in this Section 2(2) of the Act shall authorise a local authority to keep a child in their care under this Section if any parent or guardian desires to take over the care of the child, and the local authority shall, in cases where it appears to them consistent with the welfare of the child to do so, endeavour to secure that the care of the child is taken over either (a) by a parent or guardian of his, (b) by a relative or friend of his.

This expectation was made explicit because, for a long period, considerable benefit could accrue to those sheltering children and adolescents, particularly those in residential care. However, the historical antecedents of child-care law are also reflected in the only condition attached to reunion, namely that the relative or friend should be 'where possible, a person of the same religious persuasion as the child'.

For children on care orders under the 1969 *Children and Young Persons Act*, there was a similar requirement constantly to review the need for the child to remain in care. The local authority had a duty under

Section 27.4 of this legislation to review after six months had elapsed whether to make an application for the discharge of the care order, although this did not apply to children committed to care in family proceedings or in parental rights resolutions. Several other well established legal principles had implications for a child's return from care. For example, Section One of the 1980 *Child-Care Act* required local authorities generally to seek to obviate the need to keep children in care.

A further concern with the welfare of children once they have left care was re-emphasised in the 1983/84 report on children in care by the House of Commons Social Services Committee, chaired by Renée Short, although their recommendations reflect a long-standing disquiet about children's long-term welfare. For example, the 1927 report of the Departmental Committee on the Treatment of Young Offenders concluded that the value of training can be thrown away if support is not afforded after release.

The Short report recommended that legislation, which had 'become the conglomerate of centuries', should be rationalised. This was taken up by the 1985 *Review of Child-Care Law*. In its report, the Review Committee accepted the principles of returning children home as soon as the need for absence diminished and proposed that the requirement to return children to their families swiftly should become an overall duty, irrespective of the child's legal route into care, and subject to safeguarding the child's welfare. The Committee's recommendation also dropped the religious requirements previously noted and added some safeguards for natural parents when their children returned elsewhere. The review suggests that

> local authorities should seek to return any child in their care to the care of a parent or guardian or, failing this, a relative or friend, unless this is contrary to the child's best interest. In the latter two cases, the parent should be informed and consulted.

The report of the Child-Care Law Review was the first occasion that return as part of a child's care career received special attention. Naturally, as this review informed the 1989 *Children Act,* it followed that the need for successfully managing the return of children and adolescents separated from their families was emphasised in this legislation, particularly by giving local authorities a clear duty to return children from care. In fact, the Act went further than this by also including principles and requirements to facilitate the successful return of children. For example, the welfare principle requires that return be constantly viewed as an option. Similarly, the careful management of children's separations and care careers reduces the risk of subsequent return problems. These intentions are manifest in the requirement for regular reviews, the need to consider the child's wishes, the elimination of informal barriers to family contacts and the support given to children and families after reunion.

The principles espoused in legislation were expanded in accompanying regulations and guide-lines. These consider the issues of return or 're-unification'. For example, *The Guidance and Regulations on Family Placements* provides practical advice for social workers helping children to return successfully and is extremely sensitive to the stresses associated with reunion. They specify:

> The aim should be to achieve a planned ending to a placement with careful preparation and transition, whether to their family, another placement or adoptive placement.
>
> A child's return to his family may need equally careful preparation, and a child and family may need support over the settling-in period until the child is re-integrated into the family. A period of gradual re-introduction may be needed, depending on the length of time the child has been away from home and the extent of changes in the family. The need for continuity is equally critical at the end of a placement as at the beginning. Children often return to different addresses, new babies in the family, new step-parents and step-brothers and sisters. Sometimes a child must change schools and leave behind friends and interests acquired during foster placement. Parents, too, need to be prepared for changes in the child's habits, interests and routines; and for the possibility of disturbed behaviour while the child is settling in.
>
> It is sometimes appropriate for contact between former foster parent and child to continue for a time through visits, telephone calls or letters. In most cases it is helpful to foster parents to be given news of how the child has settled into his new life. Feedback of this kind can contribute to their development in the fostering role.

The regulations concerning children who return to live with parents while remaining compulsorily in care are even more extensive, mostly because of the risks associated with the return home of abused children. Following the recommendations of inquiries into the deaths of Jasmine Beckford and other children at risk, *Charge and Control Regulations* were implemented in 1989. At first, they caused some confusion, as the new arrangements seemed over-elaborate. As a result, weekly access of adolescents to their families in some CHE's was checked by zealous local authorities until references and family situations had been verified. However, the judgement in Regina v Newham, ex parte B, 1989 ruled that the new requirements need only apply when the permanent return of a child to the care of a relative, guardian or friend was envisaged and not to holiday or extended visits.

The regulations accompanying the 1989 Act on the placement of children in care with relatives introduced further changes to the conditions for returning children home. For example, short stays are included, provided they are longer than 24 hours and parents retain some parental responsibility under care orders but the placement of children with their relatives and friends is excluded, provided no previous residence order is in force, such arrangements being subject to the *Foster Placement Regulations* 1991. Considerable control has to be exercised over the return of children from compulsory care to the care of parents, to those with parental responsibility or those with residence order rights. Before the placement, for example, written views on the proposed move must be sought from a wide variety of sources and carefully considered. The child, the parent, others with parental responsibility and agencies such as the district health authority, the child's doctor, the authority in the new area to which a child might move and all those currently and potentially likely to be involved in the child's welfare have to be consulted. Indeed, enquiries have to be made about all the factors necessary to provide 'a general picture of the carers, their households and life style'.

In the same way, the child's return must be discussed by the new household, hopefully clarifying the roles, relationships and care responsibilities that will be adopted. A placement agreement then has to be drawn up and the local authority must visit the child regularly, see him or her alone and ascertain the views of both the child and the sheltering household. Interactions between the child and family must also be observed and information should be gathered from schools and other contexts in which the child may have manifested behaviours and feelings independently. Similarly, the arrangements for emergency protection of children and after-care duties are designed to promote effective rehabilitation. In the former, there is a duty on the applicant who gained the order to return the child once it is safe to do so and, in the latter, external guide-lines are provided on the support of young people up to the age of 21. Thus, return issues are implicit in many of the decisions and procedures now in operation.

While such guidance is very welcome in view of its sensitivity to children's return problems and the perspective adopted in this research, namely *return as a process,* the view offered seems somewhat limited. The recommended approach to after-care, for example, is rather child-focused in that it is predominantly concerned with linking a range of services to individual cases. Return as a process which faces all children in care, whatever their age and length of stay, and the adaptations that children and their families need to make if reunion is to be successful are given less attention. There is a risk that the human and spiritual needs of children and their families can get lost in preoccupations with services and case management. Neither is there much evidence that the passage of time and its impact on families has received much consideration. Putting this guidance into operation is going to require much greater knowledge about the return experiences of children and families, both at a macro level, such as who goes home and when, and at a micro level, such as the stress and strains faced by individuals.

Conclusion

In this chapter, we have charted changes over time in child-care policies and law with regard to the departure and return of separated children. We have seen that prior to the 1948 *Children Act,* the severance of children 'at risk' from their families was common practice, such policies being reinforced by a variety of political and religious ideologies and moralistic attitudes as well as by practical requirements and economic opportunities. Yet, even in such inauspicious situations, more children returned to their families than might have been expected.

Ideas on children's separation from and return to families were further influenced by the events surrounding the Second World War. The evacuation of children had highlighted the deleterious effects of insensitively handled departures and an increased scrutiny of child-care provision had revealed poor standards. Also, the successful returns of most evacuees questioned assumptions about the fecklessness of poor families. The 1948 Act that reorganised child-care services, emphasised the need to avoid the unnecessary separation of children from their parents and the benefits of swift rehabilitation, whenever possible. This policy still prevails, although it has since been tempered somewhat in the light of developments in child protection and preventative strategies.

The 1989 *Children Act* and its accompanying guidance and regulations, all reflect a growing awareness of the careers of children in care and the need to maintain continuities in children's lives, both features highlighted in recent child-care research. They also perceive return as an important part of that career. It is a process in itself and is an outcome of earlier decisions and separations. Thus, the implication in both the current legislation and regulations is that return is best managed as much by reducing the problems of traumatic separation, drift, isolation and poor after-care as by handling it effectively when it occurs. This policy is pithily stated in para 2.33 of Volume 2:

> The Act requires local authorities to promote contact between a child who is being looked after and all those who are connected with the child unless it is not reasonably practicable or consistent with the child's welfare. The Act also firmly addresses the re-unification of a child with his family. These are linked issues. If contact is not maintained, re-unification becomes less likely and recognition of this has to underpin all considerations in planning for a child.

Summary points

1. The 1989 Act, in seeking to simplify and give coherence to the legislation regarding children and families, particularly by seeking parental co-operation and in stressing voluntary arrangements, discourages separation and increases the sharing of care between local authorities and families.

2. A swift return is envisaged for the majority of those children who have to be separated from their families. Not only is separation of children from parents discouraged by the legislation but, at reunion, support is now an obligation on social services.

3. For those children who remain vulnerable while at home there is a duty on the local authority to advise and 'befriend' and to assist those in need up to the age of 21 years.

4. The 1989 *Children Act,* in its requirement for regular reviews, the need to consider the child's wishes, the freedom of access accorded to most parents and the support given to families after reunion, thrusts the management of return into the forefront of social work practice.

3. The return experience identified in child-care research

This chapter explores the wealth of research material that exists on children in and leaving care. Although few research studies have focused on the problems children and families face managing reunion, evidence exists on the numbers leaving care, their destinations and the duration of their reunions. In addition, different groups of children who are vulnerable to problems on return can be identified. Some of these studies provide data that merits re-analysis.

Returns are inevitably emotional affairs. The excitement, tensions and problems surrounding separation and its concommitant, return, touch our innermost feelings, whether through perceptions of home and everything associated with it or through our sense of belonging and identity. Such aspects of the human condition are almost 'too deep for tears', to borrow Wordsworth's words, let alone amenable to simple and objective analysis.

It is not surprising, therefore, that the idea of return home after an absence has long exerted a hold over the imagination of writers. Indeed, the idea of people being cut off for one reason or another from their home and the problems they encounter on their return to what has become for them an alien environment has provided the stuff of legends, such as the Odyssey, as well as given substance to both comedy and tragedy, farce and family drama, not to mention being a rich source of narrative in the Bible.

Some literary descriptions of return are simply sentimental, such as Browning's 'Oh to be in England' or Payne's 'There's no place like home' but others succeed in capturing the emotions, negotiations and adjustment difficulties we shall explore in this study. MacNeice imagines how Ulysses thinks of home, 'Here could never be home, No more than the sea around it. And even the sea is a different sea round Ithaca'. Fanny Price found Portsmouth 'men all coarse, the women all pert, everybody underbred' on a visit home from Mansfield Park. But some literary figures echo the experiences of children in care when they return to changed families and new home situations. Hamlet, for instance, returned from school in Wittenberg to find not only his beloved father dead but his mother married to his father's murderer. Wordsworth found awkwardness and lack of cordiality among former friends due to something as simple as having different clothes. Odysseus was unrecognised on arrival, and even then it was his nanny who was first to understand, while Jane Eyre's similar dismay was compensated for by the greetings of the dog, Pilot.

Adjustments, too, pose problems. War poets describe the difficulties of fitting in once back from fighting and Paul in *All Quiet on the Western Front* wistfully concludes, 'we could never regain the intimacy of those old scenes. A sense of strangeness will not leave me; I cannot feel at home among these things'. Making sense of things through reunion is a painful business, even in those studies which treat return in a light-hearted way. It is clear that those who are separated seem driven to return, either to resume things at the point at which they left off or to incorporate separation into their identity and give meaning to the rift.

But while numerous poets and authors have fathomed the deepest emotions of those who return, the event usually has some wider function, such as to dramatise tragedy or comedy. Interestingly, very few literary studies look at the return experiences of children. Thus literary comparisons with children's return from care, the focus of our interest, cannot be taken too far and, in any case, government funded research is hardly likely to put a premium on scrutinies of books that most of us reserve for either armchair or deckchair. What, then, does recent child-care research tell us about the return of separated children?

Here, the problems of a child's reunion with his or her natural family are more in evidence, although we found only one study that looked in detail on return and factors affecting its success (Simard, Vachon and Moisan (1991). Most glimpses of return are largely incidental to the main research focus, such as studies of leaving care or of recidivism. The programmes of work funded by the DHSS and ESRC in the 1980s, for example, produced much new material about children in care, although none of these studies has looked specifically at return home. We, therefore, had to extract relevant information from research into related aspects of the care system, such as studies of children placed home on trial, or from a re-working of data which include return situations. Several recent child-care studies seem relevant to the return issue and we can now see what they have to offer.

Studies of children's care careers

Let us first look at those studies that follow the experience of families and children as they become known to social services. Three studies have relevance here; the Dartington Unit's *Lost in Care* (1986), Vernon and Fruin's *In Care* (1986) and Packman, Randall and Jacques's *Who Needs Care?* (1986), all of which cover the whole spectrum of children caught up in the care experience.

Our study of the problems of maintaining links between children in care and their families, *Lost in Care*, is discussed throughout this report. Indeed, it was by studying 450 children entering care that we were alerted to the fact that, while the children have little in common in terms of personal and family characteristics, their reasons for entering care and prognoses for rehabilitation, the experience of separation is common to all but a few. Moreover, a two-year follow-up of the 450 cases raised questions not only about this initial separation and its aftermath but also about the child's return to home and family. As we have explained, it was the lack of knowledge about this latter process that led us to propose the present study.

Initially, it was clear from the follow-up evidence that most children entering care return home. A calculation in a later chapter, where the research data is re-analysed, shows that the proportion is nearly 90%. However, the evidence also suggested that the return process was fraught with difficulties and these were compounded by several factors. These included changes in the membership, structure and location of the child's family while he or she was away in care and by the tendency for links between child and family to wither during separations. Problems affected even short-stay cases, a third of whom returned to households where there had been a change in membership or location and nearly two thirds of whom experienced difficulties in maintaining contact with their families while absent in care.

For the children who remained in care for two years and were still living away from home or relatives at the end of the period, parental contact had declined to the point that nearly half of them saw no relatives at all. In addition, a further quarter of those children who were absent from home but who saw their relations frequently were experiencing barriers to parental contact. These arose either formally from the impositions of social workers or informally from factors such as distance, routine or attitudes in placements that were unwelcoming to family visits. For example, a third of the children were placed more than twenty miles away from home and a sixth more than fifty miles away.

The situation regarding parental access arose from several causes. Children's care careers had been unstable with 83% having two placements and 56% three or more. One effect of this was the separation and declining contact between siblings who had entered care together. Indeed, 54% of those aged under eleven had originally been admitted to care with a sibling, so this pattern not only increased children's isolation but also led to each child in the family having his or her own care career and return experience. For this present scrutiny of return, we have extended the follow-up of the 450 children to five years and it will be seen in a later chapter that the patterns just highlighted become even more marked as time passes.

Equally important was the declining input of social workers over time. In the second year of care, there was virtually no contact between social services and a third of mothers and four fifths of fathers. In addition, nearly half the children received visits less than once a month. Given the high proportion of children in care who return home, these research findings are disquieting. While children are away, their families change as do the children themselves and there is little social work effort made to keep contacts going and shared experiences alive. Moreover, even less time is devoted to preparation for the child's return home. It was not surprising, therefore, to find the high levels of placement breakdown described in Chapter Six.

A second study in the DHSS child-care research programme, Vernon and Fruin's, *In Care: A Study of Social Work Decision Making*, reiterates many of the points just made. Although concerned mainly with factors affecting children's length of stay in care, this research produced one additional finding significant for our study of return. Whilst many social workers are ideologically opposed to care and have considerable scope to influence children's care careers once there, they nevertheless rarely work towards children's return. Hence, factors other than social work actions tend to determine what happens to children and the social work influence on case histories is more by default than design. The returns of many children, therefore, are unlikely to be either planned or purposefully pursued by social workers. Indeed, return may only become an issue when raised by parents or children or when precipitated by extraneous events, such as the child absconding or a foster home breakdown. The authors write,

> since at the time of entry to care social workers demonstrated a basically
> negative attitude to care, it is surprising, if not a matter of some concern,
> that the balance of factors contributing to children leaving care should be
> so heavily weighted towards factors other than social work involvement.

In a third study in the DHSS research programme into children in care, Jean Packman and colleagues looked at 361 children seriously considered for admission to care. Of these, 161 actually entered care, the remaining 200 stayed put, although 45 of these were admitted later on. Six months after the initial scrutiny, 26 (16%) of the 161 admissions had left care but had been re-admitted, so suggesting a failed return after a short stay in care. Packman's study is particularly pertinent to an understanding of this latter group, a category of children that has received little research attention.

We were able to go back to the *Who Needs Care?* data and look again at these 26 re-admissions. This re-scrutiny revealed that they cover a range of child-care situations. For example, 16 of the entries were originally voluntary admissions and ten were committals to care. Of the sixteen voluntary care cases, thirteen were re-admitted voluntarily; thus only three children came back into care via legal routes such as emergency or care orders, suggesting a degree of enduring co-operation between social worker and families. Of the ten re-admissions originally on care orders, four children came back voluntarily, four on emergency orders and two on remand. A comparison of the rates of re-admission for different groups of children suggests that voluntary cases were twice as likely as committals to re-enter care but a consideration of other factors, such as reasons for care, age, gender, home circumstances and length of time in care, was less fruitful.

The reasons for these children's re-admissions arose from a wide range of circumstances including parents being unwilling or unable to provide care, abuse and neglect and continuing behaviour problems. Re-entry to care was more likely to arise from a recurrence of former problems than from new situations.

The likelihood of return for children leaving care and the risk of swift re-admission back into care identified by Packman and others is further confirmed in Rowe, Hundleby and Garnett's (1989) analysis of the patterns and outcomes of child-care placements. They looked over a two year period at all admissions, discharges and moves among children in care in six local authorities; 5,688 children were studied and more than 10,000 placements charted.

The majority of children discharged from care went home to family or their local community. Only 2% were adopted. Nevertheless, as many as 7% of all departures involved young people reaching the age of eighteen whose 'return' was necessitated by legal rather than social work requirements. Moreover, 18% of all those children who left care during the two years were re-admitted within the study period and 7% re-entered care twice, figures which confirm those of 22% and 6% found in our *Lost in Care* study.

We could continue at length drawing out the implications for return from studies of children's care careers but the exercise is likely to yield diminishing returns. Fanshel and Shinn's study (1978) of 624 children in care in New York State, for example, is worthy of consideration in its own right but largely echoes the issues raised so far. However, some other studies do make additional points relevant to our task.

Cawson (1988) provides statistical evidence about the distances from home that children in care are placed. She estimates that in March 1984, 7,363 children in care were living outside their local authority, although half of these were in London where boroughs are small. She emphasises the problems arising when children settled in one geographical area return home to another and the paradox that the more placements try to integrate the child, the greater will be the disruption caused for children by reunion. This contrast is most marked in those residential settings where, as Burford and Casson (1989) have found, there is a reluctance to include families in the day-to-day care and a general lack of awareness of how to achieve this.

The importance of continuity in children's care careers is stressed in Simard, Vachon and Moisan's (1991) Québec study of children returning to parents after an absence in care of more than 30 days. The successful returners had fewer placements while away and received consistent help from social workers. A further auspicious factor was the child's ability to integrate with peers. The impact of these variables was reduced, however, if foster families and natural parents were in competition or if step-parents in newly reconstituted families sought to discipline the newly arrived child.

To conclude these discussions of care processes, mention must be made of the research and development programme on family re-unification in foster care being undertaken at the University of Connecticut. Maluccio and colleagues are using their considerable research data to produce guide-lines and training packages for social workers and foster carers (Maluccio and Sinanoglu, 1981; Kreiger, Maluccio and Pine, 1991). Family re-unification is seen as a planned process, needing a variety of services and supports, to help each child and family achieve their optimum level of re-connection, whether it be full re-entry or other forms of contact and affirmation of the child's membership of that family. The need for commitment to such strategies, the awareness of the relationship between agencies and families and the importance of services to maintain the re-unification are all emphasised.

All of these studies of children's care careers have contributed to our thinking about children's return home from care. The benefits of a process perspective have been illustrated. It is clear that return is not a single event. It embraces a set of negotiations, the majority of which will lead to return. Even then, the process goes on, because a few children fail to settle at home and are removed yet again. Let us next look at child-care studies which focus on a particular type of return, that is placements of children at home.

Placement with parents

Several research studies scrutinise particular aspects of reunion. For example, while most children going home also simultaneously leave care, a number of children, about 10%, return to their families yet still remain legally in care. This used to be called 'home on trial', a limbo situation in which those who were to be on trial were seldom specified. Such children are included in Rowe, Hundleby and Garnett's study of child-care placements, *Child Care Now* (1989). They are also the focus of Thoburn's study *Captive Clients* (1980) and of Farmer and Parker's *Trials and Tribulations* (1991).

In looking specifically at children living at home in this way, Rowe and colleagues found that of all the placement types considered, this category was the least likely to endure for as long as social workers thought advisable and a third of these placements ended prematurely, a risk which affected all age groups. Indeed, by using the criteria of whether the aim of the placement was met and whether it endured, Rowe concludes that only 36% of placements with parents were successful.

In Rowe's survey, the placements known as 'charge and control' accounted for 9% of all the living situations experienced by the children. Adolescents were more likely than others to be so placed, with boys being more likely to return than girls, a reflection of the greater proportion of boys among the adolescents included in the study. However, many younger children were also involved, particularly if on care orders for protection or following wardship, guardianship or matrimonial proceedings. Of all the moves to charge and control, 48% were from residential placements, 26% from foster care and 10% from penal custody. The low rate of returns home on trial from foster care and high rates of return from residential and penal provision clearly surprised the researchers.

The aims of placements at home were mostly associated with providing an ambience for care and upbringing. Nevertheless, there was a wide range of other situations. Nearly a third of the children under ten were returned as part of an assessment exercise and for 26% of those aged 11 or over, the placement was viewed as a 'bridge to independence'. Social workers' estimates of the success of such placements varied considerably according to their perceptions of the aims behind the return, as the following table shows:

Table 3.1: Proportion of placements with parents meeting stated aims

Aim of placement	% met aims
Remand	68
Assessment	64
Temporary care	50
Roof	49
Care & upbringing	48
Treatment	45
Bridge to independence	33

When the two measures of success used in Rowe's study were combined, that is whether the placement lasted as long as expected and met desired aims, it was found that estimates of satisfaction fall as children's ages increase; it is 46% for children aged 0-4 but 23% for the over tens. What should be seen as a happy event for children and families, therefore, more often than not ends in difficulties and the older the child the more likely it is that there will be problems. It may be that placement with relatives is frequently a last ditch attempt at the rehabilitation of children with families whose caring abilities are poor; it may be that the placement reflects a lack of viable alternatives rather than a conscious and esteemed future plan for the child. On the other hand, it may indicate insufficient preparation for and support of the family and child from social workers.

Thoburn's study was the first to alert social workers to the large numbers of children living at home while in care and to explore the particular difficulties this placement posed. In an intensive study, she traced the care careers and family responses of 34 children living 'home on trial'. Initially, she found that such placements were rarely negotiated and that parents had little choice in what was offered to them and their children, making them the 'captive clients' of social work.

Three influences were found to bear on the decision to let children go home, although there was a difference between decisions about whether to return children and when to do so. These were: the attitudes of parents and children and their reactions to the care placement; the attitudes of the social workers and the nature of the practical and emotional support offered and the quality of the placement. She concluded, however, that the most important of all was the determination of the parents, and when old enough, the children, to stay together as a family.

Thoburn anticipates Vernon and Fruin in suggesting that where social work plans changed, it was usually in response to pressures from the parents or children or to the unhappiness of the children when away from home. However, she also stresses the importance of the social work contribution to the maintenance of children's family contacts and the preparation of them and their families for return, a factor we shall come back to in a later chapter. The availability of resources made return plans more imaginative and, in general, she praised social workers for taking risks when letting children go home, especially when abuse was a possibility. She concluded with the view that where parents wish to care for their children and can be helped to offer good enough care, they and their children have a right to such help.

A larger study of children placed with relatives has been completed by Farmer and Parker who looked at 321 children who had returned 'home on trial' in 1984. They divided the study population into two groups: children in care for protection or because families could not provide for them (N=172) and those in care to control behaviour (N=149).

Most of the 172 care cases had been neglected and abused (61%) or came from families unable to provide for them (39%). Prior to the placement, 49% lived in residential care, 37% were fostered, 2% were in their own accommodation and 1% were in custody, the remainder having stayed at home throughout. Residential care was a more common antecedent than the authors expected and was also unexpectedly high (36%) for the under fives. It was noted that, for those going home from residential care, return had rarely been part of an initial care plan.

The abused and neglected children who did well after their return displayed particular characteristics. They tended to have been in care for shorter periods, that is less than one year; they had not changed placements while in care and they returned to households where there had been no change of membership. Children who settled successfully also tended to be the only child in the household or, if they had siblings in care, to have returned with them. In addition, they tended to be young. The number of successful returns clearly falls as children's ages increase. Other factors related to success were highlighted in interviews with children, families and social workers. Among these were: the quality of attachment to parents before admission to care, contact with the family prior to return and the number of other changes the return required for the child, such as school or friends.

A follow-up of these placements revealed that further problems arise after return. As many as 42 of the 172 children were re-abused or neglected but only nine had to be removed. Generally, the more the supervising agencies were concerned about cases, the more likely it was that home on trial failed. Yet it is difficult to judge the quality of home placements, as breakdowns often occurred well after the original return, 37% after two years had elapsed, suggesting that the 'trial' element had long been superseded. Indeed, pressure to terminate the placement at home came mostly from families and children (58%) rather than from the dissatisfaction and unease of social workers (33%) or courts (7%). Moreover, in most cases, children moved to the care of another relative.

A scrutiny of the children in care for the control of their behaviour, mainly adolescents, provides a quite different picture. The stays away for these young people were much shorter, the usual absence was for only one or two years. This factor distinguishes this group from the protection cases more than any other background factor, such as age, sex or race. Another important difference was that most (80%) of these older children returned home from residential establishments, either social services or penal institutions, and only 2% moved from foster homes.

For the behaviour control group, the home placement was seldom viewed by social workers as a controversial and fraught decision, a sharp contrast to the care and protection cases. Indeed, few community supports other than intermediate treatment were offered to children and parents. Nevertheless, the researchers found it difficult to interpret the behaviour of these young people while at home. For example, on return, 55% offended, 58% truanted and 44% of the girls got pregnant but these setbacks rarely resulted in the placement ending. While such figures seem high, it is hard to know how this situation compares with other deprived and difficult adolescents in the community. Much also depends on the circumstances leading to the return; in some cases the move was purposeful, in others it was clearly *faute de mieux*.

Certainly, a return home on trial neither greatly improves young people's behaviour nor offers social workers much control over difficult and anti-social behaviour. Indeed, social services tolerate levels of misbehaviour which would be unacceptable in those living away in care. Thus, social workers were hardly enamoured of placement with parents for this group and, paradoxically, because difficult cases received most support, there is a correlation between poor results and high social work input. Independent of this relationship, however, not being able to see the child or loss of contact by social workers were particularly bad omens. Social workers' interest in the cases clearly waned over time, subsequent reviews did not take place and care orders were left to expire or to be slowly discharged. It is not clear, therefore, whether the returns reflect a treatment plan, a reward for good behaviour, a response to absconding or simply time running out.

These studies of children returning home on what we used to call 'on trial' emphasise the wide range of situations facing children and families when young people return from care. Return occurs from a variety of settings, including penal establishments, and placements at home have a number of aims. Yet, whatever the circumstances, all returners face additional difficulties and there is a high likelihood that further separations will be precipitated, particularly among adolescents. The studies also highlight serious ambiguities in return situations. Social workers have only moderate expectations of success and give variable attention to the preparation for such moves, again particularly for adolescents.

Return and independence

Adolescents raise, often in extreme form, the difficulties faced by long separated children going home. Indeed, each year as many as 8,500 young people leave care simply because they reach the age of 18, although as we shall show, leaving care is not concomitant with return. Reunions for older children are coloured by the nature of adolescents' transitions, particularly their moves towards personal independence alongside some continuing reliance on the family.

Stein and Carey (1986) explored the problems experienced by 79 leavers all aged over 16 who had recently left care. Interviews with the young people reveal many serious problems of return and of leaving care. For example, instant maturity was expected in situations where young people faced several transitions. Thus, many young people who found difficulty in adjustment sought a refuge in return to care or to quasi-care situations. On the other hand those who had a sense of identity, awareness of continuities in their lives and a preparedness for difficulties on return experienced more successful outcomes.

Nevertheless, it was abundantly clear that most young people faced a miserable time after leaving care. Happiness, warm relationships, security, relief and help were left behind and young people's low job aspirations, a reflection of their worth entertained by society while in care, led them to face continual financial difficulties. Simple survival was a challenge; to eat sufficiently and launder clothes cheaply became priorities. Loneliness was also a problem, counteracted by sad wanderings round cafes, cinemas and pubs. Enduring petty delinquency also meant that many lads were in continual trouble with the police. Movement between living situations was, therefore, common, either to survive or to relieve depression. In other instances, it was thrust upon them by circumstance.

The arrangements for the return from care varied considerably, a feature emphasised by Bonnerjea in her study *Leaving Care in London*. She found that, during a successful care placement, the field social worker had little active role except to offer support; so, an impending return to home of a child from care requires practitioners to re-negotiate a key role in the reunion. But, even for those young people benefiting from social work inputs, it was often difficult to seek social work help without being seen as a failure. The task of building future lives was much eased by their having their own accommodation, stable peer relationships and/or a specific boy or girl-friend, but unanticipated events frequently occurred, especially parenthood or the taking on of step-children, which considerably complicated return plans.

After leaving care, the young people proved very mobile. Only 20% stayed in the same place for two years. Most hated living alone and had all kinds of difficulties, from rows with neighbours to poor sleep or extreme fears. They left the lonely situations of flats or bedsits and moved quickly to group or shared situations. None undertook further education and all were fitful in employment. Former care-givers occasionally proved important sources of support, especially foster parents who were often seen as 'family'. Many young people, however, continued to be dependent on welfare agencies and viewed the decisions made about them as being largely out of their hands.

The Dartington Research Unit's follow-up studies of young people in Youth Treatment Centres provides further information on the return of older adolescents from residential care. The data on leavers' subsequent care careers is re-analysed in a later chapter but several points from these studies add to the experiences of adolescents described by Stein and Carey and mirror the findings about delinquents described by West and Farrington (1977).

A scrutiny of the living situations of the 104 young people who left the Youth Treatment Centres between 1982 and 1985 reveals instability and frequent change. While most young people eventually achieve some independence, the transition is by no means smooth, often interrupted by custody, homelessness or returns to former situations. Hence, parental relationships not only wither but periodically tend to revive and returns home may occur long after the young person has moved out of residential care. For example, twice as many leavers lived at home at some point within two years of leaving as returned there directly.

The patterns of changing family structures and enduring tensions were found again for these leavers but an intensive follow-up scrutiny showed that the depth and significance of relationships between children and relatives were greater than levels of contact would suggest. Despite continuing stresses in family relationships, parents provided considerable support for their offspring, especially male offenders and girls. However, it is wrong to assume an uninterrupted strengthening of relationships over time, for they fluctuate, reflecting particular circumstances, such as pregnancy, employment and criminality.

The returns of many of the young people studied were seriously impaired by the consequences of offending so that remands in custody frequently disrupted living patterns, social relations and employment prospects. This situation has been emphasised by Farrington (1990) in his long-term follow-up of offenders. Poor physical and mental health, in contrast, were less common constraints on young people's lives.

Despite extensive social work efforts, a quarter of the leavers failed to resolve their difficulties and remained highly dependent on welfare agencies for accommodation and support long after their return to home and community. Generally, the more deprived and fragmented the young person's earlier family care experience, the more difficult were the post-return adjustments. Young people long bereft of any family support, for example, rarely succeeded in creating a new support network after leaving. Boys who had been long in care found it especially difficult to cope and many quickly found themselves back in a residential setting, usually prison. The relative success of girls appears to indicate the importance of achieving an acceptable role in society, since many were coping surprisingly well as single parents.

Social workers' responses to the needs of these young people were more varied than for less extreme child-care cases. As the young people had posed severe behaviour problems in the past and as there is no clear philosophy of effective after-care for such cases, social workers responded to their supervisory tasks in different ways. For example, some consciously sought to discourage the dependency that can follow institutionalisation and restricted their help to instrumental areas, such as housing or jobs, while, in contrast, one local authority allocated two full-time staff to one individual. Nevertheless, despite these efforts, Garnett (1992) found that key decisions were often left to the young people themselves and Bonnerjea has emphasised that young people's requirements are equally variable and support needs to be available according to their demands.

These studies of adolescents' experiences indicate the significance not only of the return situation itself but also of people's perceptions of the reason for care, the quality of the care experience and young people's circumstances after leaving. They also highlight, once again, the complexity of the return process, the variety of adjustments and transitions that have to be made and the problems of coping with the stigma associated with being in care. In their emphasis that return takes place over time and involves negotiations with and re-evaluations of not only family but also friends and neighbourhood, they recall the social network that Whitaker, Cook, Dunne and Lunn-Rockliffe (1984) identify as easing the return home of children in residential care.

Consumers' views on return from care

Important insights into return as it affects children absent in care are offered in several studies in which adults and children describe their experiences. Triseliotis and Russell, for example, in *Hard to Place*, interviewed 84 young adults who had either been adopted or placed for long periods in residential homes. Those who had stayed long in residential care were largely critical. Their memories recall stigma, poor self-concepts, being different from other children and a lack of family roots. Former residents felt cut off in that they knew few other young people outside care, they rarely had to make decisions or establish themselves as individuals and found it difficult to revisit former institutions. They also lacked continuity of support after leaving. Hence, the demands of return came as something of a shock for those long in residence, in addition to more widespread anxiety about jobs, accommodation and general survival.

These experiences of feeling different, stigma and lack of integration into society are echoed in other consumer studies, such as Kahan's (1979) *Growing Up in Care,* Festinger's (1983) *No-one Ever Asked Us* and Page's (1977) *Who Cares?* One aspect of children's and parents' feelings highlighted in these studies has been developed in Hundelby's (1988) paper on returning children home. She confirms the likelihood of change in family structures while children are away in care and concludes that in order to effect a satisfactory reunion, social workers have to reconcile ambivalent feelings between children and their relatives. Children may not understand what has happened to them or why, they may feel guilty that they have upset or destroyed their family while at the same time they feel angry that the family has broken up. They are certain to be fearful about returning to changed situations.

Other writers have developed these points from a practice rather than a research standpoint, looking at individuals' adaptations when returning and the possible contributions of social workers. Burgess (1981), for example, echoes Stein and Carey by emphasising that the move from care to independence and work not only requires new skills but also stamina to cope with boredom and monotony. Too often, the employment expectations of leavers are unrealistically high, making drop-out and withdrawal common responses.

The work of Wendelken (1983) and Brearley and colleagues (1982) complement Hundleby's stress on the ambivalence of children's and parents' feelings about return. Parents, they argue, are the most difficult to prepare; their children will have changed while away, their feelings are confused and, instead of being happy to be at home, their offspring may be aggressive, troublesome and enuretic. Similarly the returning child has to face a new home, perhaps with a step-parent. The family home may appear small, dull, cold and poverty stricken; food may seem poor and irregular. Parents may not have much free time to spend with the child and the local school may strike the child as different, for instance in terms of expected attainments or racial composition. The honeymoon of new relationships may soon pass into a nightmare of acting out and rejection.

Several hypotheses are proposed in these consumer studies concerning the factors that help children return from care successfully. Children seem to cope best if they feel secure because they understand the past and its effect on them and if they have participated in decisions about their future and in the departure process. Recovery from the initial separation also needs to be complete. Secondly, it may be that good adaptations will reflect children's enthusiasm for and ability to function in new settings. As the care experience is neither wholly good nor wholly bad, children may gain or lose from their placements. Do children, therefore, need to be emotionally prepared for leaving, perhaps with rituals such as parties, presents or cards? In addition, what emphasis should be placed on continuity of relationships and boosting the self-confidence of children?

Adopted children seeking their roots

A slightly different aspect of return experienced by children separated from their natural parents is offered by adults who were adopted as children and who subsequently sought out their origins, an exploration facilitated by the 1975 *Children Act*.

Haimes and Timms (1985) concluded that the whole exercise centres on issues of identity. The seekers are continually asking, 'who am I?' Adopted children are marginal relative to other children and wish to overcome this problem by acquiring the right to explore without censure their backgrounds.

Here the return process has several stages. There was an initial period of mourning for the past, then dreams and fantasies had to be overcome. The revelation was more a process of disclosure than a sudden discovery. Thus, slow re-appraisal and re-examination were necessary. Because of this, some people stopped their inquiries after reading their birth records, their paper identity being sufficient to satisfy their curiosity. They did not go on to trace their natural parents for fear of rejection, disappointment or of upsetting their adoptive parents.

For some, the new knowledge simply filled in gaps in a single story; understanding the past helps us cope with the present. For others, the information linked pre- and post-adoption periods and filled a need to calculate their alternative life histories and reduce their sense of confusion. In short, the experience enabled them to place themselves better in both their own life histories and, equally important, those of other people.

These actions were best interpreted as part of the inquirer's social identity, that is their self view and others' view of them. Marginality and feelings of being different were reduced. Haimes and Timms conclude that the ideology of adoption is too much the pathology of an identity crisis whereas it is more associated with what MacIntyre (1981) has called the 'narrative self'. The difficulty is, however, that the condition for starting this process is to acknowledge that you are different. As Rowe (1986) has said,

> there has been less discussion about what adoption really is than on whether it has been successful.

Conclusion

This concludes the overview of return as it occurs in child-care research literature. Many perspectives have been described and significant areas and factors specified. There is general agreement in all studies that return cannot be understood in isolation, it is part of a process in which the initial separation is key. As return is an outcome of that separation, there are further outcomes of the return, so the process goes on. It is also clear that the care experience itself can complicate plans and expectations for rehabilitation.

Continuities of children's care careers, perceptions and feelings of participants and legal definitions of responsibility have all to be considered. But, equally clear is that, although many child-care studies have scrutinised returning children, the process of return has never been properly studied in its own right. This is a surprising deficiency in social work literature considering that nearly all children in care eventually go home. This gap in knowledge is manifest in the fact that experienced researchers have been surprised by certain aspects of children's returns, such as the high proportion of residential and the scattering of penal placements that precede it and the anti-social behaviour among older children once returned.

It was because of these research deficiencies that we decided both to re-analyse existing data on the care careers of returning children and to look prospectively at a number of cases as they returned home from care. This combination of macro and micro approaches seemed the most effective way of exploring issues scanted in the studies we have discussed. Such a design scrutinises individual cases in the context of the child's long-term care career and family situation and interprets each return experience in the light of the general return patterns we have identified.

Summary points

1. There have been several recent research studies of children in care but few have looked specifically at children's return home. Relevant information has, therefore, to be extracted from research into related parts of the care system.

2. Several available research studies highlight aspects of children's care careers, others look at the return routes taken by children, some explore the experiences of older adolescents leaving care while other relevant information is found in consumer studies of child-care services and adoptees seeking their roots.

3. All studies indicate that return cannot be understood in isolation and that it is part of a process in which the initial separation is key. There are also further outcomes of the child's return to be considered.

4.   As none of the research described has explored children's return as a process, macro evidence on the careers of children in care and micro studies of individual cases are used in this study.

4. Return in other contexts

This chapter looks at studies of children outside the care system which throw additional light on the return process. Of particular importance are investigations of children leaving hospital, ordinary boarding schools and schools which cater for children with special needs. In addition, insights can be gained from a scrutiny of other groups experiencing separation and return, the families of young offenders and those from the armed forces.

The experience of return is not confined to children in care. Indeed, many more children return home each term from boarding schools and many other young people spend time away in hospital. Moreover, certain occupations, such as the armed services, require their personnel regularly to leave home. Thus, we need to ask whether research studies in these areas offer findings and perspectives relevant to family reunions of children in care.

Hospitalised children

The separation experienced by children on admission to hospital has been the focus of many psychological and psychiatric studies and much separation theory rests on this work. Bowlby (1952) was probably the first to undertake such research systematically and subsequently used his evidence to inform general theories of attachment and child development. Much of the concern about the bad effects of separation, especially of children from mothers, stems from this work. Since Bowlby, the effects of separation have been further scrutinised and the conditions of most harm clarified, for example by Rutter (1972). Also, there have been more intensive studies of children in hospital, such as those by the Robertsons (1970), and radical changes in the hospital care of children have been encouraged by official reports, such as Platt (Ministry of Health 1959).

While many studies have concentrated on the separation of hospitalised children, few have looked at return other than in terms of a medical follow-up. One exception is *Beyond Separation* by Hall and Stacey (1979), a set of papers concerned with various aspects of the hospital care of children. This book argues that children's response levels of distress 'reflect more than the nature and severity of the child's medical condition'. An explanation of children's disturbance within hospital, they say, must concentrate on the hospital environment and that of the home and must not fragment the two. Also, the organisational aspects of the hospital are as important for understanding individual disturbance as are the insights of psychology.

Hall and Stacey attempt to integrate medical, psychological and sociological variables to explain how the behaviours and attitudes which the hospital approves can determine children's problems after leaving. However, it is important to emphasise that children in care are usually far more seriously disadvantaged with regard to separation difficulties than are children in hospital. We have seen that their families are usually more fragmented with key members spread across a number of households and, while they are away, the children are often moved around placements, making it difficult for parents to keep in touch.

Discontinuity is, however, still a common experience for children in hospital. Not only is the child's educational and social development likely to be affected by long or repeated hospitalisation but the lives of parents or siblings are also changed. Although hospitals have made enormous strides to include families in the nursing of children and to inform them about treatment and prospects, a mother's stay with the child still means separation from father and siblings. Moreover, brothers and sisters may resent the attention given to the sick child, producing wider family tensions, especially when the effect on one sibling is greater than on others. Parents, too, may face frustrations arising from restricted occupational or geographical mobility.

Both Rutter (1975) and Pill (1979) also raise a very important issue, highly relevant to children in care, namely the difficulties faced by children who are repeatedly admitted to hospital. They found that some young children were not only highly anxious but also fearful of pain on every occasion and did not seem to have developed coping strategies. Pill writes,

> little is known about the long-term psychological effects of repeated admissions and there is no evidence to suggest that this pattern is any less damaging to a child's mental health than a stay involving months. Parents are often not sure where to turn for advice concerning the management of the child and sometimes have considerable difficulty in obtaining equipment. The initiative is left entirely to them, and the hospital appears to take little interest in the patient once discharged, even though the child may be readmitted in the fairly near future.

The National Association for the Welfare of Children in Hospital has done most to co-ordinate research into hospitalised children but admits that much current practice is based on the work of writers in the 1950s, such as the Robertsons and Menzies and, later, Maureen Oswin, all of whom were alarmed about the effect on children of hospital admissions. It is difficult to find much current research on the subject although practice has changed considerably. Naturally, there are children who still spend long periods in hospital but improved practice seeks to ameliorate the risks and to make the stay as family-like as possible.

The Association's publication most relevant to the issue of return is Woodward's (1978) pamphlet *Has Your Child Been in Hospital?* She begins by discussing the problems of separation and shows how, for some children, these are exacerbated by the child's lack of time sense, confusion about their situation, difficulties of gaining comfort, view of hospital as a punishment and fears and fantasies about their fate. The children most at risk are under fives who stay in hospital for more than one day, particularly if admitted in an emergency. Temperamental factors in the child are also influential. She then considers the parents' position, noting the likelihood of anger, fears of responsibility, change of role, feelings of guilt and failure, sensitivity to criticism and the difficulties and strains of visiting.

Difficulties can also arise from the ways that children and family interact as a result of mutually stressful experiences. Children's unquestioning love for their families may have been shattered, they may find it hard to trust their mother and father and may test out parents' commitment to them. Parents are often physically tired and cannot easily comprehend the changes they see in their youngsters. The most common reaction is for the child to regress. Responses include thumb sucking, clinging, aggression, destructive behaviour, wetting, rocking, fear of the dark or of the unknown and, for older children, smoking. Woodward advises parents to see their children as needing reassurance rather than as simply being naughty or as having been spoiled by nurses. Children need help to relinquish the sickness role and parents need to know how to remain optimistic when talking to their child as well as to relatives, neighbours and friends. As sickness and disability among children are not restricted to disadvantaged groups, these problems have been articulated for a wide range of family situations rather than merely for those where children are in care. However, the difficulties described probably apply with similar force whatever the circumstances.

These studies of separated children in hospitals confirm the personal difficulties posed by return for all parties but also highlight the role of family attitudes and the need for parents to feel involved. While that involvement means delegating caring tasks to nurses and doctors, the formal power of parents, as they perceive it, remains considerable. One can only contrast this with the child-care situations we have described. Let us look next at another sizeable group of returning children, those leaving boarding schools.

Boarding schools

By far the largest group of children, over 100,000, separated for long periods from parents and family are to be found in boarding schools, the focus of the very first project undertaken by the Dartington Research Unit in the 1960s. The public independent schools and the preparatory schools that feed them have long been the subject of plays and novels but, while the isolation and discomforts of their regimes have often been highlighted, the problems of return home which children face have been little explored. In these boarding schools, we found that the pains of separation experienced by pupils and parents were considerable but that the context of separation acted as considerable compensations for children (Lambert and Millham, 1968; Lambert, Millham and Bullock, 1975).

In situations where generations of families have gone away to school and where siblings, cousins and peers undergo the same experiences, the perceived deprivations are less, even though many children are homesick and can be anxious about their families. In addition, their educational career is likely to be status enhancing and generally improves life chances, which help to ease the immediate pains of separation, at least for parents. School regimes have also become more benign and sensitive to the needs and interests of individuals in recent years.

Return for children in public boarding schools is also a group experience, the education is prized and the parents are likely wholly to support the child and school. The children leave and return as valued individuals and parents see themselves as making financial sacrifices on their behalf. Even though formal contacts between child and family during the absence are few, parents have considerable power to influence events by virtue of paying fees; moreover, children know this. This is in sharp contrast to the impotence and feelings of abandonment common among parents of children in care. In addition, the cultural continuities between school and family are likely to be consistent, which makes it relatively easy for children to move from one context to another, just as they will need to do later in life as they pass through Oxbridge, Inns of Courts or prestigious regiments to the professions. Separations and returns are still difficult in terms of personal adjustments but the wider contexts and assumed compensations for making the transitions ameliorate the situation. For these reasons, return is likely to be less difficult for children in public boarding schools than for those in care.

A group more likely to experience considerable return difficulties, however, are those children in residential schools for children with emotional and behavioural difficulties (EBD). Unfortunately, there is very little research evidence on the backgrounds of these pupils and even less on their long-term educational and care careers. What material does exist suggests that many children face problems at home which are every bit as severe and complex as those faced by children in care. On the whole, the schools do not seek to incorporate the child's family effectively into the curriculum or treatment programmes and contacts between parents and children very much follow a half-term, holidays and annual open day model (Upton, Bundy and Speed, 1986). The return problems of these children and their resolutions remain unknown.

Military families

Before drawing final conclusions from the literature, it is important to consider whether return studies of other social situations have anything to offer child-care research. Several occupational groups, such as the armed forces, merchant navy, trawlermen and light-house keepers, experience regular separation from and return to their families and it is interesting to explore how people in these situations cope.

Vivid evidence on the adaptation of families experiencing regular separation and return is found in studies of military personnel. The most extensive is Jolly's, *Military Man, Family Man: Crown Property?* The strength of her analysis is that return is placed in the context of the tensions between the modern family in terms of its structure and functioning and the expectations of the military services. She argues that the paternalism of the armed services in relation to the resolution of family difficulties is no longer appropriate for families with a symmetrical structure, as described by Young and Willmott (1973), or for the dual career families studied by the Rapoports (1977). This highlights a problem that could well affect children in care; namely, how far do we have outdated stereotypes of family structures and parenting roles and are the problems we identify merely common situations exposed by increased social worker scrutiny?

Jolly emphasises in particular the changing roles of fathers in recent years and shows how the military machine fails to acknowledge these by continuing to make demands, such as sudden and prolonged absences, that seriously hinder parenting opportunities. She writes,

> the resentment which many fathers feel in missing continuous contact with their children often surprises them. The young military father, like any other, has absorbed the ideal of 'involved fatherhood' and then seems to be frustrated at every turn when he tries to put this ideal into practice.

Fathers report feeling guilty at being away when children are born and then finding their children unrecognisable when they return. In the light of this situation, it is reasonable to ask how far the return problems faced by children in care and their families are exacerbated by the context and structure of their peculiar situation.

The father's return also poses problems for the family role and power structure. Wives having dealt with everything for several months, have to share roles, some of which they have come to enjoy. Jolly concludes,

> in most households, after an initial period of intensely difficult readjustment, family relationships return to normal. But, for some time, the returning husband remains an outsider. If he lacks the force of personality to demand his share of the decision-making, he becomes little more than a temporary lodger and his status in the family sinks, so does his sense of responsibility to them. In fact, many fathers spend time on leave away from their families, in the company of other servicemen.

This feature has been widely observed among returning war veterans; they find solace among colleagues who have shared their experiences and separate from their family again to solve the problems of return.

The difficulties of return to a family group are well illustrated in other military studies, such as Lodge's *Ginger, You're Barmy* (1962) and Chandler, Bryant and Dunkerley's (1987) work on Naval families. Lodge's pithy opening describes, my first leave was inevitably a disappointment. Three short days in London could not fulfil the expectations that had been built on them in the preceding weeks.

The process of family adjustment that follows a home-coming is long and complex. Jolly shows that for soldiers it begins with the arrival, usually joyful, sometimes emotional, always charged with underlying apprehension. And there is also shyness, some reserve. Jolly writes,

despite all the *macho* talk about what they will do with, or to, their women, when they get home, for more than a few, the first days or even weeks bring sexual problems.

These include reluctance to accept intercourse on the part of the wife and impotence for the husband. Then,

as both partners struggle to create a small space for themselves to begin the psychological readjustment of being together again, arguments, sulking and depression can occur. The family recoils instinctively from the intruder, but guiltily feeling that they should not be doing so. Father, for his part, cannot understand the children's truculence, or his wife's disappointment as her romantic illusions quietly evaporate. He loves his wife and children, he has missed them and, so they say, they've missed him, but they don't seem to show it.

Naturally, reactions vary among families from mild unease to blazing rows or stony silences, until the new way of life - inclusive of the new arrival - is re-established. At some point comes acceptance, as each member of the family stops feeling aggrieved. Rebuilding of the relationship takes place as husband and wife resume social activities as a couple and sex and rows assume more normal, even humdrum proportions.

The merry-go-round of family adjustment to loss and change is virtually continuous as the military posts its men from one location to another and sends them away on unaccompanied missions. As one would expect, the more upheavals a family has lived through, the less it comes to dread them, knowing it has coped and survived in the past, and is mature and open enough to be honest about the difficulties. As Tunstall (1962) shows in his study of trawlermen, some experiences can soften the traumas of separation and return; for instance, children may be pre-socialised for this life-style in education, by community values and by the frequent moves to live with relatives during fathers' absences. Nonetheless, people grow and change and a significant number of families do reach a point where they become tired of coping and compromising and making the best of things.

The return of fathers in well paid jobs to families they love may not appear to have many parallels for children in care. However, we shall see many similarities, for example, in the anxieties preceding the reunion, in the clashes and negotiations about family role and power, in the unease about the returner's secret activities while away, in the importance of the row for re-defining roles and power, in the gap on both sides between expectations and realities and in the slowness of the necessary readjustments. It also questions Rutter's (1975) suggestion that the separation anxieties of children in care are largely due to the disturbed families they come from and return to. Even with auspicious beginnings, return is a long and difficult process for service families of all ranks and as we shall see for children, the problems of return are often resolved by further separations.

Conclusions

This evidence brings to an end our review of the research literature. We have looked not only at child-care studies but also the experience of other social groups. What conclusions can we draw about return as it affects children in care? Initially, it is clear that return is a common experience, affecting nine out of every ten youngsters. It is also complicated, every bit as fraught as separation, a process that has had far greater research scrutiny. It is equally clear from all of the studies that a child's return from care to home and community can only be fully understood in its wider context. This is because return will have been preceded by separation and may be followed by further departures. Hence, the reasons for prior separations and the skill with which they have been managed will be important determinants of return success. A longitudinal perspective on children's care experiences would seem essential for a full appreciation of the re-unification process.

Secondly, although the studies discussed include young people who have returned from care, their main focus is on children's situations once back. Hence, the findings highlight placement sequences and factors associated with successful reunion. Snapshots are provided of prior- and post-return situations with success evaluated on criteria such as whether the placement lasts. As our review has shown, this has been a fruitful approach. For example, new evidence on the high frequency of return from residential settings and the considerable changes that occur in children's families during the child's absence in care have surprised even child-care specialists.

However, there is also a clear need to view children's returns to home and community more in the context of their care experiences and subsequent life-styles. Such a perspective sees family relationships as fluctuating and seeks to accommodate variations over time in children's emotional stability. Thus, some flexibility is introduced to the evaluations of outcomes. A prospective view of children's situations is needed to capture these dynamics and to explore the options open to participants at key moments in return negotiations.

These conclusions suggested to us the benefits of analysing existing longitudinal data further to see how children in care can best be classified to clarify their return experiences. Farmer and Parker, as we saw, found significant differences between care and control cases among children placed home on trial but this approach needs extending to the whole care population. There is also a need to weight the influential factors to see which of those highlighted in the studies have an independent influence on children's successful return from care and its aftermath. Since such an analysis is absent from the studies discussed, we decided to undertake this exercise in addition to our scrutiny of return routes and patterns within representative child-care populations. It will be seen in the methodology chapter that both these exercises form part of our re-examination of child-care research data and of the additional follow-up of the *Lost in Care* cohort.

However, one consequence of the emphasis in the research literature on children once they have gone back is the lack of knowledge about the process of return, its psychological *sequelae* and what it actually feels like to be returned. The negotiations, accommodations and conflicts experienced by children and their families have been acknowledged but little explored. Neither has much consideration been given to the adaptations required from the wider family. Children's adjustment to outside situations, such as peer group, school and community, have also been given scant attention. While we have reasonably comprehensive information on the various return routes from care taken by children and some indications of the problems that young people subsequently face, these other processes remain uncharted and their effects unknown.

There is, therefore, a clear need to explore return in its own right and to examine the variety of adjustments that have to be made by children and families. Such an exercise needs to look wider than just the relationship between child and family, for a youngster's return from care can affect other relationships, such as those between parents and grand-parents or between siblings. The child's behaviour in other contexts, such as school, may also be significant.

The literature review has sought to summarise the research information available about return home as experienced by children in care. At the same time, it has revealed considerable gaps in our knowledge and has suggested fruitful research approaches. In this study, we hope both to extend previous work and tackle issues that have, to date, been little explored. Let us now turn to consider the ways we set about these tasks.

Summary points

1. Many children other than those in care experience return. The main groups are hospitalised children and young people in boarding schools.

2. Research evidence shows that hospitalised children suffer separation and return problems but they are likely to be less severe than for children in care because of greater family stability and clear reasons for the child's absence. Nevertheless, return is difficult for children and families and disturbed behaviour by children following reunion is not uncommon.

3. The periods of separation and return are also considerable for children in boarding schools but are tempered by the cultural context of the experience. The extensive pre-socialisation for departure, the clear and predictable cultural continuities and manifest status enhancement provide compensations. Nevertheless, many EBD children in residential schools probably face similar problems to children in care.

4. Studies of occupations where separation from and return to families is frequent, such as the armed services, show enduring difficulties of readjustment. Family roles and power have to be constantly re-negotiated.

5.   To understand children's returns from care in their wider context and to fill gaps in existing research knowledge, longitudinal and prospective studies are needed both of large cohorts of children and of individual cases as they return home from care.

5. Designing the study

Here we lay out the variety of research approaches employed in our study of reunion. We rely on a re-scrutiny of data on 875 children included in three recently completed studies of children in care. Longitudinal information is available on each child from the point of referral to social services, through the care experience and the child's return to the family. This extensive data is supplemented by an intensive scrutiny of 31 children from 24 families experiencing separation and return. These families have been selected to illustrate the range of problems that can occur during reunion. We hope to identify predictive criteria which will help highlight those children likely to return, when they will go back and the success of the reunion when it takes place. These criteria have been fashioned to aid social workers in their decisions about returning separated children to their families.

We have now set the scene and placed our study of return as experienced by children in care in the context of other research. Clearly, numerous studies have explored aspects of children's return from separation but, as we have noted, few have scrutinised reunion as an issue in its own right.

It will be recalled that we intend to chart the processes and return avenues experienced by children in care for whatever reason and for whatever length of time. This study will also identify children particularly vulnerable to return problems and look carefully at the different households to which children return and the various styles of social work provided. Furthermore, the study seeks to identify predictive factors associated with successful returns and from these to develop guide-lines which will better inform social work practice.

We have undertaken two inter-related studies of return situations. The first study, A, consists of *a retrospective scrutiny of a large number of children returning to home and family from care.* This study is based upon a new data set of 875 children culled from three completed research studies. These comprise; first, the 450 children in our study of the problems of maintaining links between children in care and their families, extended to include a five year follow-up. Secondly, we have included data on the 104 young people who left the Youth Treatment Centres between 1982 and 1985 and, thirdly, Farmer and Parker's information on the 321 children placed with parents or other relatives. Each of these studies, while not specifically focusing on the issue of children returning from care, contains a wealth of material on reunion. For example, the YTC research covers the return of very difficult older adolescents and the *Trials and Tribulations* data provides valuable evidence on younger children restored to their relatives.

Thus, we have longitudinal data on several hundred returns experienced by children and we can examine the problems of individual reunion in the light of children's overall care careers. We will suggest in a later chapter how this new data set has generated evidence about the nature and consequences of return and has identified the predictive factors conducive to the success or failure of any reunion.

The second study, B, involved a *prospective study of a number of 'returning' children* identified in the first exercise as being vulnerable to return difficulties. This study complements the first investigation by examining how those caught up in the return process perceive and contribute to the experience. How, for example, are factors generally associated with return difficulties tackled and, possibly, ameliorated by the individuals concerned? This micro-study has involved 31 children from 24 families in five different local authorities. It also contributes to the identification of those factors which help us understand which type of children are restored to parents and relatives and also which children are successfully reunited.

The two studies

Let us now consider each of the two investigations in greater detail, looking first at the extensive scrutiny of 875 children who returned from care.

Study A: A retrospective scrutiny of 875 children returning to home and family from care

In view of the large amount of data available in recent studies of children in care, we believed that little benefit would have accrued from yet another large scale exploration of children moving through care and returning home. A more fruitful approach was to review the existing material and, where and if necessary, provide supplementary information on those few significant groups of children for whom there was a dearth of information on their 'post-return' experience. For this reason, we extended the follow-up of the 450 children in *Lost in Care* from two years to five. This involved re-interviewing social workers, checking files and, in some cases, seeing the young people themselves.

The extended *Lost in Care* data, the follow-up information on Youth Treatment Centre leavers recently completed at Dartington and Farmer and Parker's *Trials and Tribulations* provide information on most categories of children in care, as the following table confirms.

Table 5.1: Data on the return experience in the three data sets used in Study A

Care Category	Return Information	Lost in Care	Trials and Tribulations	YTC
Short-term care	Who returns	4	8	8
	Outcome	4	4	8
Long-term care	Who returns	4	8	4
	Outcome	8	4	4
After leaving care	Who returns	8	8	4
	outcome	8	8	4

4 = Data Available   8 = Data Not Available

The strength of this approach is that it provides longitudinal data on each child from the point of referral to social services to the return to home or community. It also contains much information on how children settle once back. This material has been prospectively gathered on a range of issues, all by a series of interviews or from care records, and thus yields more extensive and reliable data than could be obtained by a new retrospective scrutiny of case records. Naturally, the emphasis of the present analysis, preoccupied as it is with reunion, is different from the focus of the original work but this proved no deficit and was offset by other gains. Indeed, re-working the data provided a salutary reminder of how frequently under-used is cohort material on children and the lost opportunities such data afford. One criticism might be that it is several years since many of the children left care but it is unlikely that the passage of a few years will significantly alter an experience as fundamental as reunion. Any weaknesses in our approach, therefore, are more than compensated for by the quantity and quality of the material.

The exercise allows us to identify from a large study population issues surrounding the management of return, the problems that families and children experience and what happens over time. It also suggests groups of children particularly vulnerable to return difficulties, identifies factors which predict who goes home at different stages in the return process and, furthermore, enables us to see how successful such reunions are when they take place. These outcomes are explored in the following chapters, Six, Seven and Eight.

Study B: A prospective study of returning children

The study just described provides information only at a general level, relating return outcomes to aspects of the child's care experience and to children's characteristics and backgrounds. Return from care, however, is a long process involving complex interactions between children, siblings, parents, social workers and many other agencies and individuals. We needed, therefore, to scrutinise in detail children as they were prepared for return, as they went back and as, hopefully, they settled in. We have sought to explore what it is like to return after a separation and how it feels to welcome, once again, the child into the family during the subsequent period.

We therefore scrutinised 31 children from 24 families living in five local authorities who were likely to experience reunion. In selecting possible cases, social workers were asked to identify children in care for whom return was a current issue; that is children whom social workers wished and expected to return to their families and where a strategy for reunion had been clearly articulated.

In selecting the intensive cases, we were not trying to gather a random sample but rather to identify children and families who reflected the range of problems presented by children in care and who represented a cross-section of return situations. Thus, the intensive study group includes a range of return situations, such as those being reunited after short and long periods, those experiencing difficulties going home and those restored with relative ease. How was this selection made?

We asked selected social workers to identify children for whom return was becoming an issue. Eighty-six families were put forward. Nevertheless, the time between separation and envisaged reunion varied considerably. Some of the children were arriving back on their doorsteps by the time we were involved while in other cases the restoration was planned for several months hence.

We, therefore, categorised the children into early, intermediate and long-term returners. The *early returners* are children away from home for six months or less, the *intermediate group* have been away for between seven and 24 months with the *long-term children* away two years or more.

Our extensive scrutiny of 875 children returning home from care already indicated that some of the 86 families suggested by social workers had a better chance of seeing their children returned than others and some reunions were more likely to encounter especial difficulties than others. We, therefore, further categorised cases into the following four groups,

i)   Children who would be likely to go home with relative ease.

ii) Children who would be likely to experience some difficulty in getting back.

iii) Children who we felt would not go home despite the social worker's plan.

iv) Children who would probably go home but would subsequently move on.

These four options when crossed with the early, intermediate and long-term returns described above produce 12 possible categories. We selected two families in each category producing 24 who agreed to participate in the study. These families had 31 children who were expected to go home. We were thus rewarded with a group which provided us with a broad picture of the stresses and difficulties surrounding many return situations.

We began the intensive study of the return process immediately after the social worker had identified the child. We then followed the case for 18 months, regularly interviewing parents, children and other relatives as well as social workers and concerned professionals. As we shall see, some of the children rapidly returned home and stayed there, albeit with some difficulty, while for others the period between our initial involvement and the actual return was far more protracted. Indeed, an important finding from this exercise was that, despite the intentions and plans of social workers and the supposed imminence of reunion, more than a third of the 31 families did not see the return of their offspring during the 18 month follow-up period.

Research methods and issues

So much for the two studies. How did we set about the task and what problems did we have to overcome on the way?

Pilot Work

Before embarking on our second look at 875 children in care and our intensive scrutiny of 31 children for whom return was actively under consideration, we undertook a small pilot project involving people from outside child-care who, we felt, could contribute to our understanding of the issue. Members of the armed services, young men returning home from prison custody, a refugee who went back and a war veteran all participated. They helped us identify themes and experiences common to all return situations and highlighted the inherent stresses.

Discovering factors which predict return

A key element of this study is the identification of factors which predict different return outcomes and which will offer guide-lines for social workers planning the reunion of children in care. To do this, different methods were used in the extensive and intensive studies.

In the extensive study, variables statistically associated with the child's return to relatives or with the eventual success of the reunion were identified. However, there was a problem that certain variables were dependent upon others. For example, it is probable that children will be more likely to return if their relationships with relatives are good but we also found that relationships between family members are better when there are few stress factors within the home. We therefore faced the familiar methodological problem of deciding whether either of these variables best explains return patterns and outcomes or whether a combination of both is more useful.

Here, there were further difficulties in that the variables we explored were of four types. Some were categorical, representing groups of children, some were ordinal, measuring issues on a scale from high to low, the third type were nominal, such as whether or not a child returns, and the fourth group were continuous, such as age or attainments. As most multi-variate regression techniques deal only with continuous data, we needed to find an approach which teased out the complex relationships between different types of variable.

We also looked in detail at those children whose return outcomes are different from those suggested by their background characteristics. Some were simply mis-fits, exceptions or false positives, to use the statistical terms, while for others, the unexpected outcome was explicable in terms of some idiosyncratic feature, such as a death or a chance meeting. This latter group we call *outliers*. An examination of outliers is particularly useful in understanding the relationship between variables and the factors that can overcome adverse situations. Moreover, by taking out unusual cases which defied our prognosis and describing them separately, we have been able to discover the real power of our predictive models.

We used different methods to produce predictive criteria from the intensive study. The main source of data was interviews conducted at regular intervals during the return process. These were of two types; structured interviews designed to establish the facts of the case, because there can often be different perceptions about what has actually happened and different interpretations of clients' situations, and in-depth interviews which explore participants' experience of the return process.

The use of interview material collected over time raised two important methodological issues: the consistency of data collection and the reliability of the information, both of which had to be overcome.

Ensuring consistency in the interview material

Initially, we took care that the families participating in the interviews were dealt with consistently. Woods (1986) suggests that research interviews ought to be 'democratic, two-way, informal, free-flowing processes' but, on the other hand, it is important that certain individuals do not distort the picture obtainable from a wider group of respondents. For example, there is a danger that the very articulate will get a better hearing than the verbally limited.

To achieve consistency, we agreed a set of principles to guide our interviews. These covered not only the way in which we engaged with the respondent but also the actual conduct of the interview itself. For example, it was decided that in order to avoid distortion by third parties, only members of the research team would talk to respondents. The pilot work had also taught us that returns can be precipitate and, if we were successfully to capture the full flavour of the process, it would be necessary to see families at significant points as reunion gathers pace. To overcome the danger that certain returning children would capture a disproportionate amount of our interest, we assigned two researchers to each case who shared interview material with each other. These practices, we believe, ensured consistency in the conduct of the interviews and scrutiny of the evidence.

Ensuring reliability of the interview material

Such an approach to consistency also assisted in validating the interview material; after all, we faced the familiar research problem of not knowing whether the information collected was true or typical. This problem is particularly thorny in the social sciences because deception and concealment by respondents are not uncommon and although, as Hammersley and Atkinson (1983) found, a loss of accuracy may be balanced by the insights gained, reliability is still a problem.

It is our experience that distortion is less easy when the interviewer is well-versed in the subject matter. As Whyte (1982) found, the plausibility of accounts can be checked during the interview and, as Little (1990) discovered, deception seldom endures over several meetings or the scrutiny of a group of respondents.

Nonetheless, we have attempted to minimise, where necessary, the confusion that can spring from recollection. Whenever possible, interviews took place near to key moments in the return process. When people were asked to look back over even short periods of time, we attempted to avoid the systematic bias that occurs in long-term recall by using the methods employed by Quinton and Rutter (1988). They recommend,

> .... until the question of experiences, memories and reaction to childhood experiences are better understood, it is preferable to place most weight on discrete events located within broad time periods; to place more weight on clear descriptions of events and relationships rather than generalised recollections and to use the reconstructive nature of memory to locate events within a coherent life-history framework.

Observation of family life

The study of individual cases also benefited from observations of the interaction between family members and, in some instances, the actual return of the child. A considerable amount of discussion about research methods has concentrated on the ways in which researchers can best obtain such data (Giddens, 1976; Denzin, 1970; Filstead, 1970; Hammersley and Atkinson, 1983). Many are at pains to show that the researcher can become a member of the group under observation without affecting its structure, (Becker, 1958; Becker and Geer, 1960). However, in child-care research, it is extremely difficult to be a participant observer and slip unobtrusively into private family moments; nevertheless, the principles and aims of the method had obvious attractions and there was a viable alternative in *non-participant observation* (Woods, 1986).

Non-participant observation can be defined as 'participant observation where the people under scrutiny are aware of the researcher's role'. The researcher may change the dynamics of the group being studied but the effect can be minimised as participants become acquainted with and feel at ease with the stranger.' During this research, considerable time was spent with the families of returning children and we gathered data on the state of the child's home, whether the child had any belongings there and, particularly important, if a bed was available. We also looked at the physical preparation for the child's return, the buying of gifts and redecoration that took place. In addition, we observed the actual return looking at who greeted the child, whether neighbours and friends were involved and so forth. As we shall see, in some cases the return was a marked event with identifiable rites of passage while in others the actual moment of reunion was hard to place as the child gradually re-integrated with the family or drifted back home in an unplanned way.

The analysis of material from the intensive study

The information produced by both the observation of children's returns and the structured and in-depth interviews was used in two ways. Firstly, it contributed to a profile of each individual family and the changes that occurred as the return took place. The experiential evidence provided unique material about respondents' fears, expectations and adaptations, their need to negotiate role and territory, their perceptions of home and their feelings of being returned.

Secondly, both the qualitative and quantitative evidence were used to develop the theoretical perspectives discussed in later chapters. In doing this, we faced the thorny problem of generalising from case studies and the danger of considering only those cases that fit pre-established theories.

We sought theoretical generalisation for our qualitative material in the following way. Initially, we examined the qualitative material for key concepts and themes that were frequently mentioned or observed and constructed typologies. However, as we would expect, there were some ambiguities and these were examined in the light of the context of each case and the significance of the personalities of respondents. For example, misplaced optimism about a child's return can follow from the renewed interest of a parent long absent. We next applied contrasting theoretical perspectives, such as functionalism, conflict theory and also common sense to ensure that all possible explanations of the data were considered. Further checks involved bringing in external judges, including some respondents as well as academic colleagues. For example, a consultant psychiatrist commented on our interpretation of events in individual cases. The procedure seems the most effective way of ensuring rigorous scrutiny of qualitative data.

Episode analysis

One result of this approach was a realisation that there were several stages in the return process. However, long experience of longitudinal research has led us to be wary of identifying clear stages in the lives of children in care or their families as individuals' lives do not fit into neat packages and apparently distinct phases rarely accommodate the experiences of every family member. Indeed, although it became clear that the return process could be broken down into segments each of which was meaningful to the participants, it was more difficult to understand how one part of the reunion led to another. We found that some children or relatives skipped what seemed important stages for others, for example the preparations for the homecoming. Furthermore, a step towards restoration lasting a matter of days for one family could take several months for another.

We therefore needed to find a more fluid schema for analysing and presenting the intensive data. Using a procedure developed for Little's (1990) study of young men in prison, we identified the key episodes in children's returns. An episode is defined as a variable period of time surrounding a particular phase of the reunion. As Lofland and Lofland (1984) point out, episodes are by definition remarkable and dramatic to the participants and, therefore, to the researchers as well. Episode analysis has been used in several disciplines but mainly to make sense of past events. For example, Keegan (1976) describes twelve episodes in the battle of Agincourt. In this study, we have used the method in situations where, in contrast, long-term outcomes were unknown.

Even when used prospectively, the great strengths of the episode analysis adopted for this study are its contribution to our understanding of the meanings and perceptions of the children and their family members over time and its allowing us to wield control over the enormous mass of qualitative data assembled. There are, of course, some deficiencies in this approach; for instance, the reader is often left to fill in the gaps or make the links between the episodes and it does not lead to relatively straightforward, deterministic explanations. Indeed, it demands that the reader keeps a number of competing notions about return simultaneously on the boil.

As we shall see, seven episodes clearly stood out in the information given to us by parents, children, other family members and professional staff. These included the initial entry to care, the separation of child and relative, which inevitably has an influence on the prospects of re-unification, through a honeymoon period after the reunion leading to the rows and negotiations that follow as participants seek a new *modus vivendi.*

Conclusion: Linking the different studies and research techniques

We have now described the two principal elements of the research design; Study A involves a re-analysis of existing sources of data and a further follow-up of the *Lost in Care* cohort and Study B is an intensive study of 24 families and their 31 children expected to experience the reunion of a child from substitute care. It can be seen that this approach covers the most important aspects of return and uses a variety of research methods to investigate them. Concepts such as 'process' and 'career' discussed in the opening chapter and the aims of the research as described have both guided the fashioning of this research approach.

As a child's care career involves individuals making choices between available options and adapting to particular situations, the decision to use this perspective as a way of understanding aspects of the lives of children in care suggested a need for both quantitative and qualitative approaches. We have discussed the analysis of the information obtained and shown how quantitative and qualitative material has been rigorously evaluated, although the actual techniques have obviously differed in each case. Similarly, hypotheses developed from individual cases have been tested and refined by applying them to the full study group. Thus, we hope that this methodology is innovative in that qualitative and quantitative approaches have been linked in a fruitful way at each stage of the research (Bullock, Little and Millham, 1992). We also hope that a good foundation has been laid for further confirmatory research studies.

Let us now discuss the findings of our endeavours. In the following two chapters we describe the extensive study, looking at patterns of return and their various outcomes. As we shall see, this results in sets of indicators which predict who goes home at successive stages in the return process and the success of such reunions when they occur.

Summary points

1. To achieve the aims of the study, two inter-related studies of the return situation were undertaken. The first is a retrospective scrutiny of children returning from care to home and family. The second is a prospective study of individual cases as they return.

2. For the first study a new data set of 875 children was constructed from existing research data. In the second, 31 cases were selected to be representative of children's return experiences.

3. Each study faced special problems. Statistical approaches had to be developed to identify factors which predict return success and procedures for ensuring the consistency and reliability of interview material had to be fashioned. Observation data had also to be incorporated.

4. The qualitative material was analysed using episode analysis and several techniques have been fashioned to ensure reliability of data collected.

5. As quantitative and qualitative research material has been rigorously evaluated and as emerging hypotheses have been applied across both study groups, the methodology seeks to combine qualitative and quantitative approaches in a fruitful and complementary way.

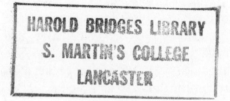

6. Patterns of return

Here we explore how long children stay in care and the destinations of those who leave. While the majority swiftly return to the family, some do not. We distinguish between early, intermediate and late returners, identifying their characteristics and the complexity of their reunions. But return rarely means reunion with families which are unchanged in the interim. Not only are many children's care situations unstable but on return they have to accommodate major changes within their households. These changes greatly complicate reunion.

We have already seen that most children who are looked after by a local authority and are separated from their families return home after the rift. We have also established the principle that if preventative work fails and the child has to be removed from the family, every effort should be made to ensure a swift reunion. We shall also see that some children go home more rapidly than others and with more success. In this chapter, we shall scrutinise which children go back to the family, how their returns are organised and when they are reunited. In later chapters, we shall identify those factors which best predict who will return, when they are likely to go back and, particularly important, how successful are these reunions.

Here, we are using new data from 875 children drawn from three sources; *Lost in Care, Trials and Tribulations* and Dartington's recent research into leavers from Youth Treatment Centres. The strengths and weaknesses of this approach have been explored already, however it should be stressed that at no point do we offer data on all 875 children; this would be misleading as only certain children in the cohort are relevant to particular issues. For example, the Youth Treatment Centre leavers can only reveal the reunion problems of difficult adolescents long separated from home. Nevertheless, the study group of 875 children, variously used, will provide an authoritative national picture.

We begin with a re-examination of the 450 children first studied in our scrutiny of the problems of maintaining family links. Later, we include the 104 young people followed up in our retrospective study of YTC graduates; this provides a wealth of information about the return experiences of older children who have left care. When we turn to the success of children's returns, the 321 placements with parents studied by Farmer and Parker make an important contribution.

General return patterns

It will be recalled that at the outset we have defined return as going home to live, but the restoration does not necessarily involve the same home or the same relatives involved in the departure. Moreover, some of those returning also leave care but, as we shall see, not all of those leaving care go home. In the case of the 450 children from *Lost in Care* we have looked at those returns which were intended to last; thus weekend leaves and placements preliminary to the final reunion have been excluded. Because of the greater fluidity in the careers of older adolescents, we have been more generous in our interpretation of their reunions. They include brief periods at home, the shortest of which was a stay of four days.

Who then are the children going home to relatives and when do they go back? Initially, it is encouraging to report that most children looked after by a local authority enjoy a reunion with parents and most go home quickly. Indeed, social workers can draw considerable comfort from our findings as many of the children we scrutinised clearly benefited from social services' intervention which provided short periods of respite care and an uncomplicated restoration of offspring to relatives. In the frequently voiced criticisms of social work, it is rarely acknowledged that the majority of children and families greatly benefit from the help provided and are appreciative of the service offered.

Of the 450 children looked after in five local authorities in 1980, 78% returned to relatives during a five year follow-up period. In addition, there was a small proportion of children, 4%, who came into care but never left home. Most of the separated children were reunited very swiftly with their families, the majority (71% of these returners) going back within six months of separation and a third of them being restored within a week. These findings suggest that the length of time a child is accommodated or in care is significant in predicting when and where eventual return takes place.

As we can see from the following diagram, if we categorise children according to the length of time they are looked after, we find different proportions of children returning and different rates of children leaving substitute care in each of the selected time periods. Of the 450 children coming into care, 58% of possible returners were reunited with relatives within six months of entry. However, of those still in care and away from home at two years, less than a third went home in the following three years.

Figure 1: Number of children returning in different time periods

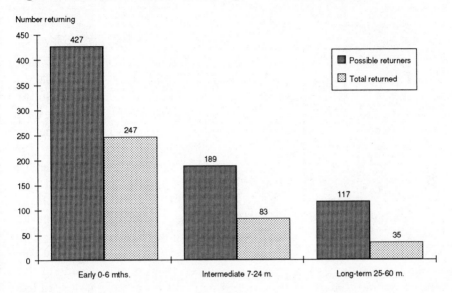

We can also see from the following diagram that return is not always concomitant with leaving care or local authority accommodation. Although 88% of the 247 children returning within six months of separation also left care, nearly a half (41%) of these reunited between seven and twenty four months remained subject to a care order.

There were, however, 81 (18%) of the 450 *Lost in Care* children who never returned during the five year period. What happened to them? When our longitudinal scrutiny came to an end, half (48%) were still being looked after, most in relatively stable placements, but hopes for the child's reunion with family were entertained in only one-third of cases. Of those who had left care, a third had been adopted or remained with foster parents but the rest had graduated to living independently, were in youth custody or in residential education. All of these children experienced tenuous links with natural parents and the wider family but social workers felt there was little prospect of future reunion.

Figure 2: Proportion of children returning who also leave care in different time periods

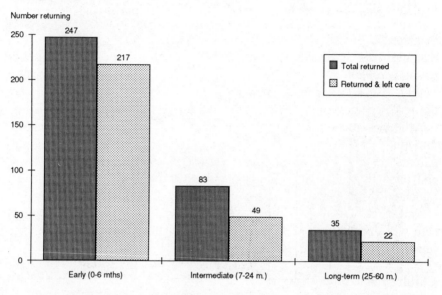

Number returning

However, when we look at the post-care careers of the older adolescents leaving Youth Treatment Centres, we found that social workers' gloomy prognoses were ill-founded. Over two-thirds (70%) of the YTC graduates were reunited with relatives despite severe problems in late adolescence and after prolonged separations, most having been away from home well in excess of two years. Indeed, the YTC returners included in their number a few children who were homeless on entry to security; the reunion took place in a completely new household with relatives with whom they had never lived before.

Thus, we can use this data to calculate how many of the 450 children looked after in the *Lost in Care* study eventually went home. Three-hundred and forty-nine children were reunited at least once within five years. For another 39 children still in care after five years, social workers had hopes of reunion in a third of cases but, as professionals can be over cautious, we would predict that half of the 39 children, that is 19, eventually went back to relatives. Of the remaining 42 children who left care but who had not been home since separation, our YTC data on the adolescents leaving the Centres would suggest that 25 (60%) would return.

Thus, we can predict that 393 (87%) of the 450 children coming into care are likely to be restored to their families, for a short period at least.

These findings should not surprise us if we recollect the normal family experience of children. A glance at the general household survey reveals that, for 16-24 year olds, the likelihood of marriage is much greater than that of living independently and that by far the greatest proportion of young people in this age group remain at home and dependent upon their family. The conclusions to draw from this analysis are clear and reinforce the research messages which helped inform recent child-care legislation. For the great majority of children in care, family members are the most important resources available to social workers, for it is parents, grand-parents, siblings and wider family who are likely to provide continuing and unconditional support. It may be true that some children in care reluctantly go back to relatives because they have nobody else. Nevertheless, whether professionals like it or not, almost all children in care will eventually be restored to their family and our perspectives and interventions need to accommodate that fact.

Children who do not return

As we shall see, children returning do not form a homogeneous group; they enjoy a variety of experiences. However, before we consider the different routes back home, it is helpful to look at those who never returned to relatives during our five year follow-up. It will be recalled that all but 81 of the 450 *Lost in Care* children were returned to relatives at some point. We separated the above 81 who did not return into two groups; 39 who were still being looked after by social services after five years and 42 who left care for destinations other than home.

The situation of those still in care five years on is difficult to assess. In only a quarter of cases (26%) did the social worker entertain any hope of a return home to parents or relatives although a third were aged 6-10 years and two-fifths (38%) 11-15 years. Nonetheless, most (72%) of those being looked after who had not returned home were in a foster family when our scrutiny ceased, while the rest were living in residential settings.

The situation of the 42 children who left care but did not return home is more clear-cut. Eight of this group left care within two years of entry with the remaining 34 waiting three to five years before departure. A third of the 42 leavers, 13 children, were adopted and another three left care but remained with the foster parents who had sheltered them for some years.

We might assume that the future of these children is relatively secure. However, the situation of the other 26 leavers is less satisfactory. As we can see from Table 6.1, most left care to various forms of independence, although a handful moved on to youth custody or residential education. All of these children enjoyed poor links with their natural parents and return home was not envisaged in the near future.

Table 6.1: The destination of children who left care but did not return

Situation on leaving	Left care 0-24 mths	Left care 25-60 mths	Total
Adopted/with foster parent	N=4	N=12	N=16
Lodgings/bedsit	0	7	7
Sheltered accommodation	0	7	7
Youth custody	2	3	5
Own flat/house	0	4	4
Residential education	2	0	2
Hostel	0	1	1
TOTAL	8	34	42

The return experiences of children in care

So much for those who fail to find a niche at home, what about those who are reunited? As we have seen, children returning to relatives do not form a homogeneous group and present problems of categorisation. Indeed, we might classify the children in a variety of ways. Initially, we have found that children are not always reunited with the same household from which they departed and it is helpful to understand what happens at home during their absence. Secondly, we might categorise returning children according to other characteristics, for example their age, gender and race or by the reasons they were originally separated. Thirdly, children going back to relatives enjoy a variety of experiences in care during their separation from home, for example in type of placement, frequency of movement and so forth. Do children returning from foster care fare better or worse than those going back after residential care?

After considering all these options, we have found that one variable, the length of time the child is looked after, subsumes and overrides other categories. We found it most useful to distinguish between *early returners* who go back to relatives within six months of entry to care; *intermediate returners* going home between seven and 24 months after entry; and *long-term returners* who are separated for two or more years prior to reunion. This latter group includes young people who return several years after leaving care. Let us look at the situations and different return experiences of these three groups.

Early returners

Six months after entry to care, 247 children in our *Lost in Care* cohort had returned to relatives. This number comprised 217 children who left care on the day of reunion and 30 children who were placed beforehand with relatives. What were the circumstances of these children?

Less than a quarter (23%) of these children had previously been looked after by social services, a proportion far lower than for the intermediate and long-term returners discussed below. This finding cannot be explained by the age of the children as there were similar proportions of young and old returners. Equal numbers of the 247 *early returners* were boys and girls which again sets this group apart from those being reunited later on.

Most of the children accommodated were in care because of a temporary breakdown at home. Parental illness is the most common reason for care and is the primary factor in nearly a third (31%) of cases. The behaviour of the child is also important, being the principal reason for one-fifth (19%) of *early returners'* being looked after, although only one in twenty of this group was delinquent. Given these characteristics, it is not surprising that nearly three-quarters of those going home swiftly are accommodated voluntarily. These findings contrast with other groups of returning children.

Table 6.2: The primary reason for early returners coming into care

Primary reason for being in care;	%
Breakdown in family care due to;	
mental illness of parent	13
physical illness of parent	18
neglect or abuse	20
abandoned/deserted	7
unwilling/unable to care	17
other family problems	5
Behaviour of child	19
TOTAL	N=247

The situation of these *early returners* becomes clearer when we look at their family circumstances. Nearly half (48%) of the children came from single-parent families and less than two-thirds (63%) had a mother and father who were married to each other at the time of their birth. These findings are surprising even in the context of the particularly disadvantaged situation of children looked after by local authorities. Three-quarters of the 247 *early returners* came from households which were dependent upon social security. Whilst these data highlight the type of problems which lead to a child's coming into care or being accommodated, we are also reminded that none, not even poverty, forms barriers to reunion.

Having looked at the background characteristics, what happens at home once the child is away being looked after? In the *Lost in Care* study we found that children in care, particularly those under the age of 11 on entry, are likely to experience a major change in the membership of the household to which they belong. What of those who leave care quickly, who opens the door in welcome?

As we can see from table 6.3, 199 (81%) of the 247 short-stay children are reunited with the same adult family members from whom they were initially separated but the idealised nuclear family of natural mother and father only features in two-fifths (39%) of cases. Indeed, step situations feature in 12% of early returns.

For the remaining 48 children, some of whom have been separated from home for only a few weeks, the reunion is with different adults, although most go back to the same households. As the following table illustrates, for those returning to different adults, it is much more likely that step-parents, relatives or others outside of the nuclear family will assume some responsibility for the child's care. These 'other adults' appear in over two-fifths (42%) of all separations and returns.

The tables suggest considerable fluidity in families with members leaving during the child's absence and new adults arriving. However, as the following pages reveal, family re-constitution does not prove to be a barrier to the success of a child's return, although family reconstitution may have been significant in propelling the child into care. Indeed, in some instances, such as in the 12 situations where a child returned home after father's departure, changes in the household membership may be the very essence of a fruitful reunion.

Table 6.3: The family structure of the 199 early returners going back to an unchanged household

Adult membership of family	Children leaving care	Children placed at home or with relatives	Total %
Natural mother only	N=85	N=1	43%
Natural mother & father	72	6	39%
Natural mother & step-father	22	2	12%
Natural father only	7	2	5%
Other relatives	2	0	1%
TOTAL	N=188	N=11	N=199

Table 6.4: The patterns of movement of the 48 early returners going back to a changed household

Child separated from:	Child returned to:
Lone natural mother (11)	Mother & step-father (5) Mother & father (1) Mother & relatives (1) Father & step-mother (1) Relatives (2) Father alone (1)
Natural mother & father (15)	Mother alone (12) Mother & step-father (1) Relatives (2)
Natural mother & step-father (8)	Mother alone (3) Father & step-mother (1) Father alone (1) Relatives (3)
Lone father (2)	Mother & father (1) Mother alone (1)
Other relatives (7)	Mother alone (4) Mother & step-father (2) Father & step-mother (1)
Other adults* (5)	Natural mother (3) Father alone (1) Mother & step-father (1)

* Private fostering arrangements (N=3); friend of child (N=1);
   boyfriend of child (N=1)

Summary of adults in the home to which the child returned

Natural mother alone	N=24
Natural mother & father	2
Natural mother & step-father	9
Father alone	4
Father & step-mother	2
Other relatives	7
TOTAL	48

So much for changes within the family during the care sojourn. What happens to the child during the absence from home? Probably because of their short stays, we generally find *early returners* and their families attract considerable social work attention during the separation. This is evident from the high proportion (87%) of plans which encourage family links and the higher than average parental participation in the care process. Over half (54%) of those swiftly reunited with relatives are first placed with siblings, once again illustrating the inclusive nature of the social work intervention with such children.

The placement patterns of the 247 *early returners* reveal the equal contribution made by residential and foster care settings and that the use of either type of placement need not hinder a child's swift reunion. The following diagram describes the major routes taken by children returning home within six months of entry to care. Whilst a slightly higher number of children are first placed in foster care and considerably more experience such a placement during their sojourn in care, residential settings are significant and feature in two of the three principal routes home. This pathway accounts for 97 of the 247 children reunited. Indeed, residential placements feature in over half (51%) of the early return careers.

To summarise: the *early returners* are largely made up of children whose families were temporarily unable to care for them. Their disadvantage is self-evident yet there is a clear commitment from social workers to keep parents on the scene and to re-unite children with the family as soon as possible. During the child's absence from home little has changed except that in a fifth (19%) of cases there has been the arrival of a new parenting figure.

Figure 3: The career routes of the 247 children returning home within six months of coming into care (First three placements only)

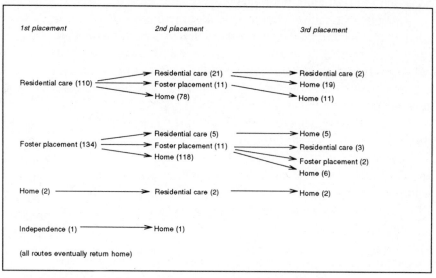

1st placement | 2nd placement | 3rd placement

Residential care (110) → Residential care (21) → Residential care (2)
→ Foster placement (11) → Home (19)
→ Home (78) → Home (11)

Foster placement (134) → Residential care (5) → Home (5)
→ Foster placement (11) → Residential care (3)
→ Home (118) → Foster placement (2)
Home (6)

Home (2) → Residential care (2) → Home (2)

Independence (1) → Home (1)

(all routes eventually return home)

Intermediate returners

We have seen that a high proportion of children return swiftly to relatives after coming into care or being accommodated. What of those who fail to get home quickly? Let us now turn to those reunited with relatives between seven and 24 months after entering care, i.e *the intermediate returners.* Of the original 450 children first scrutinised in *Lost in Care,* 222 were still being looked after six months on. Some of these 222 children, 33 in all, were living at home and remained with relatives throughout the follow-up period. Of the remaining 189 children, 83 returned during the following 18 months, 43 leaving care and 40 going home without a change of legal status. What were the circumstances of these 83 *intermediate returners,* particularly their characteristics, family structures and care experiences?

In contrast to the short-stay children just discussed, the *intermediate returners* are predominantly adolescents who display behaviour difficulties and for many there is an identifiable family problem to which the child makes a considerable contribution. Nearly two-thirds (65%) were aged 12 years or more on entry to care and three-fifths were boys.

The nature of the problems they posed is reflected both in their legal status (over two-fifths (43%) were committed to care) and in the lack of a family focus in the social work intervention.

Although, the family circumstances of the *intermediate returners* were noticeably less fragmented than those found for children who left care early, nonetheless, two-fifths of those going back to relatives after between seven and 24 months had single-parent families and the amount of turbulence within families during the child's absence in care was still considerable.

However, the most noticeable aspect of the families of the *intermediate returners* was the variability and sometimes poor quality of relationships between relatives and children. In only two-fifths (39%) of cases did social workers feel that the relationships between mother and child was warm, accepting and affectionate and for as many as a fifth (22%) of the 83 children, they felt the mother was downright rejecting. The commitment of other family members to each other was similarly uncertain.

The different circumstances of the *intermediate returners* was reflected in their care experience. The emphasis upon family links was less than we found for the *early returners* and over a third (36%) of these children had restrictions on access to parents imposed at some point in the care sojourn. Levels of parental participation in the care process were also reduced and there was a more exclusive attitude taken by social workers towards family members. Indeed, in going home, many of these *intermediate returners* defied the prognoses of social workers who originally gave over a third of the 83 children only a slight hope of reunion within two years of entry to care.

The children's ages and circumstances were reflected in placement patterns. Only a quarter were admitted to care or local authority accommodation with siblings and fewer still were placed with their brothers or sisters. Residential care was much more common among this group with three-quarters (74%) being placed in such settings on entry to care and 86% experiencing such a placement during the time they were looked after. This contrasts noticeably with the 47% of *intermediate returners* placed in foster care at some stage in their care career.

Obviously, *intermediate returners* are children whose problems have weakened family bonds. However, despite social workers being hesitant in keeping parents and other relatives involved in the child's life, there is little to suggest that reunion, even for this recalcitrant group, is out of the question. Eventually, the child grows out of his or her problems or social workers exhaust viable placements and re-unification follows, often as a child's 16th or 18th birthday present!

So much for the *intermediate returners.* Let us now turn to the child who stays long in care prior to reunion.

Long-term returners

After two years had elapsed, 170 out of the original 450 *Lost in Care* children originally admitted to care were still there. Of these 170 children, 53 were placed with relatives and stayed with them for the remainder of the study period. This left 117 children, of whom only 35 returned to relatives at some point in the following three years: 22 left care for home and another 13 went back but the care order remained in force.

However, before looking at these children, we have also to mention another group of *long-term returners,* those who go back home at some later point after leaving care. It will be recalled that there were 81 children who never returned home during our five year follow-up including 42 who left care for destinations other than home. With the aid of data from our Youth Treatment Centre study we would suggest that 35 of these 81 children eventually return to live with relatives. Thus, adding these to the other group of 35 returners just discussed, the total number of *long-term returners* in the *Lost in Care* cohort is likely to be 70 children.

Let us look at the first group of 35 *long-term returners* whose re-unification took place from or in care. We have found more boys than girls in this group, indeed three-quarters (74%) are male. They are also older than the children previously considered, with none being under six on entry to care and nearly two-thirds (63%) being 12 years or more, although just under a third (31%) had been in care on a previous occasion. Given their age and gender, it is not surprising to find that the child's behaviour was a contributory factor to the decision to enter care in a half (48%) of cases and that two-thirds (65%) of the 35 children had been convicted or cautioned for delinquency.

However, the situation of these children is more complicated than that of the *intermediate returners* and we find that neglect and/or abuse was a contributory factor for nearly two-fifths (37%) of the 35 children coming into care and the principal reason for a quarter (26%) of their admissions. Moreover, many of the less severe problems such as single-parenthood and poverty which press upon *early returners* equally afflict these *long-term returners*. The chances of family reunion, given this sad combination of child, family and wider social problems, were always low.

Nonetheless, social workers had been optimistic about reunion during these children's long stay in care. On the day they came into care or were accommodated, social workers had entertained strong hopes for restoration within two years for over four-fifths (86%) of these 35 children. Furthermore, despite the prolonged separation, usually in residential settings, social workers had encouraged family links in two-thirds (63%) of these situations and regular contact between mother and child was maintained in four-fifths of cases.

Now we turn to the situation of the other group of 35 *long-term returners*. These are children who leave care for destinations other than home, but who are reunited with their families several months later. To predict their likely circumstances, we looked at the 68 Youth Treatment Centre graduates who, during the two years in which they were under research scrutiny, had the opportunity to go home. How many of these young people does this exercise suggest eventually went back and what was their situation?

Despite prolonged periods of living away from home, including a mean length of stay at the Youth Treatment Centres of 2.1 years, over two-thirds (N=47) of the 68 young people studied in this research were reunited with relatives at some point during the two years after which they left the Centres. More boys returned home than girls and, as might be expected with those in late adolescence, there was considerable movement in and out of the family and widespread use of siblings, friends and extended kinship networks for temporary shelter. Indeed, the importance of the family, even for those long separated and in late adolescence, should not be under-estimated.

The YTC evidence suggests four points relevant to the reunion of adolescents long in care. Firstly, when a child goes home as an adolescent or as a young adult, the return is different from that of other children in care. The reunion is more likely to be negotiated informally between relatives and offspring even in defiance of social work decisions. Once at home, few entertain the belief that reunion implies permanent residence. Indeed, the 47 young people reunited with home after leaving the Youth Treatment Centre enjoyed between them 63 sojourns at home. A quarter of these returns lasted three months or less but the same proportion were over a year in duration. As we shall see in the following chapter, a termination of the reunion for these young people seldom indicated its failure.

Secondly, because of the extended periods of separation experienced by *long-term returners,* the level of household and family change taking place during the child's absence is far higher than that recorded for our other return groups. Nearly half (47%) of the 47 young people going home did so to a home with different family members than on the day of departure. As we can see from the following table, the comings and goings within families are quite complicated and, for older children, are more likely to involve wider family members. We also found that some children without a home on arrival at the Youth Treatment Centre later re-discover family members and the study included one young man who had been adopted returning to his natural mother.

Thirdly, the perceptions of family members of the child's situation and the child's view of the family prove important in decisions about reunion in late adolescence. The willingness of parents, wider family or friends to offer accommodation, financial and emotional support smooths the way for re-unification and can triumph even when the circumstances at the point of separation were dire. Indeed, given changed priorities and the passing of time, relatives frequently accept the young person as being well adjusted and viable even when his or her current situation is less than satisfactory. For example, young adults' drugs problems and girls' unplanned pregnancies can evoke a tolerant, even positive, response from parents who turned away from similar problems during the early adolescence of the child.

Fourthly, young adults' reunions are often co-incidental with a change in other circumstances. More stable home circumstances can lead to better relationships with others outside of the home and improve job prospects. Just as crises have a knock-on effect and cluster around collapse, so can small successes engender stability and acceptance.

This is not to suggest that long-term returns should be viewed optimistically. Many are fraught with conflict and some occur in the absence of any alternative for the young person; living with an abusing father can be better than the shelter of a cardboard box, especially in the short-term. The Youth Treatment Centre data have proved a useful supplement to our re-scrutiny of the *Lost in Care* material in that they remind us first of the special nature of long-term reunions, particularly those occurring after the young person has left care, and, secondly, of the enduring significance of the family for even the most disadvantaged among them.

Table 6.5: The patterns of movement of 22 long-term returners going back to a changed household composition

Child separated from:	Child returning to:
Natural mother (6)	Mother & step-father (4)
	Relatives (2)
Father alone (1)	Relatives (1)
Mother & father (3)	Mother (1)
	Relatives (2)
Mother & step-father (7)	Mother (5)
	Mother & step-father (1)
	Mother & father (1)
Father & step-mother (1)	Step-mother (1)
Other + (4)	Mother* (2)
	Mother & step-father (1)
	Relatives (1)

* Child moved to mother and grandparent in one case.
\+ No home (N=1); foster parents (N=2); adoptive parents (N=1).

Summary of adults in the home to which the child returned

Natural mother	N=8
Natural father	0
Natural mother & father	1
Mother & step-father	6
Other relatives	6
Step-mother	1
TOTAL	22

Conclusions

We now have a much clearer view of what restoration means for children. We have found several groups returning in a range of situations. Some have been long in care, others have barely been away. Some are adolescents whose personal perspectives greatly influence events, others are delivered in a pram no doubt bemused by the world changing around them. There is no single message which could improve or speed up the returns of all children in care, although to accept that most will go back certainly changes our view of their circumstances.

For the *long-term returners,* those whose length of stay in substitute care exceeds two years before reunion, family and child behaviour problems are complicated by the vicissitudes of separation, including placement breakdown and poor family links. Some of these *long-term returners* leave care for destinations other than home, only to be reunited with family several years later. The pull of home is considerable, even after the passage of years and the family remains a resource for hard-pressed social workers attempting to manage return.

Return is *not* the stereotype of the separated child being returned to a nuclear family of natural mother and father or a return to the *status quo ante.* Indeed, over two-thirds (68%) of children restored within six months of entry to care do so to lone parents or to step-parents and one-fifth (19%) go back to family members different from those at the point of separation. The longer relatives and children are apart, the greater the chance of household re-constitution, this being a feature in almost half (47%) of the long-term reunions. We also note that relatives, grand-parents, aunts, uncles and siblings play an important role in return situations.

We have found that not all children going home leave care and that not all children leaving care go home. There is a complexity to return which means that when we attempt to predict who returns several groups need to be considered. In this chapter, a range of possible indicators of a child's likely restoration have been suggested and factors which do *not* seem to be important predictors of reunion discussed.

It is noticeable that certain characteristics of the children, their age, sex and ethnicity are of little use in determining whether reunion takes place. Many children are restored to households which would score badly on any scale of poverty but deprivation does not form a barrier to reunion. Nor can we say that children's placement experience hinders their way home as there are several routes back to relatives. The fact that these factors, either alone or in combination, seem unimportant comes as something of a surprise.

However, going home, as we learned from our glance at the considerable literature which deals with reunion, is only part of the negotiations. We have seen that many children looked after by local authorities are swiftly restored to relatives but interesting questions remain. Do the young people stay at home and is a lengthy duration in the bosom of the family to be regarded as a success? Let us now, in the next chapter, explore how children fare once they have been reunited with their families.

Summary points

1. During the five years which follow entry to care, 78% of children go home to relatives, some several times. Indeed, most (71%) returners go back within six months of separation and a third are back home before a week has elapsed.

2. Some children leave care for destinations other than home. However, a scrutiny of their subsequent careers reveals that they, too, are likely to be reunited. By including these late returners in our calculations, we find that 87% of children in care are eventually restored to their families.

3. Of the 450 children followed up, 81 did not return, including 39 who were still being looked after five years after entry and 42 who left for destinations other than home. The situation of many of these children is less than satisfactory.

4. Three groups of returning children have been identified; *early returners, intermediate returners* and *long-term returners*. Early returners, those going home within six months of entry to care, are largely younger children whose families are temporarily unable to care for them. Their disadvantage is little assuaged during separation.

5. *Intermediate returners* (going home between 7 and 24 months after entry to care) included children whose problems have weakened family bonds. Older adolescents predominate with two-thirds (65%) aged 12 years or more on entry to care and three-fifths were boys.

6. *Long-term returners* (going back between two and five years after entry to care) comprise two groups; first those being reunited from a substitute care placement and, second, those going home several motnhs after leaving care.

7. Children vulnerable to problems after return

Here we explore the success of the child's reunion although success is here defined, somewhat simply, as remaining at home and avoiding a precipitate breakdown. Nearly three-quarters of children seem to settle back successfully on return, although some groups of children are particularly vulnerable. These are children whose placements break down in the short term, children who repeatedly re-enter care, some adolescents seeking independence and homeless, skill-less young people. The outcomes for different groups of children as they return are highlighted.

How many reunions could be considered a success, indeed, what do we view as a satisfactory return? Is it warmth and reciprocity clustered around the family hearth or is it the chilly nod of recognition, the grunt from behind the newspaper or the tepid supper left in the oven?

To answer these questions, we shall look at the outcomes for the 247 *early returners* identified from the *Lost in Care* study. For the success of intermediate and long-term returns, we shall consider the Youth Treatment Centre data as these give the most reliable information available on outcome. But, given the small number of returns in the YTC study and the unusual qualities of the children involved, we have also incorporated the evidence on the 321 children placed with parents and other relatives first scrutinised by Farmer and Parker. We have been fortunate in being able to re-analyse their comprehensive data.

What is a successful return?

Before embarking on a scrutiny of what happens to children once back home, it is helpful to define what we mean by a 'successful' return. As we shall see in following chapters, outcomes of returns are difficult to assess. Many children may elude the gaze of social workers, who then feel confident that the child is safely integrated once more into the family. In recent years, several scandals in child-care have demonstrated the sad consequences of such assumptions. In fact, as we shall see, reunions can be the source of considerable disharmony and dissatisfaction, even when the child remains under the parental roof. Moreover, as we saw in the previous chapter, many adolescents go back precipitately.

Choosing the baseline against which outcomes are judged is also important. Should we compare the child's progress back at home with the situation prior to the child's being looked after or with the circumstances on the day of reunion? We have also to consider the perspectives entertained by the various participants in the restoration, looking not only at the social worker's assessment but also the views of relatives and of the child. Selecting an appropriate time period for following up the outcomes experienced by those returning from care is also important. An apparently satisfactory scenario at six months can become a nightmare a little later on, while success in one area may not be matched in others.

The following measures of return success have been used in this re-analysis of existing sources of data. When dealing with large sample groups and using complex statistical procedures, it is most practical to use unequivocal outcome measures. In assessing the success of younger children, therefore, we used the following general criterion: 'did the child stay at home during the 12 months following the restoration?' However, as we were specifically looking for returns which broke down, each case was examined individually so that children moving between relatives anxious to provide respite care or leaving a household in a planned way could be excluded from the analysis. But, in fact, none of the younger children met these latter requirements; all either continued satisfactorily at home or the return broke down in some way.

As we have already seen, any assessment of success of reunions enjoyed by older adolescents poses additional problems. For example, the majority of the 47 young people who went home during the first two years after departure from a Youth Treatment Centre subsequently moved on. But our research information showed that this did not always mean that the young person or the family had 'failed'; many of the leavers graduate to more independent situations, secure in the knowledge that further retreats to the family are possible if plans go awry. Other youngsters returned with low expectations of life at home, simply seeking shelter or temporary protection from a harsher life on the streets. If these young people move on after a few weeks, can we really judge the restoration as a failure? A sense of success or failure in reunion depends largely on what you expect from the *rapprochement*.

We, therefore, chose to assess the success of older adolescents' returns using further qualifying dimensions. As above, we looked at whether or not the young person moved on after going home but we then applied a stricter test of whether the period at home led to a breakdown in relationships between relative and child. Breakdown was defined as the young person wishing to stay at home but where relatives discouraged and terminated such an arrangement.

Finally, for all children included in this study, young and old, we have been able to make use of additional information, namely the researchers' independent assessments of long-term outcomes on each individual child. Taking into account a range of indicators concerning the family, the child and the social worker's perspective, placements at home have been classified on an ordinal scale from positive to negative. In two of the studies used in this analysis, the researchers' assessments had been checked independently by a social worker and psychiatrist.

So much for the way in which we estimate the success or otherwise of returns in this quantitative exercise. What did we find? First let us take an overall look at the success rates of children returning home after a separation.

The general picture

First impressions on re-analysing the data are most encouraging. The majority of children going home stay there; moreover, their stays are tranquil and unremarkable. If we measure success as the proportion of children who stay for 12 months following reunion, we find 72% of the *early returners* stayed put. In other words, 28% broke down prematurely. As we have seen, some of those going back to parents also leave care at the point of reunion whilst others stay officially in care and parental responsibility remains with social services. As the table 7.1 illustrates, the success rates for both groups are similar.

How do these findings compare with the success rates of substitute placements for children in care generally? If we look at the proportion of placement breakdowns experienced by the *Lost in Care* children who returned home early, we find an overall rate of 26%. Further comparative evidence is provided by Rowe, Hundleby and Garnett's (1989) study which asked whether placements lasted 'as long as was needed'. They found an overall rate of 62% for placement stability although again this was higher for the under fives (75%) and lower for adolescents (56%). Thus, a success rate of 72% for those returning early to home after separation and its converse, a breakdown rate of 28%, can be viewed in a favourable light.

Table 7.1: The success of early returns; children leaving care compared with children placed home while in care

	Nature of returns		
Success of return	*Leaving care*	*In care*	*TOTAL*
Success	73%	67%	72%
Failure	27%	33%	28%
TOTAL	N=218	N=30	N=247

The situation of those who stay longer in care, that is the *intermediate* and *long-term returners* identified in the previous chapter, is more complex. Our follow-up of the Youth Treatment Centre graduates would suggest that the majority (70%) of adolescents and young adults going home subsequently move on within two years. However, many of these moves took place in a planned, amicable way and less than a third (30%) of those leaving as young adults could be said to have experienced a breakdown in relationships at home within two years of leaving the Centres. Indeed, having tasted the fruits of independence and finding them unexpectedly sour, a quarter (24%) of the young people subsequently went back to relatives for a second time.

The complexities surrounding the return of adolescents is further amplified when we look more closely at the situation of the 47 YTC graduates who went home within two years of leaving the Centres. Ten went on to live independently whilst maintaining good relationships with home. Three of these children subsequently returned once more, including one girl whose mother ejected her after a row, then allowed her home five days later and greatly helped her move to a council flat several months later. Twelve young people left home because of a remand or sentence to custody. Nevertheless, even here parents were anxious to have their offspring back. Indeed, in four of these 12 cases, the young person did return again after a sojourn in custody. There was also one child who moved between parents during our follow-up scrutiny. Thus, 33 young people moved on after their initial return home but could not be said to have experienced a breakdown in home relations. Indeed, these adolescents seem to display much of the footloose behaviour, the comings and goings, characteristic of young people generally.

However, in another ten cases the situation was less tranquil. In five families, the family had simply endured enough and decided to evict their offspring, although it was clear that the young person wanted to stay. In the final five instances, the young person's departure to custody was the last straw in a line of disappointments and frustrations for the parent and further reunions were thought to be unlikely.

We have also been able to look at the outcomes for children who went home in the *Trials and Tribulations* study. This information crosses our categories of *early, intermediate* and *long-term returners*. Nonetheless, the results are also encouraging, although as with previous evidence there are some caveats and qualifications to the good news. Of the abused and vulnerable children, mostly under 11 years of age, who returned in Farmer and Parker's study, only a third (37%) subsequently moved and independent assessments suggested a positive outcome for the child in over two-fifths (44%) of cases with less than 15% being viewed as detrimental. The rate of movement among children who need control, most of whom are teenagers, is higher; half of such returners leave within the two-year follow-up period, but once again independent assessors gave a positive view of events in 42% of reunions.

All of these findings show that a high proportion of children return to relatives and establish a relatively stable relationship. Indeed, we have found that, even where children have been separated from parents in quite desperate circumstances or where links between family members have been allowed quickly to wither, restorations have had a positive outcome in the sense that the reunion endured. Furthermore, the most serious of abuse cases can have positive outcomes if the perpetrator of the abuse is removed and the family receives added support from social workers.

Children vulnerable to return problems

Whilst we have been gladdened by the smaller than expected proportion of return breakdowns, we are nonetheless concerned for certain children who fail to find a niche back at home. A scrutiny of the *early, intermediate* and *long-term* returns described in the previous chapter revealed four groups who could have benefited from additional oversight after re-unification. However, as vulnerability to difficulties following return does not coincide with the length of separation, there is an overlapping of categories.

The first group of concern are the children who return home after a short separation only to break down within 12 months of reunion. We have called these *short-term breakdowns*. While three-fifths (62%) of these children are later successfully reunited with relatives, some of the remainder become long-stay cases. In addition, some *early* and *intermediate returners* continue to move in and out of care and form our second vulnerable group of *oscillators*.

Among the *intermediate* and *long-term returners* described in Chapter Seven, two groups also concern us. Initially, there is a need to anchor those older adolescents who return to relatives many times in their attempts to establish autonomy. This group of *adolescents seeking independence* remains unsettled and much more could be done for them by accepting that the young person will use the family, however unsuitable, as a base for forays into independence.

The final group, however, needs much more than a change in attitude. We have identified in the outcomes of the *long-term returners* a small group of adolescents who not only fail to find succour in the family home but who are also bereft of the social skills which enable them to survive alone. For them, a breakdown of the return is likely to result in homelessness and social isolation and will almost certainly be accompanied by unemployment and difficulty in gaining adequate social security benefit. It is for this reason that we have named this group *homeless, skill-less adolescents*. As we describe below, of greatest concern to us is the finding that these youngsters are frequently precipitately pushed towards independence or are reunited with families without sufficient preparation.

As we have seen, the four vulnerable groups are not coincidental to the return categories identified in the previous chapter. Some children are susceptible to return problems no matter how long or short their separation from home. The following table illustrates the overlap between the various groups.

Table 7.2: Groups vulnerable to return problems

Return group	Short-term breakdown	Oscillator	Adolescents seeking independence	Homeless skill-less adolescents
Early returner	4	4		
Intermediate returner		4	4	
Long-term returner			4	4

If we apply the findings from our scrutiny to national statistics, how many children each year fall into the four vulnerable groups just identified?   Of the 30,000 admissions to care or local authority accommodation in England per annum, we have found that, within six months, over half, about 16,500 will be reunited with relatives. Most of these returning children settle without any apparent difficulty but over a quarter, that is about 4,700, will experience further problems and will move back into a substitute care placement. While the majority of these are eventually successfully reunited with families, those that are not either become *long-stay* care cases, which we identified as highly vulnerable in *Lost in Care,* or *oscillators*, as we have just described. When applied to a national picture, we estimate that more than 1,700 children annually join these groups. We know from the research literature that the increasing instability of such children's careers makes their long-term prognosis poor.   We need to know much more about them and their swift identification should be a social work priority.

How many children are there in the final two vulnerable groups, that is *adolescents seeking independence* and *homeless, skill-less young people?* For these calculations we have used the numbers of young people discharged after extended periods of being looked after. Our estimates are complicated by the fact that some young people leaving care do not immediately go home and others will have been living at home for several months before the care order is discharged. Nonetheless, every year some 9,300 children leave care having been the responsibility of the local authority for two or more years.   The following figure indicates the numbers who will experience difficulties after departure and for whom continued support and provision seem essential.   We have based our calculations on the numbers leaving care each year after extended care sojourns.

Figure 4: The estimated number of long-term care graduates who go home, seek independence from a home-base or experience a further breakdown in relations with relatives

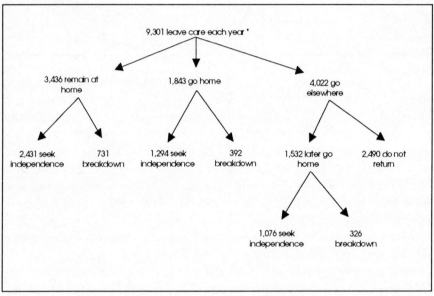

Summary: 4,783 move on from home including 3,334 who seek independence from a relatively stable home-base and 1,449 who break down at home and experience difficulties elsewhere

* leave care after being in care two years.

As we can see, over a third (37%) of the 9,301 graduates are at home on the day the child ceases to be looked after. Another fifth leave care or local authority accommodation to live with a relative. As such, 5,279 of those leaving care are at home on the day they graduate leaving 4,022 who depart for other destinations. However, as we saw in the previous chapter, nearly two-fifths (38%) of young people leaving care from home are, in fact, reunited with relatives during the following two years.

In total, therefore, we find 6,811 long-stay children eventually restored home. The table indicates that 4,783 of these returners subsequently move on. Included in this group are 1,449 young people whose reunion ended in breakdown and who fail to establish social and family relationships, job skills or any security in the outside world. We thus conclude that of the

9,000 *long-term* care graduates each year, about 3,300 eventually achieve reunion and a secure place at home but over 1,400 join the ranks of *homeless, skill-less* young people who cannot go home and also fail to find a niche elsewhere. It is not surprising that Stein and Carey (1986) in their scrutiny of children leaving care found such a high number of young people swiftly joining the transient populations of the inner cities.

To summarise, while most children in care going home do so with relative ease, evidence from our studies of *short* and *long-stay* cases indicates that over 11,000 each year experience significant return problems. Most of these are adolescents but many are young and the disruption of failed restoration is, for them, particularly acute. Indeed, one of the aims of this study will be to more easily identify these vulnerable children early on in the care process so that resources can be more successfully deployed to help them.

The circumstances of children vulnerable to return problems

So much for national trends among children returning home after a separation in local authority accommodation. Let us now look at the situation of the four groups we have identified as particularly vulnerable to problems after reunion. These are *early returners* who fail in reunion and quickly move back into a substitute placement; *oscillators* who shift uneasily between home and care situations several times; *adolescents seeking independence* from a home base and, finally, the *homeless, skill-less young people* who are wanted neither at home nor by others in the outside world.

As in the previous chapter, we shall focus on three aspects of children's circumstances. Firstly, we examine their personal characteristics, their age and gender. Secondly, we scrutinise their family situations, for example, the quality of relationships at home. Thirdly, we look back at the child's care experience, the frequency and duration of separations, the placements experienced and his or her links with the family during absence from home. We begin with the *short-term breakdowns*, that is those children who returned to relatives within six months of separation only to come back into care during the following year.

Short-term breakdowns

Whilst aspects of the child's family, their personal characteristics and different types of social work intervention can be used effectively to predict which of the *early returners* went home, the same variables prove to be of less use in selecting which arrangements broke down. Indeed, it is remarkable how similar are those children who went home swiftly and smoothly to those who experienced problems. On many dimensions they are identical. Thus, the characteristics of the failed returners are very much the characteristics of the *early returners* previously described.

It will be recalled that 69 of the 247 *early returners* experienced a short-term breakdown. The majority (57%) of those having return problems were male, three-quarters (75%) had been received into care under voluntary arrangements and over two-fifths (45%) came from single-parent families. Yet none of these characteristics distinguishes a child suffering short-term breakdown at home from one who returns without difficulty.

Few differentiating factors of *short-term breakdowns* are apparent from an examination of the family structure. Again, we find that this vulnerable group has not suffered unusually high rates of family re-constitution and that over half go back to a lone mother and two-fifths are reunited with both natural parents. In fact, a much higher proportion of those going home 'on trial' to the same relatives break down when compared with those placed with new family members. Neither is there a pattern to the 13 short-term breakdowns who were restored to a different family structure. Clearly, a change in family membership need not imperil the success of a child's return, at least in the short-term.

However, the reasons for the child being looked after as well as the arguments advanced for reunion do seem to be more closely linked to success or failure on return. Only 10% of the *short-term breakdowns* had been admitted to care because of neglect or abuse, suggesting that children returned in such circumstances are well prepared and supported by social workers and by others during restoration. Possibly, the sad and public consequences of professional error in these cases increase social work zeal. If we turn to the principal reasons given for the restoration, it is children going back to previously ill parents, children returning to initially reluctant and ambivalent parents and delinquent young people who predominate among those who break down on return.

Previously, we have emphasised the importance of family links when the child is absent in care. However, all but three of the 69 *short-term breakdowns* enjoyed regular contact with the natural mother and access had been restricted in only a quarter (28%) of cases. Indeed, many relatives who had faced severe restriction on access to their children during the short period of substitute care subsequently welcomed their offspring home and displayed no further problems. Such a finding does not call into question the value of maintaining links between family and absent child but suggests that regular contact, in itself, cannot solve the problem. Obviously, the damage done by isolation is not so extreme in these short-stay cases as it would be for those children who linger long in care.

Table 7.3: Principal reasons given for the short-term breakdowns' return

Reasons for return	*%*
Family illness ends	35
Reluctant parents resume care	28
Child's behaviour improves	26
Reduced risk of neglect/abuse	7
Family problems improve	4
TOTAL	N=69

Our data would suggest, therefore, that once the child is back home she or he is likely to stay, even in situations when children have been separated from parents in desperate circumstances or when social workers have failed to sustain regular contact between children and families. However, as we shall see in subsequent chapters, the home circumstances of many such youngsters may be less than satisfactory and, having lost their children once in difficult and stigmatising situations, many parents are reluctant to lose them again.

To summarise, the first of our four groups vulnerable to return problems, the *short-term breakdowns*, share many of the characteristics of the *early returners* described in the previous chapter. They tend to be younger children accommodated by a local authority under voluntary arrangements although there are also recalcitrant adolescents who pose problems for parents before, during and after the separation. There is nothing remarkable about the care experience of *short-term breakdowns*, indeed social workers' efforts on the family's behalf is often exemplary. However, when we look in the following chapter at the way adverse factors cluster in particular situations, we may be more successful in predicting which *early returners* become *short-term breakdowns*.

Oscillators

Of the 69 children experiencing a short-term breakdown after reunion with relatives, 43 went back to their families for a second time and settled down. However, the remaining 26 young people failed to find a niche at home during the follow-up period. Six simply stayed in a substitute placement after the failed reunion and never went home again but most oscillated between residential care, foster homes and moved back unsuccessfully to live with relatives several times. Although small in number, these are the children who concern us most. What are their characteristics?

The group of *oscillators* in this study consists of several types of very vulnerable children. Two-fifths are adolescents aged 12 years or more on entry to care but a quarter were infants aged two years or less. Most (80%) of the children had been voluntarily looked after but nearly all of the committals came into care under emergency proceedings. The social work focus was upon the whole family in just over a half (55%) of cases but on the child only for the rest. Thus, contrast rather than similarity characterises those children who oscillate. All they seem to have in common is their failure to settle.

The *oscillators* clearly engender some anxiety on the part of social workers. Although there was no opposition to the reunion in 70% of cases, reservations were expressed prior to one-fifth of their first restoration. Moreover, in nearly half (45%) of these first returns the social worker expected the child to come back into a substitute care placement.

These findings lead us to conclude that, if we are to predict which *early returners* will be vulnerable to problems at home, it will be more fruitful to categorise the children by other means, for example age or reason for entry to care. Indeed, we shall see in the following chapter, when we do this with the cohort first described in *Trials and Tribulations,* our efforts are rewarded.

Adolescents seeking independence

So much for the *early returners* who meet difficulties at home. What about those long looked after and their reunion problems? It will be recalled that two groups of *long-term returners* enjoy a less than tranquil restoration. The first comprises adolescents who move on from home, secure in the knowledge that relatives will have them back. The second, which we discuss shortly, experience a breakdown in relationships at home and have difficulty in establishing an alternative base.

As we described in the previous chapter, 47 young people from the YTC cohort returned to live with relatives during our follow-up and 33 of these eventually moved on. Let us compare their characteristics and experiences with the 14 children who stayed with relatives.

Initially, it is found that the young women move on with greater alacrity than the young men, reflecting the increased likelihood of the girls setting up their own homes. The younger leavers moved on more often than older leavers but statistical comparisons proved inconclusive. Other features, such as the young person's ethnic background or social class do not differentiate between *long-term returners* who stay with relatives and those who move on.

Because of their problematic behaviour, all of these children have experienced long periods of separation, intensive treatment and are reunited with families which are under stress. More important for predicting success on return than stress factors within the family, however, is the view of the young person's situation taken by adult relatives. A powerful indicator of success, more important in many cases than the prognosis of professionals, were the perspectives of close family members; if they felt that their offspring was doing well and was well adjusted to family expectations, then the young person was more likely to stay after return. Indeed, all but one of the 22 leavers failing to match family aspirations moved on after return.

What happens when the young person is at home; does this influence his or her propensity to move on? Clearly, many young people remain with and are dependent upon their families because they find it difficult to fashion an independent life elsewhere. However, this characteristic can be a two-edged sword when poor survival skills outside the home lead to tensions within it. As we shall see, an imbalance between dependence on and independence from relatives contributes towards instability following reunion for *long-term returners*.

Young people with poor survival skills outside the family home were more likely to move on after reunion with relatives. These children comprise a doubly disadvantaged group who leave home and yet are ill-equipped to live independently. We also found that those who move are less likely to hold down a job and are more likely to be offenders, although some of the delinquents are reluctantly separated from the family by a remand to custody.

To summarise, our findings suggest that *long-term returners* separate into two groups; the first seeks independence from a relatively sound home base in the knowledge that respite is available if and when problems occur. The second, however, does badly at home and is not expected to do well away from home. Let us now explore the circumstances of this latter group which comprises the 10 young people whose relationships with relatives broke down when they moved out of the family home.

Homeless, skill-less adolescents

Breakdown at home for *long-term returners* is associated with many of the same personal and care characteristics which predict those adolescents prone to move after reunion. However, levels of contact between parent and child during the separation were sparse for those young people leaving home under a cloud. Indeed, the relationships between family and offspring before separation were generally very poor and many of the *long-term returners* experiencing a breakdown in relationships at home originally left extremely stressful situations.

It is clear that the aftermath of severe difficulties at home can take many years to overcome. This is evidenced by the finding that all ten of the young people concerned had been referred to child guidance when young, compared with less than half (47%) of those enjoying more tranquil family situations. Indeed, a multi-variate analysis of the relationship between children's backgrounds and their present situations shows that past difficulties are inextricably linked to relatives' current abilities to provide financial and emotional support, the failure of which is also linked to return breakdown.

These long-term negative continuities conspire not only to bring a premature end to the young person's restoration but also cause considerable problems while he or she is away from home. Those whose return ends in a breakdown of relationships at home usually have a poor capacity to make effective lasting relationships with people outside it. This, in turn, affects their abilities to get a job or to stay in employment. Indeed, none of the ten leavers experiencing a breakdown was ever employed. None entertained the idea of further education or training. They were also more likely to move into temporary living situations, such as lodgings or squats, and, whilst the support of statutory agencies is essential, lacking the skills and persistence to go and ask, they often failed to harness the help they needed. Neither is this sad group highly delinquent; indeed, a few minor offences would at least attract the notice and support of social services or probation. But, what is really worrying about the ten leavers who experienced an acrimonious return and subsequent breakdown is that they are much younger on restoration than those whose reunion ends more satisfactorily.

Conclusions

In this chapter we have highlighted those children who are vulnerable to return problems. However, this scrutiny also reveals that many children are swiftly and successfully reunited, confirming the continuities in the lives of children in care. Most of these continuities are positive and they ease the swift return of the majority of separated children in care and ensure the eventual reunion of most others. It is evidently difficult to break the continuum of family life.

These continuities in family life suggest an early reunion whenever possible and, indeed, we have found that many children go back with few complications. Neither the Scylla of an abusing relative nor a Charybdis of new family problems threaten the swift and successful return of 22,000 children every year, a major contribution to the welfare of vulnerable children and their families which is often overlooked. For these, social services provide successful and important respite care. For several thousand other youngsters, positive continuities also encourage reunions, for living with relatives is the norm even where poverty and family dislocation make it a painful experience. Like Odysseus, many children are delayed on their return journey, although the detention is seldom as pleasant as Calypso's home. But, as in the classical legend, these children in care eventually get back.

However, some 11,000 children every year experience return problems, some more severe than others. The *oscillators* in care and the *homeless, skill-less adolescents,* bereft of any support, should provoke the most anxiety. Unfortunately, as they are few in number and unremarkable other than in their poor care experiences, these high-risk young people are difficult to spot and can drift by unnoticed.

The breakdown rates for early returners are similar to those in other child-care placements. The rates of movement among adolescents and young adults are much greater than for the younger children scrutinised and, whilst much of this has been found to be a healthy pursuit of independence, it is helpful to compare these figures for children graduating from care with those for the general population of young people, the majority of whom, it will be recalled, live at home with parents.

We have also witnessed the negative continuities which affect the child's life. We have seen that there are changes in the family situation of children in care during separation but we have rarely witnessed great improvements in their circumstances. Indeed, it is noticeable that the majority of disadvantages, such as poverty, unemployment, financial and housing problems, parental rows and poor child-care persist throughout the care careers of young people and things did not improve much when they were reunited with their families.

Some negative continuities, however, hinder a child's progress home or lead to a failure of return if it occurs. Once again, we have found these outcomes are largely consequent upon the quality of family relationships. The relatives have to like the child and the child has to like the relatives. Such factors are not altered by separation and they probably change little over time. If the parents are reluctant to have the child at the point of separation, they are likely to be equally reticent when efforts are made at reunion. What then can social workers do?

As we shall see in the following chapters, giving the child a role, building his or her place and finding a niche in the family identity undoubtedly helps. If the adult relatives can be convinced that the child is a part of their world and is behaving normally when measured against their own standards, then both return and a positive outcome are more likely. This is not an easy situation for social workers to influence but such a strategy might be pursued with greater zeal if we all accepted that the great majority of children separated from their parents will go home, sooner or later, for better or for worse. Nevertheless, there are great advantages in identifying those prone to return problems, not in order to scant the support of those who are more resilient but to intensify social work support for those who are not. We shall see that there are many opportunities to pin-point the children vulnerable to return problems. In the following chapter we will identify factors which help predict the success of restorations. As we shall see, many of these are in the direct control of social workers, for example family involvement and, for adolescents, the need to provide unambiguous future plans.

Summary points

1. Clear outcome measures have been devised to meet the requirements of the complex statistical procedures used. For the younger children we asked 'did the child stay at home in the 12 months following the restoration?' Given the fluidity of older adolescents' lives, we looked more specifically for breakdown.

2. Several groups of children are vulnerable to return problems. Among the *short-term returners*, two groups are of concern. There are short-term breakdowns who come back into care after return but settle successfully second time around. *Oscillators*, on the other hand, move between substitute care placements and relatives several times.

3. The intermediate and long-term returners also comprise children who do not settle at home. Firstly, there are adolescents seeking independence. They use the home as a base for forays into independence. There is, however, a further group of adolescents who not only fail to find a niche at home but who also lack the social skills to establish a stable alternative. These *homeless, skill-less adolescents* should cause considerable concern.

4. Of the 30,000 admissions to care per annum, over half, about 16,500, are returned to relatives and most settle without any apparent difficulty. This represents a considerable contribution by social services to the welfare of deprived families.

5. However, each year there are also some 11,000 children going home who fail to find stability. Of particular concern are the 1,700 children who annually join the ranks of the *oscillators* and the 1,500 *homeless, skill-less* youngsters.

8. Predicting return outcomes

In this chapter we lay out those factors which best predict which children go home and when they return. We explore the ways in which these factors differ for particular groups of children in care. In addition those factors which correlate with a successful return are indicated and case studies are provided which demonstrate how an exception regarding reunion can prove the rule.

In the preceding two chapters, we have explored the general patterns of children returning home from care and identified the different groups among them; we have also highlighted those who are vulnerable to problems after reunion. From our re-analysis of the data set of 875 children, it was clear that several variables were associated with different return outcomes, such as who goes home and the success of these reunions.

In this chapter, we take this analysis a step forward by identifying those variables which best predict return outcomes. What is the value of such predictive exercises and what do they add to the evidence previously described? Principally, we have chosen to predict outcomes for particular groups of children because the procedure gives focus and salience to the most important of the indicators described in the preceding chapters.

For example, we have found that over twenty variables are statistically associated with a child's early reunion, that is within six months of separation. But these variables are diverse and include the type of placement experienced by the child, whether or not the child is delinquent and the mother's feelings for her absent offspring. It would be difficult for a social worker to accommodate and plan in all of these areas, especially when a change of strategy on one front can easily impede progress on another.

Our predictive exercises have involved a type of multi-variate analysis which selects two, three or, at most, four variables which, in combination, best predict a particular outcome. This group of indicators would make a significant contribution to a social worker's understanding of a child's progress even if they were used to the exclusion of all others. As such, we are able to weight the relative contribution of different aspects of the family situation to the child's future.

By predicting outcomes in this way, we are also able to see how factors cluster. As we have been repeatedly reminded in this study, it is not one risk factor which reduces a child's chances of reunion or of success when returned but several factors in combination. These may, in turn, be offset by protective factors which increase the likelihood of positive outcomes. The way in which indicators react with each other is evident from our predictions.

We also feel that the selection of predictive factors takes forward our knowledge on children's care careers. The statistical exercises we have used to make a prognosis are common in medical research and are *de rigueur* for insurance companies seeking accurate calculations of risk. Their application to meeting the needs of deprived children, in contrast, is much less developed.

There are, however, weaknesses in the predictive exercises. There is a danger that results will be misinterpreted. The prediction is never 100% right: indeed, there are several 'false negatives' and 'false positives' and *outliers* who defy the prognoses. It would be wrong to send a child home or blindly to accept that everything would be rosy in the post-return period on the basis of a few indicators highlighted by this study as being important. The aim has not been to diminish any aspects of the management of children's reunions with home or to reduce professional judgements to that of a check-list but to provide for social workers guidelines which can reliably be taken into account when making decisions about each child's restoration. Hopefully, they will provide an *aide-mémoire*, with the additional advantage that such predictive exercises can be easily and swiftly applied.

In this chapter we summarise the results of our predictive exercises. They are described in more detail in Appendix A. We deal separately with two sets of outcomes; first, whether or not particular groups of children will go home and, second, the likely success of any reunion. For each outcome, we describe the general factors which can be taken into account when planning for all children in care. We then look at the groups of variables which are helpful in understanding outcomes for specific groups of children. Finally, we also introduce two case studies, chosen because they defied our predictions and took an opposite course. Let us begin with the first group of outcomes and make an attempt to forecast who will go home.

Predicting the likelihood of return

General themes

In each of the categories of returning children scrutinised, it is certain aspects of the family situation which are most useful in distinguishing between those who go back and those who do not. The stress factors within the family home, the way in which family members view the child and the level of contact between them and the absent child during separation have all been found to influence rates of restoration at different stages in the care career.

Clearly, families suffering multiple problems find it difficult to find room for a returning child or to maintain regular and meaningful contact. Nonetheless, in our multi-variate analysis, although family stress factors were important, they made little independent contribution to the child's chances of reunion, particularly for the younger child. Thus, individual barriers to re-unification can be overcome.

We have found consistent evidence across all groups which links the quality of relationships between relatives and offspring to the likelihood of the child's return. If the relationship between parents and child is strong, particularly between mother and child, the chance of return increases. More importantly, in the case of those long separated from their family, we have found that when the child, as measured against the child's and parents' own standards, is well adjusted and well adapted, then he or she will likely be restored even if family circumstances suggest a contrary outcome.

Of course, many of these family variables are linked to the level of contact between relatives and child during separation. The evidence gathered in this second look at data on 875 children reinforces the messages of *Lost in Care*, that keeping the family involved, keeping siblings together whenever possible and in regular contact with each other when it is not, making sure that relatives visit, phone and write to their absent offspring will all help to ensure a rapid reunion. Moreover, whilst some older adolescents go back despite enjoying poor family links during prolonged separation, as we shall see, the success of their restorations is often adversely affected.

How important a contribution does the social worker make? The ways in which the professional perceives the case and its likely outcome has the greatest influence early on in the care career of younger children. Thus, we found that the reasons for the child's entry to care, the different types of social work intervention, including the attitude taken towards family links, and the care experience itself all influenced whether or not a child went home. However, the care careers of very difficult and disturbed adolescents show that, with increased age, the young person will go back to relatives sometimes in spite of the professional view. These findings hold good even when family circumstances are taken into account.

It is also helpful to remember those factors which were not found to be associated with return. For example, poverty does not appear to be a barrier to reunion nor does family re-constitution. We should also be aware that considerable numbers of children go back home despite adverse circumstances. For instance, we have seen that half of those suffering neglect or abuse prior to being looked after are restored to the family within six months and a similar proportion experiencing a breakdown in their physical and/or emotional care also enjoy a swift reunion.

To summarise, there are several factors which seem to be important in all return situations and which influence the likelihood of children's returns, no matter how long they have been separated. Three factors, in particular, are associated with a likelihood of a child's reunion.

1. There are relatively few stress factors within the family (in the context of children in care).

2. The social work plan is 'inclusive' (ie. the family have maintained a caring role and have been involved in decisions).

3. The family relationships as assessed (using the factors described in Appendix B) are of a relatively high quality.

Early returners

So much for the general factors that are helpful in making return decisions about all children in care. Let us now consider which indicators best predict whether or not children in care will return home quickly after their separation. It will be recalled that we defined *early returners* as those children who go back to parents within six months of coming into care or being accommodated. As the full analysis described in Appendix A describes, there were several variables closely associated with return within six months of entry to care but three in combination proved the most cogent. These were:

1.   That the child enjoys regular contact with family members during his or her absence from home.

2.   That the social worker encourages family links with the absent child.

3.   That the child's separation is arranged on a voluntary basis.

Thus, a child who has regular contact with parents during separation in care, has these links encouraged by social workers and lives away under voluntary rather than compulsory arrangements has a much higher chance of reunion than had contrary situations existed. The expected odds of return given this model and this combination of events are 3.4 to 1.

The significance of these three indicators emerged from an analysis of those 391 children in the *Lost in Care* cohort on whom there was adequate evidence about the child's family experience. Those cases where knowledge was lacking or where the child never left home were excluded.

Of the 391 qualifying for the multi-variate analysis, none who experienced irregular contact with mother *and* had family links discouraged by the social worker *and* were compulsorily committed to care returned to relatives within six months of entry. However, there were 14 *outliers* who, as we saw in Chapter Five, despite having two of these adverse features, were eventually reunited with kin because of extraordinary or unpredictable events. If we remove from the multi-variate analysis these 14 children who would not normally have returned, we find that the odds of a reunion taking place, given the selected criteria, then rise to over 4 to 1.

To summarise, we can see that some benign decisions affecting the chances of reunion can actually be made before the child enters care. Making voluntary arrangements, that is in the use of local authority accommodation as specified in the *Children Act* 1989, by explaining to parents how they can keep in touch with their child and seeking their involvement in future plans, all encourage a speedy reunion, especially if such strategies inform the separation interlude. These findings are also a reminder of the difficulties that can occur if a contrary plan is pursued, that is using a court order to remove the child, if parental access is restricted during separation and if their participation in the care task is minimal. The longer the child stays in care, the more detrimental these factors become.

Intermediate returners

What of those children who fail to get home quickly? Some will become *intermediate returners,* those going back to relatives seven to twenty-four months after coming into a substitute care situation. The multi-variate analysis of this group revealed several factors which were associated with reunion during this time period. Three variables in combination proved a very powerful predictor of a child becoming an *intermediate returner.* These were:

1. There is no history of abuse and/or serious neglect at the time of the child's separation.

2. The child has no siblings or, if there are siblings, they are separated from one another during the child's absence from home.

3. Relatives of the child (especially parents) participate in care decisions.

A child enjoying all three of the identified factors is more than five times as likely to return to relatives between seven and twenty-four months after entry to care than a child displaying different characteristics.

Two of the variables selected by the multi-variate analysis are self explanatory but the contribution of a child's placement with siblings deserves further elaboration. The power of this variable stems from the proportion of half-brothers and half-sisters in this group who go home, leaving their siblings in care. Very often this reflects the changed circumstances of one parent who is able after this length of time to take home 'his' or 'her' child but remains reluctant to take on the fruits of other unions. Anxious to rehabilitate at least one child, social workers will often, in these circumstances, separate brothers and sisters.

These findings are a reminder of how adverse factors, such as the separation of siblings, need not obviate the reunion of parents and offspring. Moreover, even where original plans drift, the importance of keeping relatives involved in decisions about the child is again emphasised. The situation at home may rapidly change and, by keeping key participants involved, reunion can be achieved as soon as is possible and not just when care plans run out of steam. Neither should we lose sight of positive aspects of the case, such as the absence of abuse and/or neglect. The three factors were arrived at by analysing the circumstances of 189 children on whom there was sufficient data to make an accurate prognosis. Only three children from two families defied all three predictors and returned to relatives during the seven to twenty-four month period and there were no children meeting all of the specified criteria who failed to return. We shall describe two of the three unusual cases, Melanie and Michelle, below. Naturally, as the number of exceptional cases was small, there were few *outliers* and the exclusion of these from the statistical calculations made only a marginal difference to the power of the predictor; leaving them out increases the odds of predicting return to 5.5 to 1.

We have now looked at the factors associated with the restoration of early and *intermediate returners* who are all back home within two years of entry to care. For some children, however, reunion is considerably delayed; what factors predict return for this long-term group?

Long-term returners

At this late stage in the care career, heterogeneity in those that linger in care becomes very marked. Therefore, we looked separately at those *long-term returners* who were reunited during or at the end of the care sojourn and those who left care for destinations other than home but who went home later. Let us look first at those prodigals being reunited directly from a substitute care placement.

The multi-variate analysis confirmed the findings described earlier that the return of children long in care is more influenced by the child and family situation than by aspects of social work intervention. After careful scrutiny of the evidence, we concluded that the following three variables in combination made the best predictors of return during the two to five year period:

1. Mother is the main provider of the child's emotional support.

2. The child is a boy.

3. The family receives income support from the DSS.

The statistical calculations showed that, in the long-term, boys belonging to poor families which included the natural mother were 4.7 times more likely to go back to parents than children displaying other characteristics.

It will be recalled that some of the *long-term returners* who left care for destinations other than home subsequently lived with their families.

Can we predict on the day of their departure from care whether or not they will eventually be reunited with relatives?

The multi-variate analysis revealed that, for these children, there was no combination of indicators which best predicted reunion. Instead, we found that either of two variables proved good independent predictors of return for such young people. Firstly, a question asked at the moment of departure 'where does the young person refer to as home?' provides a relatively simple way of discovering whether or not he or she will return; if the answer is the home of relatives then the chances of reunion are greatly increased. If it is elsewhere, then *rapprochement* with the natural family is unlikely.

Secondly, the quality of family relationships is also significant. In our studies of extremely difficult and disturbed young people, we attempted to measure the depth and significance of relationships between relatives and children long absent in care. Described in Appendix B, this instrument identifies the likelihood of reunion in situations where family links have been weakened by prolonged separation and the stresses of adolescent behaviour. The general message from this exercise is that we should not underestimate the sense of belonging young people feel for relatives and *vice-versa*. Members of inadequate, chaotic, abusing and delinquent families mean much more to each other than we often credit. Moreover, however long the young person has been away, unless there are clear social work reasons to take a contrary course, we should not abandon the nurturing of family links, the visits, the telephone calls and the exchange of photographs described in our previous studies.

Cases which defy our predictions

We have attempted in our multi-variate analysis to highlight those factors which will help professionals in their decisions about the return of children previously absent in care. The statistical models presented represent the best mathematical fit possible but they are not, by any means, fool-proof. As we shall see in subsequent chapters, qualitative factors must be taken into account; moreover several cases defied the predictions of our multi-variate analysis.

We shall now describe two of the *outlier* cases, that is exceptional cases where the failure to predict the outcome is explicable in terms of idiosyncratic factors or events. Such examples reveal the vicissitudes in the lives of children in care which cannot be built into statistical models used to predict their future life chances. The two children are sisters called Melanie and Michelle. They looked extremely unlikely to return, even in the long-term, but despite our prognosis that restoration was unlikely during the two years after they were first accommodated, they were reunited with their father after twelve months.

Melanie and Michelle, a case study

Melanie was eight years old when she was first separated along with her sister, Michelle, who was two years younger. The children were accommodated under voluntary arrangements with their half-sisters, Karen and Kim, who were aged four and two years. If we look back at the circumstances which led to the children's being accommodated with the local authority, we find that the family structure is rather complicated.

The older children Melanie and Michelle were abandoned by their mother, exhausted by years of making do and rows with Gary, her shattered, listless husband who was as disorganised and unreliable as the mobile fish and chip van he occasionally drove. Indeed, both Gary and the van were well known in the local community for their immobility.

With the departure of his wife, the absence of rows and disputes and with two children to look after, the gloom lifted and Gary pressed himself into action. The 'fryer' was wondrously re-assembled from its parts once scattered between bedroom, bathroom and garden. With the help of a neighbour, the tyres were inflated and, phantom like, the van lifted from the pile of bricks on which it had rested. It emerged resplendent from the garage; 'Gary's Grill and Fry-up' was back in business.

Trade, at first slow, soon picked up. While there were undoubtedly times when Melanie and Michelle were left to cope alone, neighbours and grand-parents rallied to help. As Gary slipped back into the routine of regular work, he sought a baby-sitter. One cold night, as the pubs closed, he got talking to Alison who, anxious to share more than the salt and vinegar, swiftly volunteered to help.

Soon, Alison's care of Melanie and Michelle became continuous. The girls awoke to find her preparing breakfast, she was there when they came out of play-school and, as time passed, she was there more often than Gary. The house brightened up, spare parts for the van were evacuated to the home of paternal grand-parents and Gary all but disappeared. Not that Alison and the girls were ever lonely, for they were joined first by half-sister Karen and, soon afterwards, by half-sister Kim.

For nearly four years all seemed well and a domestic bliss based upon Gary's inadequacy and regular absence from home prevailed. But the parental relationship coughed and spluttered to the tune of the mobile van. With time it died altogether and Gary withdrew to his parents who welcomed him back sympathetically.

However, left alone and largely unsupported, with four children and no relief, Alison, too, fell into periodic depressions. She began to neglect the children and on two occasions social services were called after neighbours complained that the children had been left alone while Alison went down to the pub. On a cold November night Michelle was picked up by the police after being found, somewhat ironically, asking passers-by for money to buy fish and chips. She was dressed only in her dirty frock.

The pressures mounted on Alison, the gas was cut off, albeit temporarily, and she took an overdose of anti-depressants. She finally agreed to let all the children be accommodated by social services for a while, something she had resisted despite her ever-worsening situation. Gary, on the days he could function, was wholly pre-occupied with building a re-conditioned engine for the chip van, once more consigned to its brick stilts in the garage. This preoccupation, unfortunately, lessened the attention he might have paid to his children entering care.

The four children stayed together, first in a temporary placement then, when Alison's situation failed to improve, in a long-term foster home. The social worker, delighted to find a place which would take all four girls, put a lot of effort into keeping things going. However, a year after the children's reception into care, the pressure of bringing up four girls aged two to eight years became too much. The foster parents asked for a major review of the situation and intimated that they had put up with enough. Melanie, in particular, was behaving badly and her younger half-sister, Kim, was enuretic.

Links with home had become tenuous during this time. Alison, overwhelmed by her health problems and anxiety over the children, was evicted from her home for non-payment of rent. She was understandably preoccupied and largely uninvolved in decisions about the children. Her visits became infrequent and, at the time when the resilience of the foster parents was sinking, she was at her lowest ebb. The girls' family contacts eventually consisted of uneventful, routine visits organised without reward by a long-suffering social worker who patiently sat with the grand-parents while the girls and Gary sat in the gloom of the immobile chippy in a cold, oil-ridden garage.

If we recall the factors which we found to be the best predictors of a child's reunion between seven and 24 months after the children were accommodated, we find that Melanie and Michelle were deficient on all three. Firstly neglect was a feature of the children's reception to care. Secondly, the siblings, remarkably, had stayed together during the 12 months they were away from home. Finally, there was no evidence to suggest that relatives of the children had participated in care decisions. Natural mother was living away, the step-mother appeared to care little. It was all Gary could do to leave it all to social services and nobody bothered to ask the grand-parents what they wanted. Return seemed very unlikely. The social worker faced long-term involvement.

However, there followed a series of happy coincidences which confounded our predictive criteria. Two weeks before the 'review' requested by the foster home, Gary's parents, who had put him up since his precipitate eviction, decided it was time that they moved into sheltered accommodation. Beside the sense of claustrophobia as the detritus of the van washed up on the living room floor, both were frail and living with Gary was more than exhausting. His parents were almost eager to hand over their three bedroomed council house to their son and to head for something more manageable. Thus, Gary found himself with a house and furniture and the wherewithal to keep it going.

Once more freed from apparent responsibility, Gary's depression eased. Reluctantly, he was persuaded by his erstwhile rival, Brian, to merge businesses and between them they cobbled together a mobile chippy that moved. When the girls failed to appear for their bi-monthly access, Gary, once more on the road, decided on a surprise visit to the foster parents, blissfully unaware that it was Melanie's birthday.

And so it was that, as the social worker hurried down the foster parents' garden path, eagerly clutching Melanie's card and present, around the corner sped the mobile chippy. It was instantly recognisable to the social worker, for whom hunger suddenly became more of a driving force than the need to keep professional distance. Soon Gary and the social worker found *rapprochement* over cod and chips and a cuppa. They talked about the impending review of the childrens' situation and Gary mumbled consent when asked whether he would like to come along and see how things were going.

It was only at the review that Gary really became aware of how difficult the girls had become to manage. On their visits the children were always on their best behaviour and the social worker, as worried for the father as she was for his offspring, felt it was wrong to spoil the occasion with her concerns. Somewhat to his surprise, he felt guilty; completely out of the blue, Gary blurted out that he would take the girls home with him, if everybody thought that it would be all right.

It was not, of course, 'all right' but, given the limited options open to the social worker and the need to react to the foster parents' demands that something be done, a plan was hatched which involved the reunion of Melanie and Michelle with their father. A family *aide* and a volunteer were arranged to support them at home and six weeks later the move took place.

As this case was selected from the retrospective study, we were able to chart its progress for another four years. During this time, the children's situation improved and was satisfactory when our follow-up was completed. After the reunion, Gary was married again, this time to Eva, a widow ten years his senior who, through bitter experience, was skilled at keeping the inadequate afloat. With just the two children, who were now older, to manage, they got by. Karen and Kim stayed with foster parents and the bi-monthly visits continued as before. However, having already lost touch with their natural mother, Melanie and Michelle seemed unlikely to see their step-mother again. Their fortunes, apparently tied to those of the chip-van which struggled along in an unsteady liaison with the remnants of Brian's 'mobile', are never likely to be rosy, but the children are, nonetheless, 'at home'.

Melanie and Michelle defied our predictions and went home. Why was our prognosis incorrect? At a critical moment in the children's separation, when the social worker was faced with a change in placement, the parting of the siblings and a long care sojourn for all four children, she was presented with another opportunity, albeit not very promising. Care plans had never entertained a return to the father, now he offered a slim chance of much-needed continuity and stability in a context where upheaval and the splitting up of the four children was inevitable. Despite doubts and considerable concerns, the social worker grasped this nettle and the children went back.

However, the unpromising scenario stimulated the social worker to make exceptional efforts to ensure the success of the reunion. No doubt spurred on by the fact that return was to a lone man, she provided the family *aide* and volunteer; she visited daily in the days leading up to the reunion and encouraged the grand-parents to be very supportive, albeit from a distance. Gary, anxious to overcome his guilt for previous failings, was only too glad to seek help and advice. As we shall see later, these factors can occasionally brighten up an apparently bleak prospect.

We will, indeed, come back to Melanie and Michelle later in the study but let us now summarise our predictions of when and how swiftly children go home after entry to care.

Summary of predicting who goes home

As the predictive factors have shown, there are several things social workers can do to encourage a child's reunion. Most important is the need to keep the family involved in the care task and to foster that sense of belonging that binds together even the most damaged of households. Evidence would suggest that we should entertain a more optimistic view about adolescents' chances of restoration, especially for boys who closely identify with home. The failure to keep relatives in the picture or to discourage drift will certainly delay the child's return and indecisions when the child is away are likely to cause problems once she or he is back.

The findings echo those in North America by Hess and Proch (1991) and Block and Libowitz (1983) who stress the importance of the behaviour of children, families and social workers. Clearly, the chances of reunion are reduced if parents are ambivalent about wanting to care for their child, if they refuse to help, do not attend meetings and spurn invitations to participate in social work plans. However, these may only be symptoms of the failure of social work interventions to address family problems. Despite providing clear outcome indications, the multi-variate analysis used in this part of the study has deficiencies: the use of clear outcome measures such as 'went home or stayed in a substitute placement' is crude, a point well illustrated in the case study of Melanie and Michelle. We will address these questions shortly, but let us first conclude our attempts to predict outcomes from the extensive data with a scrutiny of the factors associated with a child's successful reunion.

Predicting the success of children on return

Can we know on the day the child comes into care or at the point we decide to send him or her home who will do well and who will fare badly? The study *Trials and Tribulations* has been used to answer these questions. The data for this work is drawn from 321 children placed with parents in four local authorities. Farmer and Parker were able to follow up the child's progress for two years but, of greater value, they also assessed the quality of the placement on a range of criteria. The 'home on trial' was evaluated by several professionals who offered independent advice.

It will be recalled from the literature review that *Trials and Tribulations* is a study of two groups of children living at home whilst in care; first there are 172 younger children whose entry to care usually followed neglect or abuse or an unwillingness on the part of families to continue to look after their offspring; we refer to these as the *care and protection* group. Second, there are 149 young people who had been taken into care for reasons of offending, not attending school or failing to respond to parental guidance; these are described as the *beyond control* group. While the first group comprises children of all ages and lengths of stay in care, the latter consists mostly of adolescents who have been relatively long in care.

However, it should be emphasised that Farmer and Parker's work is not simply a study of return; it is an investigation of children placed 'home on trial'. Indeed, nearly one in ten (9%) of those scrutinised never returned to relatives because they had not been separated; their 'home on trial' status simply represents a continuation of existing arrangements. These children who stayed at home have been excluded from the re-analysis, leaving 153 in the *care and protection group* who had experienced separation and 138 youngsters *beyond control*.

When we exclude these 30 children who never left home from the analysis, we find that variables which correlate with a satisfactory outcome in home placements are not the same as those associated with a positive return outcome. That is to say, the criteria found by Farmer and Parker to predict the success of these placements do not produce a reliable prognosis for all of the return outcomes we considered. Moreover, we found different variables were associated with whether or not the reunion endured, on the one hand, and whether or not it was considered to be satisfactory on the other.

Let us now look at those factors associated with successful or unsuccessful reunion. We looked first at general factors which should be borne in mind in all return situations and then we considered variables specific to the vulnerable groups we have identified.

General factors

Most factors associated with a child's successful return concern family circumstances and, unlike our prognoses of whether or not children go back to relatives, these factors are less influenced by social work intervention. But, we need to beware of 'false positives' for even the most damaged families change over time to allow a successful reunion to take place. Similarly, many apparently well integrated families fail to keep their children at home after the return.

We found that within general limits, care experiences and family circumstances provide the best combined indicators of the success of children's returns. For example, if family links with children absent in care are maintained, then the chances of a successful reunion are increased. But, of course, family links can also bring into focus the family circumstances, patterns of reconstitution and stress factors, such as unemployment, poor housing and so forth.

As far as successful return is concerned, the earlier social services are involved and the greater the participation of the family in the care task the better. Nonetheless, the quality of family relationships can sometimes prove an independent influence on outcome, for strong links between relatives and offspring can offset even the most stressful family situations. This helps to explain why many children do well after return despite an apparently poor outlook. They simply turn to others in the family for support.

For those long in care who go home, the importance of their family situations is clearer still. In predicting success for an older adolescent's reunion, the quality of relationships among family members during and after separation and the maintenance of links and contact with the absentee were consistently found to be important, even when we applied the criteria to the difficult and disturbed young people who graduated from a Youth Treatment Centre. With the older adolescent there needs to be a balance struck between the young person's dependence and independence. As far as the success of reunion is concerned, there is a need to allow the young person to make mistakes, to try and find his or her own feet whilst, at the same time, providing the support necessary to a tranquil situation. Even then, success cannot be guaranteed. External factors can upset the best laid plans; offending and pregnancy particularly pose threats to young people recently emerged from care.

For all, a social work strategy which keeps the family involved in the care task will increase the success of reunion. We would acknowledge, however, that such a plan requires considerable flexibility on the part of social workers as many of the factors we have identified only become apparent once the child is back at home.

This study would suggest that two factors previously found to be influential in whether or not children are returned also assist in predicting the success of reunions. These indicators apply to all children leaving care, the young, the old, those at risk and those posing behaviour problems. The two factors are:

1. The social work strategy has been inclusive (as previously defined).

2. The family relationships as assessed (using the factors described in Appendix B) are of a relatively high quality.

So much for the general factors, let us now consider the indicators which can be used to predict the success of returns for particular groups. We begin with children who need care and protection, that is youngsters whose entry to care was preceded by neglect, abuse or reluctance to parent.

Care and protection children

Several variables correlated with successful return outcomes for children in care for neglect and abuse. We have studied first whether children move on after the return and secondly whether the reunion was deemed satisfactory. We have separated predictive criteria into three groups; one, those which were known prior to the entry to care; two, aspects of family functioning which emerge after the child is reunited with relatives; and, three, types of social work intervention attempted post-restoration.

As tables 8.1 and 8.2 make clear, the distribution of variables in each of these categories is fairly even and there are many opportunities to pinpoint those vulnerable to a return breakdown. We can also see that less than two-fifths (37%) of children returning subsequently move on and that 44% of the reunions were thought to be positive for the child. This is not to say that all other outcomes were negative, in fact less than 10% of the home placements were deemed to be detrimental to the child.

Table 8.1: Factors associated with care and protection children moving on after reunion

Factor	% moving on	Level of association
a) *Known before return*		
Child previously home on trial	57%	$x^2=15.1842;p<0.0001$
Child twice previously in care	68%	$x^2=8.077;p<0.005$
2 or more other children at home	49%	$x^2=7.41;p<0.006$
b) *Family factors post-return*		
Further family difficulties	62%	$x^2=12.60;p<0.0003$
Neglect/abuse of child	63%	$x^2=12.306;p<0.0005$
Irregular school attendance	58%	$x^2=7.38;p<0.007$
c) *Social work intervention post-return*		
No other agencies involved	43%	$x^2=8.17;p<0.004$
TOTAL (N=153)	37%	

Table 8.2: Factors associated with a positive outcome for the care and protection children

Factor	% positive outcome	Level of association
a) *Known before return*		
Child never previously returned	57%	$x^2=14.8;p<0.0001$
No other concerns when order made	54%	$x^2=4.785;p<0.03$
Rehabilitation planned at outset	59%	$x^2=11.271;p<0.0005$
Only one substitute placement	57%	$x^2=7.35; p<0.007$
Foster placement preceded return	58%	$x^2=7.06;p<0.008$
Return to same family members	54%	$x^2=4.95;p<0.03$
c) *Social work intervention post-return*		
Child's progress reviewed regularly	53%	$x^2=6.95;p<0.009$
Other agencies unconcerned	51%	$x^2=7.74;p<0.005$
Discharge of care order considered	60%	$x^2=11.325;p<0.0008$
Highly competent social work	84%	$x^2=17.07;p<0.00004$
TOTAL (N=153)	44%	

If we take the second of the two outcome measures used: whether, in the eyes of independent experts, there had been a positive outcome for the child, can we select two or three variables which best predict a successful reunion?

The log-linear analysis reveals that the following three variables in combination proved the best in predicting which of the *care and protection* children are successfully returned.

1. There is evidence of highly competent social work (ie. that options are considered, a plan is created and social workers are highly committed to its implementation).

2. The child has never previously been returned after being looked after by social services.

3. The social worker is sufficiently confident about the situation to consider discharging the care order or is entirely satisfied with the voluntary arrangements.

However, we also discovered that one variable, evidence of good social work, overwhelmed all others. Clearly each of the three variables is useful in predicting positive outcomes for the protected children studied in *Trials and Tribulations*. However, for the vulnerable, abused or neglected child, special social work efforts can make a unique difference to the outcomes of returning children. Indeed, good social work practice can overcome all of the negative aspects of a case, factors which would otherwise suggest a poor prognosis. Whilst these findings would dishearten a mathematician in pursuit of the perfect statistical model, the messages should be very encouraging to those seeking to rehabilitate vulnerable children.

The multi-variate analysis showed that a child who had not previously been returned *and* simultaneously enjoyed the support of a good social worker, confident enough to entertain the prospect of discharging the care order, was over six times more likely to enjoy a successful reunion than one who went back under different circumstances. There were, however, eighteen *outliers*, children who either met all of the criteria yet, for some exceptional reason, experienced problems at home or who failed to meet any of the positive factors associated with successful outcome and, yet, did well on reunion. If we repeat the analysis without these outliers, we find the power of the prediction rises to 7 to 1.

Children beyond control

As we might expect, following our evidence on the careers of older adolescents just reviewed, the proportion of youngsters moving on during the two years following reunion is greater for the children studied in *Trials and Tribulations* who were *beyond control* (50%) than for the *care and protection* youngsters (37%). However, two-fifths (42%) of the *beyond control* children enjoyed successful reunions, reinforcing the finding that many adolescents re-integrate with their families even when their behaviour or aspects of parenting lead to disharmony.

Table 8.3: Factors associated with children beyond control moving on after reunion

Factor	% moving on	Level of association
(a) Known before return		
Child previously home on trial	79%	$x^2=32.242;p<0.0001$
Control problems lead to care	57%	$x^2=3.87;p<0.05$
Three or more substitute placements	61%	$x^2=6.523;p<0.01$
Child not admitted with siblings	57%	$x^2=7.806;p<0.005$
(c) Social work intervention post-return		
Infrequent social work contact	61%	$x^2=5.699;p<0.02$
TOTAL (N=138)	50%	

Table 8.4: Factors associated with a positive outcome for children beyond control

Factor	% positive outcome	Level of association
(a) Known before return		
Child never previously returned	58%	$x^2=9.204;p<0.002$
(b) Family factors post-return		
Regular school attendance	63%	$x^2=9.827;p<0.002$
Social worker has no difficulties in access to the child or family	51%	$x^2=13.327;p<0.0002$
Discharge of care order considered	55%	$x^2=6.405;p<0.02$
Child does not offend	58%	$x^2=10.716;p<0.001$
(c) Social work intervention post-return		
Child's progress reviewed regularly	53%	$x^2=6.866;p<0.009$
TOTAL (N=138)	42%	

Once again, several variables are found to be associated with the two selected outcome measures and all can be taken into account by social workers making decisions about return for the more difficult adolescent. However, our multi-variate analysis has been able to reduce the number of indicators to three, which, in combination, predict successful outcomes for 'difficult to control' children who are returned home. Although all three can only be gauged once the child has been reunited with relatives and reflect the relative harmony in the family home after the reunion, the criteria, nevertheless, should also alert social workers to return contexts which are becoming fraught. They are:

1. The social worker does not experience difficulty in gaining access to the child or family.

2. The child has never previously been returned after being looked after by social services.

3. The child is not an offender.

If social workers are welcomed into the home, if they feel confident enough to consider a discharge of the care order and if the child is not an offender, then the prognosis for the successful return is good. Indeed, a young person meeting these three criteria has a greater than five to one chance of enjoying a successful reunion. We can also report that there were no unusual cases which defied our prediction.

A case which defied the predictive criteria - Kelly

The evidence just described concludes the first stage of our attempts to highlight factors which will help us predict how children and young people will fare when they have been returned home. As we have found throughout this chapter, when we applied the above criteria, we discovered some children who defied our prognoses. These unusual cases or *outliers* have been removed from our analysis. However, as they reveal the unexpected changes of fortune which predictive criteria cannot accommodate we shall now describe another of these cases.

This time we look at Kelly, who was expected to return home rapidly and settle but, as we shall see, oscillated between her mother and various foster homes. Kelly was accommodated on a voluntary basis on the day before her first birthday. Her mother, Madelaine, was only seventeen herself and was finding it difficult to cope alone with a new baby.

Madelaine was born to parents who migrated to England from the West Indies in the 1960s. She was the youngest of seven children and was well adjusted to city life, indeed, somewhat too well adjusted and restless in a religious and authoritarian household. Nonetheless she gave as good as she got, looking over everyone and everything with one object in mind, escape. During adolescence Maddie spent increasing periods away from home. She dabbled in minor drugs, she was cautioned several times by the police for shop-lifting and, by her own account, she 'slept around'. Her parents, worn out by the large family, retreated into the gospel hall.

On finding that she was pregnant, Madelaine set herself up in a small flat and looked forward to the life of a single mother, despite being supported by her partner. In this she was initially fairly successful, although the health visitor had constant concerns about the flat, which was cold and damp. Social services also kept a watchful eye.

But looking after the baby soon became too much for Madelaine who missed the bright lights, those few left in her run-down neighbourhood, and to her unease she found that she was again pregnant. She wanted time to sort herself out and asked social services to look after the baby for a few weeks. Somewhat relieved, the social worker took Kelly into care and placed her with Afro-Caribbean foster parents. Her mother was admitted to hospital and had an abortion, a decision which outraged the grand-parents and reduced the prospects of their subsequent support.

The reunion of mother and daughter was carefully managed by the social worker until two days before the planned date of return when Madelaine, feeling lonely, decided to remove the baby from the foster parents. While the supports organised by the social worker and regular visits by the health visitor were only a partial success, as they relied much on mother's intermittent co-operation, things held together and Kelly, the baby, stayed at home.

Indeed, using the criteria identified above, we predicted Kelly's reunion to be successful. The social work had been highly competent, extra supports had been arranged and Madelaine was well prepared, even anxious, for her daughter's return. The baby had never before been separated from her mother, which was a good sign, and there was no hint of compulsion or constraint in social work plans.

The prognosis, however, was confounded when, eight months later, Madelaine again fell pregnant. Kelly entered care once more, ostensibly for a short time. But this time Madelaine went through with the pregnancy and, preoccupied with the new arrival, she repeatedly delayed Kelly's restoration until, finally, she asked for her to be placed for adoption. Uneasily, the social worker sought a foster placement with a view to this end. Eighteen months later when the foster placement broke down, renewed efforts were made to achieve the reunion of Kelly with mum and the new baby. A home placement was arranged and initially it worked well. But, unable to take care of two children, Madelaine once more asked for Kelly to be returned to care.

Kelly exemplifies a situation which might have swiftly led to reunion with few complications: she shares all the characteristics of early returns and meets the criteria for a successful reunion earlier described. In particular, her social worker made gallant efforts to achieve rehabilitation first time around and, after the foster home breakdown, tried hard the second time. Throughout, social services remained sensitive to the family's race. However, as we have seen, cultural factors rather than race proved more important. Most significant of all was the unpredicted arrival of Madelaine's baby and it was this that put paid to Kelly's prospects of reunion.

We shall return to Kelly later on in this study when we have gathered more factors which help predict the success of reunion. Nevertheless, the case demonstrates that child-care can never be reduced to the application of simple check-lists and guide-lines. Not only does the unexpected outcome of this case add caution to our hopes of predicting return, it emphasises the importance of sensitive and flexible social work with families, once the child is actually back home. It also reminds us that a gathering awareness that things are not going well can rapidly lead to a change of plan and re-entry to care. Naturally, when these exceptions to the general patterns of return are excluded from statistical predictions, the reliability of forecasting increases considerably, but just as we fasten our seat-belts on aeroplanes and giggle uneasily at the prospect of donning a life jacket, it is salutary to keep in mind that one could suddenly find oneself amongst those exceptions that prove the rule.

This re-analysis of data from *Trials and Tribulations* has sharpened our understanding of return outcomes. We have seen that those variables associated with a successful home placement are not necessarily as helpful when we seek to understand the success or failure of reunion, although naturally there is some overlap.

Conclusions

This concludes our attempts to highlight factors which will help us to predict how children and young people fare once they have been returned home. As Melanie, Michelle and Kelly have illustrated, our predictive factors do not always hold the answer to success. The unexpected remains a distinct possibility, particularly with children in care. We must also look more closely at what constitutes a positive reunion for returning children. In this chapter, we have relied on clear outcomes such as placement breakdown or movement of child but we accept that these may conceal rather than identify difficulty. Just as the most successful marriages are not necessarily those that last, so a child who sticks at home may suffer while the footloose adolescent might have a marvellous time. Taking alternative perspectives and using different measures, we may find that factors in our predictive models change.

It is also important to look more closely at the different stages in the reunion. As we shall see in the following chapters, whatever the return group, be it short or long-term, babe in arms or recalcitrant adolescent, boy or girl; for each of the groups there are clear episodes in the return. These need to be recognised, for some provide the opportunity for applying the predictive factors just described and for the social worker to take stock of the situation. By looking at these episodes in more depth, we can better understand aspects of restoration and think again about the factors which lead to its success or failure. Let us begin by describing the intensive study group and the general themes which emerged from this aspect of the investigation.

Summary points

1. By identifying groups of variables which predict particular return outcomes, we have begun to assemble indicators of a child's return which can be used by social workers in making decisions about children.

2. Regardless of children's length of separation, it is aspects of the family situation which are most useful in distinguishing between those who go back and those who do not. Levels of contact between the child whilst absent in care and the family members are especially important.

3.   Several groups of variables specific to different return groups and situations have been identified.

4.   The way in which variables interact has been explored in two case studies.

5.   In addition, we have seen the way in which idiosyncratic factors or events, for example, a chance meeting between father and social worker, turn a bleak outlook into one which is more optimistic.

9. General themes from the intensive study

Here we turn to an intensive scrutiny of 31 children returning from 24 families, each of which characterises common reunion situations. In later chapters the process of reunion will be explored through a sequence of episodes which highlight key moments and issues as return gathers momentum. We have selected children a) who would return with ease; b) those who would have difficulty in getting back; c) those unlikely to return in spite of social work optimism and d) those who would not easily settle. We also explore several themes, continuity, role and territory which, as return unfolds, haunt each of the episodes in the process.

In the preceding chapters, we have described the findings from the extensive study involving 875 children in care. From this, we have been able to produce predictive indicators of reunion. Now, we must complement our extensive study with more intensive material to see if we can add to the factors which predict return.

We described earlier the ways cases were selected for the intensive, prospective study but it is helpful to remind ourselves of the ways in which it was done. Twenty-four families were selected from 86 proposed by social workers as having children likely to return from care. Eight of these families were expected to welcome back *early returners*, children who had been away less than six months; eight were looking forward to *intermediate returners*, those coming back between seven and 24 months after separation; with the remaining eight families having been apart from their children for two or more years on reunion, our *long-term returners*. As some families contained more than one child relevant to our study, 31 children were scrutinised in this part of the research.

Whilst we did not seek a sample that was representative of all young people in care, we attempted to include the wide range of situations and circumstances which separated children experience. In addition, we also sought to select cases according to the ease with which they might return. To do this using the predictive indicators fashioned earlier in the extensive study, we chose children who seemed likely to (i) go home with relative ease; (ii) experience some difficulty in getting back; (iii) not to go home despite the social work plans to the contrary; and (iv) to return but not easily settle.

Although we looked at 86 possible cases, we were not able to get a precisely even distribution of all these return situations. Nonetheless, we feel we achieved a satisfactory combination. The factors used to choose both children and their families can be summarised as follows.

Table 9.1: The distribution of cases selected for participation in the intensive study

Research team predicts:	*Early returner*	*Intermediate returner*	*Long-term returner*	*TOTAL*
Easy return	2	2	2	6
Difficult return	5	5	3	13
Unlikely to return	3	2	2	7
Return & breakdown	2	2	1	5
TOTAL	12	11	8	31

What were the characteristics of the 31 children? The intensive study included more boys (22) than girls (9) but the age distribution was evenly spread among the 31 children, including four babies aged two years or less and six adolescents aged 16 years or more. Just over half (16) of the 31 children had been looked after voluntarily with the remainder being subject to care orders.

If we use Packman, Randall and Jacques's (1986) classification of the circumstances which lead to being looked after, we find that six of the 31 are *victims,* for example of abuse and/or neglect, 11 are *villains* in that they are beyond parental control or are offenders, leaving 14 who were *volunteered* by their parents. The intensive study also included four children from minority ethnic families, one of whom was Asian, a characteristic which, as we shall see, was influential in his return, and one girl whose mother was Irish and whose father had come to Britain from the West Indies.

Thus, it can be seen that the children participating in the intensive study show the range of factors displayed by children in care and also cover the various return scenarios that are possible.

As we described earlier, we followed up the 24 families for 18 months, regularly interviewing all the participants in the return. We soon became aware that return is not a single event but is a process comprising many stages. Indeed, the exploration lent itself to the episode analysis previously described in Chapter Five and suggested for consideration several which were key:

1. the initial separation;

2. subsequent changes in family circumstances;

3. the point at which return becomes an issue;

4. the point at which return occurs;

5. the honeymoon period;

6. acrimonious negotiations between family members and

7. the point at which a new *modus vivendi* is established.

Clearly, certain events may overlap several episodes and some episodes may be missed altogether. Nonetheless, this approach to the qualitative material has considerably helped with the analysis and presentation of findings.

In the following chapters, we shall look in detail at the above episodes. In each, evidence from the various participants to the return is offered and the main themes drawn from the analysis are presented. We shall also add new factors suggested by the intensive study to those predictive factors already identified from our extensive data, helping us better to predict whether or not children return and the success of such reunions. This will confirm the value of a qualitative dimension in our study and effectively link macro and micro data.

In addition to the factors specific to particular episodes in the return process, we found certain general themes which applied at all stages of return. These deserve closer examination because they haunt all separations and returns and have already been glanced at in the literature review which opened this study.

Continuity

Implicit in much of the work on separation is the concept that for satisfactory development, children and families need continuity, security, belonging and even a sense of history. For example, Maluccio, Fein and Olmstead (1986) open their study *Permanency Planning for Children* with the words in order to grow up satisfactorily, children need to know that life has predictability and continuity. They need the reliability of knowing where they will be growing up.

Continuity is also stressed by Kellmer Pringle (1975) who writes,

a child is most likely to develop to a maximum level if he has an enduring relationship with at least one person who is sensitive to his individual needs and stages of development.

Several writers have explained that families and wider social networks provide children with that sense of continuity and security from which to plan and help fashion their identity and sense of worth. Kahan (1979) in her perceptive study of young adults recollecting their careers as children in care comments that

families and what they mean to individuals not only as children but in adult life were of great significance to all, whether their families were related by blood-ties, by remarriage or by adoption.

She also highlights young people's need

for a pattern and for that pattern to be an orthodox one, it is vitally important for the child that everything is done to avoid any thought of being different from any other child.

Whitaker, Cook, Dunne and Lunn-Rockliffe (1984) in their study of children in residential care comment

the most important areas of concern from the point of view of the children were families and friends. This pre-occupation was present in a wide range of circumstances.

Indeed, the authors go on to emphasise the importance of the wider family and social networks of children in providing a sense of belonging for the child and offering explanations for present situations. They comment

persons in the child's network and, of course, the child him or herself, form opinions and hold views about key issues, such as the reasons for entering care, or on a child's history and its likely influence on present and future. Network members are inclined to identify certain turning points in the child's life and emphasise subsequent events in terms of them.

The research team found that interviews helped reconstruct the child's history in network terms, as in time-lapse photography, one could see those points in a child's life at which significant network changes took place.

Indeed, the value for the child of strong family links and the sense of continuity and belonging that these provide are all explored at length in the Dartington Research Unit's studies *Lost in Care* and *Access Disputes in Child-Care*. For most of us a sense of continuity is so omnipresent that it is taken for granted and hardly thought about but for those without it, the past and its meaning become constant pre-occupations. Continuity and security are viewed as particularly important in satisfactory child development and any child who fails to enjoy such a birth-right faces considerable difficulty.

> 'I had three foster home placements in the two years after I was taken into care and then I ended up in a children's home. I hadn't much clue as to where I came from and none about where I was going. Nobody seemed to care about me, they never asked me what I wanted or what I felt, never showed any interest in what I did, either in school, in sport or in anything. Unless, of course, you nicked something or kicked up rough, then there was hell to pay and everyone put their nose in.'

Another boy comments,

> 'I was at an O and A centre for months waiting for a foster home but nothing came up, everyone needs to belong somewhere and to somebody. How can an observation centre replace your parents?'

Indeed, if continuity and a sense of belonging do not materialise, then children will create them and fantasize a past which usually bears little relationship to fact. Many observers have also commented on the value of possessions, photographs and other mementos to help maintain links with those absent and continuity with the past. Whitaker and colleagues comment that

> while all concerned constructed explanations for events, for example why a child was in care, the children themselves had little life experience to bring to bear and sometimes accepted or ascribed blame inappropriately or held incompatible views.

Thus, children comfort themselves with fantasy and myth.

> 'When I leave care I'm going to go back and find out exactly who my father is. Maybe he's a Duke or Lord or something and then everybody will be sorry and want to know me.'

Indeed, Kahan offers us a most poignant example of a child seeking continuity and a sense of belonging.

> 'About three years after I went into adoption, I used to go down to the children's home, River-Side, to see if there was anyone there I remembered and took a big chunk out of the wall and I've still got it. In fact, I've heard the place is going to be pulled down, I think I'll get in first and ask for the name-plate. The chunk of wall is out in the shed somewhere, I wouldn't part with it.'

But a need for continuity, a sense of belonging and the security that comes from a sense of place are not only needed by children; adults also seek to maintain continuities and to put separations and returns into context. Talking to Yitzhak Kashti, a survivor of the holocaust, we were reminded that middle-aged Jews long settled in Israel remained haunted by the villages and towns of central Europe from which they fled, often under terrible circumstances, fifty years before. They frequently revisit their origins. He comments on his own return to Hungary,

> 'You go back alone, it is the loneliest of experiences and everything floods back, very little things trigger off memories you've entirely forgotten. But in the end, you realise you cannot really return, all you can do is integrate the separations and returns into the battered identity you present in everyday life.'

A middle-aged woman who with her sister fled from the Warsaw Ghetto in 1940, recollects the experience long after and the way return helped make sense of the present.

> 'I went back to Warsaw with my younger sister, it was heartbreaking, absolutely nothing remained, nothing that is except the bitter anti-semitism of the Poles, everything had gone, now my sister's gone as well. Yet, in some ways there is comfort, we did go back together and the hatred itself provides some sense of continuity. Jerusalem makes much more sense to me now even though we have lived here fifty years.'

Hence, when writers raise the needs of belonging and family links for children, there is often implicit in their writing this greater sense of order, sequence and continuity which we all seek to impart to our lives.

However, even these brief illustrations would suggest that authors differ considerably in their ideas on continuity. Generally speaking there is a contrast between definitions of continuity produced by academics seeking to refine theory and the ideas developed by those working with children to describe family and child situations. There are also contrasts between ideas about continuity produced by sociologists and those of social psychologists and psychiatrists, although all would agree that disruption and abrupt change in life patterns can be damaging.

We might define continuity as that sense of meaning and order which we impose on a sequence of life events. These events may be unexpected or random, they may even be traumatic experiences such as a child entering care or the loss of a parent. Therefore, our sense of continuity is a way of maintaining our psychological health. One can also perceive different types of continuity, for example, there are 'expressive continuities', those that endure over time and change very little. Some of these have macro aspects, such as national and regional identities and perhaps religious, moral or political beliefs, but they also come in the form of feelings for those long departed or the rights of 'family' over friendship. Secondly there are temporal continuities which do change over time. Indeed, such continuities may wither and be replaced by others such as changes in career or marriage. One might even suggest that there are conflicts between expressive and temporal continuities. As we shall see in the coming pages, return can cruelly expose these contradictions.

In asking children what going back is like, two themes constantly emerge. Firstly the complexities and difficulties in the resumption of roles and, secondly, the problems they encounter during the re-colonisation of lost territory. We have already seen how much these concepts of role and territory are part of the continuity sought by those who are separated, whether child or adult. The ideas that both separation and return are not discrete events but part of a process and that separation from home for the majority of children is negotiated with return in mind are very important. Both for eventual return to home from care and for the success of any reunion, the existence of strong links with family, particularly with the mother, is of great importance. We will subsequently explore whether stressing these continuities to the absent child, highlighting continuities of relationships with family and neighbourhood and emphasising the likelihood of eventual return will facilitate reunion and lead to a successful adjustment.

On return, children's sense of continuity and security are likely to be much affected both by changes in the roles they are expected to make and by the space they seek to re-occupy. First, let us explore what roles are resumed.

Roles

Many years ago, we studied the Byzantine world of the English boarding school, a set of institutions which would have warmed the heart and stimulated the pen of Goffman, institutions beside which other asylums pale. While the relevance of schools to the return of luckless children from local authority care might at first sight seem rather distant, the complexity of the roles children played within the boarding schools, the demands made upon them and the skills necessary for adequate role performance were of great interest to us.

We classified roles in three distinct categories which may have some transfer value to the roles played by children within families. First of all, there were *instrumental roles*, those concerned with acquiring skills and proficiency. Secondly, there were *organisational roles*, those concerned with oiling the wheels of the organisation, keeping the show on the road and, thirdly, there were *expressive roles*, those which were concerned with beliefs, states fulfilling in themselves and roles which had a spiritual dimension. Now within the school, children performed and moved between these roles swiftly, but not quite effortlessly. Their role performance often conflicted with others and there were tensions within a particular role.

This classification of roles is not quite as complicated as it sounds. For example, a parent taking a cookery class might be part of an *instrumental role*; cleaning the kitchen floor an *organisational* chore, a role which hopefully prevents children from breaking their necks; and, thirdly, counselling, supporting children and offering pastoral care are *expressive roles*. Neither should such a classification of roles be viewed as exclusive. For example, one may invest either the balancing of accounts, the stacking of supermarket shelves or even a gleaming kitchen floor with expressive dimensions.

Roles often overlap and, in many role performances, *instrumental*, *organisational* and *expressive* dimensions are closely interwoven. Indeed, one of the problems families and children face on return is that many apparently *organisational roles* within families, such as washing up, making the bed, cooking the chips and taking the dog for a walk, have expressive dimensions which pass largely unnoticed and family members have expectations and investments in these roles which can easily be violated. For example, a mother comments on a returning daughter,

'I thought she would be delighted that I had got a second-hand dish-washer, because we used to row about whose turn it was to do the washing up. But she wasn't pleased at all, she moaned about being done out of her job and actually hardly ever used the thing.'

Very often within families certain roles have considerable status and power, as anyone clasping the television's remote control well knows. Thus, on return, the child finds many seemingly trivial actions deeply invested with other significances; who lays the table, feeds the cat, turns on the fire, answers the phone, each invested with rights and obligations, all forgotten or ignored at considerable risk. Indeed, we would suggest that when *organisational roles* in a family are invested with the expressive dimensions, conflict and tension are likely. An armed services' wife said,

'A moment comes when I know that he is gone and that everything, kids, home, finance, everything is up to me. That realisation comes last thing at night when I go round closing the windows and bolting the door, I hate it, I feel guilty and angry at the same time. It's his job and he should be here to do it, I say to myself, he should protect me and the children. In fact, locking up at night can easily bring on tears and then I feel bad and stupid and say to myself, 'you wimp, without him you wouldn't have children to love or even a door to lock up.'

Hence, part of the management of return should be a keen awareness of the different dimensions operating within each role and that even the simplest of roles have expressive dimensions. It is also true that various family members, including the returning child, will have different perspectives on the meaning implicit in role performances.

Not only can we view roles as having different dimensions but we have already seen that roles conflict. Naturally, the holder of the television's remote control reminds others of the power dimension behind any role performance but he or she is highly likely to conflict with others when football coincides with *Coronation Street* or *Top of the Pops* and the arbiter of the evening's viewing will be reproached with comments from others such as 'well I bought the damn' thing,' 'who paid for the licence anyway?' 'I thought it was my Christmas present', or deftest strike of all, 'but Mum I'm supposed to watch *Panorama* for my homework.' Naturally the more key the role, the more derelictions in performance are noted. 'It's never worked properly since you let the dog gnaw the damn' thing.'

Not only do roles conflict when different individuals simultaneously seek to play the same role but also within roles there can be conflict, for example, between the parents' need to control, to be fair, yet to encourage and empathise with their children. In addition, conflict can be omnipresent, built into roles. For example, the role of an adolescent or of a step-parent or step-child has built into it conflicting loyalties and difficulties in meeting the expectations of others. This glimpse of the complexity of family roles no doubt would encourage the socially sensitive to take refuge in the role of the recluse or anchorite. But, actually, the gradual way in which roles are learned and changed and the loving environment in which performance takes place mean that most families are not arenas of endless dispute and tension. Nevertheless, the complexity of family roles illustrates how a child long separated from home will find reunion difficult and amply reinforces Winnicott's (1984) comment that

> insecure children can have all the feelings they can stand within their families or within a few yards of the doorstep.

Obviously, separation and return cause difficulties in any role performance. If absence is lengthy, children forget those signals which direct and reward appropriate behaviour. On return these signs have to be re-learned. While away, the child may adopt role behaviour very different from that expected at home and on reunion find an unappreciative audience. As one mother described,

> 'He came back from the assessment centre swearing like a trooper and throwing his weight around, that was at least until his father heard him and then gave him a belt.'

It is also true that things have moved on both for children and their families, although separation tends to freeze the picture for those apart. We have noted elsewhere how the families of children who enter care display a wearisome procession of arrivals and departures, a turbulence and movement which make reunion difficult. The households from which children were removed may not be those to which they return; going back may involve them in reunion with siblings also separated by a care experience. In addition, during the interim, families may have welcomed new members or may have had lodgers thrust upon them. The passage of time means that there is a gap between the roles the children wish to take up on return and those that the family are willing to accord them. Their

departure may have encouraged others to usurp their role and occupy their
territory at home, thus resenting their return, particularly if the welcome
proffered at reunion seems disproportionate to the trauma and reasons for
the original separation. Indeed, the Bible's finest parable says it all with
admirable brevity:

> And he was angry and would not go in: therefore came his father out and
> entreated him.

> And he answering said to his father, "These many years do I serve thee,
> neither transgressed I at any time thy commandment; and yet thou never
> gavest me a kid, that I might make merry with my friends. But as soon as
> this thy son was come, which hath devoured thy living with harlots, thou
> hast killed for him the fatted calf".

> And he said unto him, "Son thou art ever with me, and all that I have is
> thine. It was meet that we should make merry and be glad: For this thy
> brother was dead and is alive again and was lost and is found".

Children and adolescents, unprepared for the tensions and difficulties
of return, will react aggressively and appear to the family to be recalcitrant
and even less attractive than they were at the initial separation. As a
thwarted adolescent girl illustrates,

> 'My new step-sister took the kids off to play group like some mother hen
> and Mum said 'there, that Angela is really good with them. You never
> liked the job and she does it without any fuss'. Well there was a fuss 'cos
> I burned that little shit's bus pass and she had to buy a new one.'

But there are ways in which the role conflict inherent in return can be
managed and minimised. When counselled and assisted, separated
children and young people can become more objective about the roles they
and others play in family life and more accommodating to the needs of
others. Distance encourages a cooler look. In the same way the arrival of
step-parents and step-siblings, although initially threatening, can stimulate
new interests in family members. Families can do much by their efforts to
keep alive the image of the absentee within the household, remain mindful
of his or her preferences and, where possible, seem anxious for the return
and be instrumental in its achievement.

A girl removed with her younger sister from a depressed mother
comments,

'It was difficult when I was at home, I couldn't understand why Mum was lonely or depressed or what to do about it. She just used to sit in the pub or lie in bed. We used to row all the time. Being here makes me realise how little she has to look forward to while I and my sister have a lot, so now when I go home at weekends I try to be different to Mum. We go shopping together, watch T.V., sometimes it's quite a laugh. Now I'm looking forward to going home. Nicest thing is that Mum has been on to the social worker asking if we can go back.'

In a similar way, a returning adolescent becomes reconciled to his new step-brother.

'I didn't like the idea of a step-brother at all and things were a bit dicey at first. We both liked football and I was much better than he was. We go to matches and we have just bought a motorbike between us to go racing. Most of the time it's in bits but now we get on fine and Mum is over the moon about it all.'

A lad returning from youth custody comments,

'Going back was easier than I thought. I felt bad about the trouble I caused everyone and they, I know, were none too happy at kicking me out in the first place. But when I went through the door everyone was smiles, my photo in the army cadets was in its old place and Mum had my favourite meal ready. My step-dad offered me a can of beer, so even he was trying hard. It's been like that now for a couple of months, I've got a job bringing in some money and they look at me different now.'

Of course, what children find most distressing is inconsistency in parenting behaviour, a lack of forewarning and unreliability in adult role performance. This uncertainty is manifest in families where key members suffer from the mood swings associated with depression and/or the aggression and unpredictability inherent in alcoholism.

While re-negotiating a new set of roles on return may present problems, we should not forget that children also have to re-adapt to familiar places. In some cases they enter new households and other unfamiliar territories. Let us now look at the ways in which 'territory' affects their return.

Territory

In terms of outcome the mystery of criminology has not been among the most productive of social sciences. Nevertheless, one of its more interesting by-ways has been geographies of crime and the territories of offending. Intriguing, possibly even useful, is the knowledge that one is most likely to be murdered, not by some mindless thug, but by one's nearest and dearest. In addition, the kitchen and bedroom, where presumably our keenest appetites are aroused, are territories of maximum risk. Should we in moments of high family tension abandon eating and sleeping or, like children, retire strategically to the toilet?

Although these issues might seem adult pre-occupations, territory and the personalisation of space are of equal concern to children. On return, if having one's roles usurped is also accompanied by the seizure of one's territory then tensions will quickly mount. As a mother swiftly learned,

> 'I thought he would be grateful the boy next door had looked after the rabbits. Well, he wasn't. He said he'd built the hutch, the rabbits were his and nobody else would look after them properly.'

It is accepted good practice that separated children need to take something of home away with them, mementos and keepsakes, the loss of which can be very distressing. In the same way, during separation children's private places, their bed, cupboard, drawer, cluster of photographs and prized possessions should remain undisturbed and inviolate. Change can immediately be recognised and resented even after an absence sufficiently long to have contributed to forgetfulness. Neither does age act as a filter to a sense of violation, as adolescents are quite as sensitive to changed territories as younger children. Anyone managing return should explore the young person's expectations of what his or her territory is going to be like, what changes might have occurred, in order to forestall disappointment. Naturally, bountiful additions like a new chair or bedspread may be welcome if the chance to retain what has gone before remains open, but the disposal of anything, varying from a pair of odd trainers to a pile of battered colour supplements, is fraught with risk. A naval wife copes with an upset child,

> 'I was amazed. Anne is only six and we had been in Gibraltar for three years. When we came home she was in tears because her bedroom was different. All that our friends had done while they stayed was to move the wardrobe and chest of drawers a bit. Anyway, she was inconsolable until we moved them back again. I didn't even realise they had been shifted, but Anne did and didn't like it one bit.'

The gradual re-colonisation of lost space is also a strategy to ease return, as a mother recollects the designs of her adolescent daughter in seeking reunion.

'I knew she was worming her way back in, each weekend she would leave more and more stuff behind, shampoo in the bathroom, clothes, magazines, anything. Gradually she took over the bathroom shelf and all my stuff went on to the window-sill.'

The scattering of one's property not only helps regain lost territory but possessions themselves are symbolic of one's rights and place in the home. Indeed, possessions can be sacrosanct and the unauthorised borrowing of gear, however trivial, can allow tensions to focus upon the culprit. As a returning adolescent girl comments,

'That scrubber my dad brought home had the cheek to borrow my skirt, then she complained it was too short, too tight and needed cleaning. 'Wash it yourself' I said 'then it will be even tighter for all your friends, like dad, with wandering hand trouble.'

Winnicott (1984), slightly less acerbic, neatly summarised these issues fifty years ago as the dust of war settled on parents awaiting the return of their children. He reminded them that the child who came back would be different from the waif, brown label round the neck, that tearful mothers had seen off several years before.

In two or three years of separation, both mothers and children will have altered, more especially the child out of whose life three years is a big chunk. After three years, he is the same person, but he has lost whatever characterises the six year old because he is now nine. And then, of course, even if the house has escaped bomb damage, even if it is exactly as it was when the child left, it seems much smaller to him because he is now so much bigger. It must also be difficult to come back from a farm to a room or two in a block of flats in a big city.

Thus, the re-occupation of lost territory is as important as the resumption of family roles on any return from separation. In addition, we can see that role and territory are often closely associated, sometimes they are invested with considerable expressive significance. So, it is not surprising that, after a brief honeymoon period, rows and tensions between family members and the returning child manifest themselves. Far from offering forebodings that *rapprochement* is not working, quarrels are likely to signify that reunion is on course.

Conclusion

Clearly, reunion with parents and the wider family will not be easily accomplished by the child or adolescent and going home is likely to be as stressful for those who afford a welcome as it is for those who return. Hence, careful management of return should be part of any social work intervention and the same effort that goes into smoothing the pains of separation should also characterise return.

It is also clear that separation and return are part of a continuing process which may take long to complete. Indeed, they may never be accomplished, but, like so many relationships, hover in a limbo of uncertainty. Seeing the child back through the door is not sufficient because we have seen that breakdowns in reunion are not necessarily rapid, clustering in the first few weeks. Rejection and withdrawal take time to negotiate and hope dies long after going back.

Far from being a moment in time, it is difficult to say when a return has actually taken place, just as not being with someone does not necessarily imply separation. Is return the thudding of one's heavy boots on the doormat? Is it the passionate, unfeigned embrace? Is it the inevitable row when tensions over role and territory become explicit and, hopefully, lead to rapid re-definition? Is it when everything is back to normal and the separation can be recollected with nostalgia and a guilty smile?

If we take a process perspective then separation and return cease to be discrete events but colour each other. What happens at the outset will influence the ways participants view subsequent events, as the parable of the prodigal son beautifully illustrates. What happens on return will alter perceptions of and give meaning to the initial separation. Each episode informs the other and an exploration of 'return' can benefit from the adoption of this longitudinal perspective. For example, looking at the episode of entry to care we might ask why was separation necessary in the first place? Who, if anyone, was deficient? How much was everyone a victim of circumstance? The answer to these questions will obviously colour the ways in which links are maintained over time between family and separated child and will also affect reunion.

Thus, it is best if we cease to view moments of separation and return as discrete events but perceive them as part of a continuing process of adaptation in the child, as he or she strives for continuity, meaning and identity. After all, there may be many separations and several attempts at reunion, the return itself will be blurred by preparatory visits, by subsequent departures and by the uneasy mobility of the young person even after re-unification with the family. There is a difference between 'returning', which is a process brimming with fraught possibilities and 'being returned'; indeed, many of our respondents in their interviews suggested that long separation fundamentally alters the ways in which they perceive others and themselves so that reunion is never quite the same as the union which preceded it. In that sense, return is never possible.

While, on return, a voyager may expect people to be the same as at the moment of departure and they similarly expect a facsimile of him who set out, time and experience irrevocably change any actor's performance. In some, such as those returning from ordeals and trauma, such as hostages and servicemen, the gap in comprehension between those coming back and those who stayed cosseted in domestic trivia can lead to breakdown.

This perspective is reinforced as we realise that to return home, children and adolescents have, once more, to separate from those carers and friends with whom close relationships may have been forged during separation. Adolescents are highly likely to have reciprocated relationships with other young people far from the home front. Even the prodigal son might be forgiven for occasionally twitching in nostalgia for past harlots and riotous living. Thus, however welcoming the natural family proves to be on return, some oscillation in the young person's involvement and contentment is to be expected. There is also evidence that separation and withdrawal are effective strategies for coping with stress and that, once learned, such devices are not unattractive. Thus, a young person's movement round the wider family, the succession of comings and goings, may not be particularly detrimental; indeed, in late adolescence movement is a characteristic and well-tried avenue of breaking away from the nest.

While return may be problematic, we have seen that most children and adolescents achieve some sort of reunion with their families; in fact, the majority of these are successful in that few young people return to state care. Even those who do break down and seek placements elsewhere are likely eventually to achieve reunion. Neither should breakdown among those who go back necessarily imply a failure of reunion, in the same way as divorce does not necessarily signify a marriage devoid of satisfactions.

This chapter has alerted us to the difficulties a returning child may experience in resuming lost roles and territories within the family. Nevertheless, for most young people, return also involves re-entry to the neighbourhood and re-integration with friends, whose mobility and transience will complicate re-acceptance. The majority of children and adolescents will go back to school, to employment or to some form of training. It is unlikely that these looms of youth will provide an entirely smooth passage for those who shuttle to and fro. The greatest challenge to those seeking resettlement may not lie within their families but in seeking jobs, in resuming school and community membership. Indeed, when the difficulties inherent in family reunion are compounded by re-adjustment problems outside the home, then return may swiftly end in defeat and flight.

By looking at those episodes significant in the process of reunion, beginning with the stresses and perceptions engendered by the initial separation, we will be able to understand more fully the clusters of adaptations, both within and outside the family, that all returners have to face.

We will see that continuity, role and territory are important at several points in the return process and the messages learned can be used to plan for children's restoration before, during and after the separation. We hope to identify new factors influential in the return process and to fashion guide-lines for social workers making return decisions. Already, three factors suggest themselves which can be applied at successive moments during restoration. We would suggest that children meeting the following criteria are more likely to be reunited with relatives and will have a greater chance of success when:

1. There are continuities in the child's life (including family relationships, education, cultural identity and social networks).

2. The child retains a role within the family at each stage in the return process.

3. The child retains territory in the return home either by having a room, a bed or by the leaving of toys and other personal possessions or by the retention of keepsakes.

As we shall see as we describe the different episodes in the return process, different factors become apparent at successive stages. Let us begin this task with a look at the first episodes in the process, the events surrounding a child's entry to care and early negotiations after separation.

10. Separation from home

Many subsequent negotiations, including reunion, between parent, child and social workers are coloured by early events in the care experience. Here, we look at early episodes in the care career, both entry to care and the first few weeks of separation. These are explored and the significance of these experiences for families and children as they negotiate reunion is illustrated. From this scrutiny of the early days in care we can add several factors to those predictive indices already highlighted in earlier chapters.

We could see in earlier chapters the increasing focus in both child-care policy and legislation on speeding the return of children separated in local authority care back to their parents. Today, ideas of child rescue are unfashionable and families are now seen as the mainstay of children's lives, even of those children who are abused, neglected or beyond control. Thus, preventative work which obviates the need to remove the child from home has once more become a high priority and where this fails, the sharing in the care of the absent child between families and social workers is obligatory. After all, it is to the family that the child will eventually return and any improvements made in the parents' capacity to care will be a considerable bonus.

Getting the child home quickly has high priority with social workers and a strategy for return ought to assume considerable salience in a 'care plan' for the child, just as, in the halcyon days of the reformatory schools, 'after care' was supposed to start as the boys came through the gates. Hopefully, for children in care, this ideal should come closer to realisation than it did for young delinquents.

The alacrity and success of any return is bound up with the processes by which the child entered care and the reasons he or she needs to remain away. We have seen elsewhere the complexity of issues surrounding a child's entry to care. Children will have been referred for help by a wide variety of agencies, such as schools, police or health authorities, all of whom maintain some interest in the solution of the problem. Some candidates for care present themselves or are identified by families and neighbours. While most of those who come to notice merit little action and remain 'known to social services', a minority of referrals are swiftly removed from home, often in crisis circumstances. In previous studies we have seen the ways in which these precipitate departures colour the way parents perceive the intervention and feel able to share in subsequent events.

As we described at the beginning of this study, the outcomes of welfare or educational interventions with children and adolescents can only be evaluated and understood if antecedents are explored. It is important to take a long-term view when scrutinising the situations of children and adolescents because what is a disaster at one moment can easily herald subsequent success. In considering return, therefore, knowledge of the antecedents of the care situation and key moments in the separation process are very important. After all, the unexpected resurrection of Lenin would certainly re-awaken many issues which surrounded the dissolution of his empire. Roles and territories would have been occupied by others, possession of which would be unlikely to survive longer than the evening of his return, and temporal continuities would most certainly wither. Thus, the swiftness and success of any reunion is likely to be much influenced by what has gone before, by the preparations made for return, by the legitimacy of the original separation and by the resolution of problems while the families are apart. Like the young men of Alsace, who long kept two uniforms in the cupboard, one German, one French, successfully coping with any return implies a keen awareness of and accommodation to preceding events.

We will now turn to key moments in the process of reunion and to the 'episodes', the function of which has been previously described. Initially, however, it is helpful to describe the situation of the 31 children and 24 families who participated in the intensive study.

Episode One: Separation

Children enter care for many reasons and by many legal routes. We have seen among the 31 children in our intensive study that 16 were accommodated under voluntary arrangements, leaving 15 who were on care or emergency protection orders. The expected lengths of children's stay in care varied depending on these and other factors.

Short-stay admissions are usually voluntary arrangements between social workers and families and most follow temporary family breakdowns, usually a mother's illness or confinement. In the majority of these cases families view social services in a very positive way. Such admissions involve many younger children, often sets of siblings, most of whom are placed in foster care. This mode of entry to care characterised eight of the families we scrutinised in this part of our study. Their needs were short-term and social workers hoped that reunion would be possible within six months of entry to care. Indeed, in two cases, the child was already at home by the time we first saw the family. As might be expected, these short-term separations posed fewer problems on reunion than others.

The intermediate and long-stay returners, in contrast, included more children who had experienced severe abuse or neglect as well as adolescents seriously beyond control. Residential care and placements at home under 'charge and control' were more common for these young people and, in these cases, social workers viewed returns as a more delicate task.

We know that children rarely come into care unexpectedly. While the actual admission may be precipitate, 16 of the 31 children we studied were well known to social services and ten had been in care before. These proportions closely mirror general care admissions. Prior to admission, therefore, considerable negotiations had taken place in many cases between families, children and social workers. These initial contacts were also likely to colour the ways in which family and children perceived entry to care, particularly when, as Packman, Randall and Jacques (1986) have demonstrated, the degree of choice for families is restricted.

So much for the characteristics of the 31 children involved in the intensive study. Let us now turn to the circumstances of their separations and their effect upon subsequent return experiences.

We have seen elsewhere the complexity of issues surrounding a child's entry to care. The admission of a child poses a variety of immediate problems. Social workers have to choose the appropriate legal route into care, decide where the child should live and, wherever possible, negotiate access between families and absent children. Our research would suggest that in making these plans, much will depend on the length of time the separation is expected to last and on factors such as the reasons for entry to care, knowledge of the family and the availability of resources. In addition, the involvement of outside agencies, such as police or courts, not only complicate social work decisions but affect the ways in which families and children perceive the legitimacy and wisdom of the separation. Police intervention is highly likely to outrage families and sour subsequent events, while health visitors, for example, are more amicably accepted.   Subsequent decisions crystallise these initial perceptions, emphasising certain options and closing others.

As the child enters care, parents have to cope with the loss of their offspring in circumstances that are generally stigmatising. They have to handle a mixture of feelings, such as failure, anxiety, mourning and anger, and develop coping strategies, such as what to tell relatives and neighbours. In most contexts, their views will be forceful.

'If I could stand up in court and tell the judge everything, he'd understand and let me have my babies back,'

said one resolute mother whose access had been restricted.

'My daughter is ill and needs help, it was quite wrong to take the children from her,'

appealed a grand-mother in a letter to us. While another aggrieved parent added,

'I went to social services for help and what did I get? They took away my children and made me feel like a criminal. When they come back I'm clearing out somewhere else where social workers will never find me.'

For children, too, an entry to care involves major transitions, even traumatic upheavals, with all the disorientation, stress and adjustments associated with such moves. Even for them, tears are not necessarily a barometer of feelings.

'They took me to a foster home. I didn't know where. I still don't know why. Everything I knew went and I've never got it back.'

In contrast, some children see the changes as necessary and find them easy and enjoyable.

'When Mummy's ill, we go to Mrs. Fraser's; we love it. They've got a hamster and a goldfish there and Mr. Fraser acts silly and makes us laugh.'

Before and after the admission, various negotiations have to take place, some reassuring, some less so. Two mothers told us:

'I didn't know what to tell my mother; we meet in Kwik-Save every Tuesday, so I said I'd got the 'flu and didn't go but she'd heard about the kids being taken away from our Pamela (my sister)'.

'They said Amanda would go to a special centre where experts would get her back to school. They said it was a treatment place and she'd stay for six weeks. I was so worried that I just nodded. But after they'd gone, I thought how the hell will they get her to school when I haven't been able to for a year? They came back after a fortnight and said she needed intensive care and now I don't see her at all.'

In all these negotiations, return will be on the agenda from the start, either as a clearly expected outcome or as a generally desirable aim; on the other hand the issue may remain significant simply because everyone ignores it, as the following examples show.

One mother recalled,

'I went to this meeting and they explained where the twins were going and it sounded very nice. It was all about how I could visit and what the foster parents were like. I got home and Stuart (partner) said 'when are they letting them come back?', I just looked blank and said, 'No-one mentioned anything about that'. He said I was an idiot and we had a row.'

The social worker in talking to the above parents at a subsequent meeting said reassuringly,

'Of course we want the children back, Mrs. Campion. We're not being critical but we have to be sure it's right for them and that might be some time. You need to sort yourselves out first.'

In an interview with us, the social worker elaborated,

'I can talk to Karen (the mother). She knows I'm on her side. She knows that I opposed the adoption when the psychiatrist suggested it and recommended work towards rehabilitation as soon as possible. Basically, she loves the children and vice-versa. She's a bit unstable mentally but the most she's ever threatened was that she'd once felt like she might harm them and when I said 'how?' she replied, 'by hitting them.' It really annoys me when the senior talks of child protection because I've never seen any evidence they need it.'

The response of families

Our previous study of children, *Lost in Care*, showed that there were several routes into care. Naturally, all of the 31 children in this intensive study were separated and they too illustrate the wide variety of situations that can lead to a child being looked after. Some left home willingly, while two left swiftly under emergency arrangements. Six of the families involved groups of siblings but the others departed alone. We recorded the distress of weeping parents who felt their child's departure as a bereavement, others viewed separation as a familiar recurrence and three mothers could not face the event at all. Similar variations were seen in other aspects of the care admission, in the role taken up by social workers, the receptions offered by carers and the style of interactions that accompanied the children's initial separation.

How should we interpret all these observations? We know that the way separation is handled has important consequences. Indeed, it is quite clear from our follow-up work that initial perceptions colour future relationships between families and social services. Aggrieved parents can respond in many ways but bad early experiences rarely lead to cooperation and, even less, to participation in social work plans. Similarly, difficulties encountered in early visits cause parents to withdraw from their child's life, engendering problems for later returns. At the moment of separation, parents are highly likely to be preoccupied with their own problems and changes at home, particularly new relationships and reconstituted households. They may find the traumas of separating from their child overwhelming or may use the stress of separation as an excuse to avoid facing the problems that necessitated the child's removal.

The child's entry to care and the separation that accompanies it is, therefore, an outcome of a long and complex family history and much of what follows, including the eventual return, is affected by both the reasons for the child's entry to care and its style of implementation. Thus, the management of return is specific to each case and needs a thorough understanding of all the antecedents leading to a child's separation.

Bitterness can endure long as this poignant quotation from a child's letter to a dying father shows:

'I am sorry you are gone. I wish we could have had some more good times together. In some ways I am glad it is over. I wish you could have been a good adviser like the staff here. I have a lot of complicated feelings and I do not know how to put them. From your loving son, Dan.'

The response of children's relatives is particularly affected by the way that the separation was seen to have been handled. If the child's departure was well managed, there was less anxiety and there was less chance of parents and social workers becoming bitter. One social worker explained why he had overridden parents' request for fostering with relatives and outraged the wider family.

> 'It's all very well them talking about the extended family. Mother's relationship with her mother was explosive. So suggesting that Darren might have gone to his grandparents opened up all the old wounds. Putting Darren with grandma and grandad would be like sticking him in lodgings and he's only six.'

It was clear from the cases we studied that some families and children were far more prepared psychologically and culturally for separation than others. This anticipation had several aspects: in three cases, parents had been in care themselves and the pre-socialisation took the form of inter-generational awareness.

> 'I and my sisters were in care six times. I think my gran was in an orphanage in Ireland as a girl as well. I was fifteen before I realised that every child did not have a social worker.'

In three other cases, there was a cultural tradition either of private fostering or of high geographical mobility of wage earners and a sharing of care amongst female relatives.

> 'You must realise that in the Caribbean the family structures are different on different islands. In Jamaica, the men worked away and the women looked after the children.'

As a consequence, preparations for care varied considerably. One mother shopped in Boots as if her child was off on a school trip, while seven others claimed to have been neither consulted nor informed until the day of separation.

Certainly it would seem that the ease and success of return are influenced by the quality of social work offered at the time of separation. Many parents are numbed by numerous anxieties not all associated with the loss of their children. When the problems leading to separation are perceived as likely to be ameliorated or resolved by a separation and the intervention is seen by the family as legitimate and in the best interests of the child then, we would hypothesize, return will be less difficult. Reunions chill when the issue of return reopens unresolved difficulties.

Nevertheless, at this stage, there is still a great deal that social workers can do to obviate problems later on. By bridging the two worlds of the child and keeping parents involved in decisions, social workers can ease participants' sense of personal failure and reduce the likelihood of fantasy which, as we shall see, can complicate reunion. Particularly important is to avoid the sense of mutual loss. This means helping relatives and children anticipate and interpret what the return will be like, for example by getting parents to chart the changes in their household and the consequences of these for the home-coming.

Does a successful separation affect return? For all parties, the separation brought about by the child's admission to care proved extremely stressful. This was more because of expressive failure rather than poor organisation. The actual dynamics of the child's entry to care were viewed as well-handled in the majority (70%) of cases and, although most children were understandably anxious, most found the experience less stressful than expected. In fact, while a few families spoke of a sense of release, many families and children found the event something of an anti-climax.

It was the affective component of separation that raised most anxiety. Parents felt guilty, especially that they had failed their child and let down their wider family. In the eyes of others they had fallen short. Children felt rejected, partly because of the rift and partly because their families seemed powerless to help them. Their worries focused on matters, such as territory, that may seem trivial to an outsider, 'Will my brother get my toys?' 'I bet she'll pinch my gear'. But such apparently superficial concerns reflect much deeper insecurities about their situation. Often, the long-term viability of their family is questioned. Is it a family in anything but name? As one child recalled,

> 'One night I dreamt the phone rang, I picked it up and it was Auntie Kate. She just said 'Your mother's dead'. I woke up sweating and couldn't get back to sleep. Did I have a family or was I like some orphan in story books?'

Return also has an affective dimension. It tests our perceptions of whether people really want us back and whether they are keeping our memory alive while we are away. Unfortunately, during this episode, return was rarely discussed as part of the care plan, other than in very general terms of how long the child would be away and what home visits should take place. But for most children it was the only question that mattered. All kinds of symbols indicated to them the priority afforded by parents and social workers to return. One eight year old, Jason, correctly interpreted his mother's casual comment to a neighbour about taking in a lodger as a sign that his speedy return from care was not wanted, despite the social worker's repeated assurances that this was far from true. Another six year old was reassured by his mother's romantic suggestion that at bed-time they should both look at the moon and they would know that each was thinking of the other. Return is built into the strategy of separation and its possibility and imminence should be honestly faced by everyone. Expressive continuities are, for youngsters, constantly threatened by temporal continuities and we should not underestimate children's sensitivity to the symbols, actions and expressions of adults, siblings and peers. Children, like us, only too easily get the wrong messages. Anxiety makes them distrustful.

The stresses caused by separation also vary; they arise for different reasons at different points in children's care careers. On the first occasion, there is considerable fear of the future, but as time passes the focus of anxiety changes. But, the distress experienced by children does not seem to diminish on repeated separations, an anxiety noticed by researchers studying children who oscillate in and out of hospital.

Why do repeated separations feel more difficult? It may be that the failures and disappointments of previous reunions suggest to children and parents that their problems are insuperable. Separation, far from being an unwelcome incident in life's rich pattern, is likely to become the pattern itself. On the other hand it may be that the focus of anxiety changes; the threats posed to children by the mechanics of separation fade with familiarity, allowing feelings of insecurity, discontinuity and rootlessness to assume greater salience.

The initial separation can be viewed, therefore, as a key moment in the process of return. Sensitively managed, the rift need not hinder eventual reunion but all too often the anxieties and violations of the episode linger and magnify. On departure, roles change as the absent adolescent becomes the prodigal and as parents face up to feelings of bereavement.

Of course, the absentee rapidly learns that emotional and physical territories are vacated and may be occupied by others. There are many rites of passage in this process. Some of these are overt, such as case conferences, the signing of papers and the packing of clothes; others are covert, such as the moment when entry to care emerges as a possibility, gaining importance as the family's problems refuse to budge. These moments of truth are very clear to children and families and markedly contrast with the few signposts which characterise and ease return.

In order to ease the pains of separation, continuity is stressed both formally and informally as children leave for care. Social workers mollify all parties, stressing that the absence will be as short as possible and that contacts between children and families will be frequent. In all too many cases these reassurances markedly contrast with what actually happens. Families and children feel betrayed. Other continuities of experience may also be promoted, such as keeping the child at the same school or maintaining the child's racial identity. Even at this early stage, the extent to which expressive continuities are maintained lays the foundations for the ease of later returns.

The separation experiences of children in care, therefore, should not be viewed in isolation but as part of a sequence of events in which family and children have had to accommodate many disintegrating experiences. Entry to care may solve the immediate problems facing a family and child and, hopefully, should promote or protect the young person's welfare, but for some, particularly for those whose stay in care is extended, the care experience can open the door to new problems - the secondary difficulties of coping with separations, managing new relationships and mastering changed living situations. Indeed, interactionist psychologists have suggested that these can prove overwhelming, even displacing the primary problems for which care was originally deemed necessary.

> 'Jason came here for assessment but we're now thinking of at least 18 months in our treatment unit,'

said one group worker, reacting to the discovery referred to earlier that Jason's mother had let his bedroom. The fact that his sister had entered care with him and was also likely to stay as a result of this decision aroused little concern from relatives or social workers, despite the fact that her needs were somewhat different.

As our review of recent research has shown, the changes which follow an admission to care have been well documented. Indeed, it was anxiety over the instability of many children's placements and relationships while in care that encouraged the development of concepts such as 'drift' and 'permanency planning' in the 1970s. But it is only in recent years that their extent and complexity have been fully appreciated. We have looked at the separation in the context of return and have highlighted areas where sensitivity to the experience of child and family may subsequently ease reunion.

There are several factors which might be rewarded by further exploration in a predictive exercise but we would hypothesize that return will be eased and is likely to be more successful when,

> Family and children perceive the problems necessitating the original separation to have been resolved or to have been much assisted by the child's admission to care.

Episode Two: Changes in circumstance

So much for the entry to care, what happens in the days and months following separation? The histories of the children included in our intensive scrutiny confirm the patterns noted earlier. In Chapter Six, for example, it was found that the composition of the natural family was highly likely to change during the child's absence. New babies and step-parents greeted returning children while previous household members well-known to the child departed. Children also often returned to new and radically different households and experienced considerable movement both while in care and in their home circumstances.

Changes highlighted in our previous research were also common. Links between families and absent children declined even in situations where everyone wished them to flourish, siblings in care were separated, parents felt de-skilled and played a diminishing role in their child's life. Social work contacts with the natural family became infrequent or were lost altogether.

This cluster of events, we concluded, characterised the histories of children who had become 'lost in care' and affected as many as one in seven of the long-stay group. These residual cases were highly dependent on the welfare system. For example, they had no friends outside care and they were culturally and socially anomic. Unfortunately, many of the adverse effects of separation do not become apparent until the child's return home becomes an issue.

To the points raised in the research, several factors highlighted by our intensive case studies are important. First, there is a tendency for new information to emerge about children and families as a result of the increased scrutiny which accompanies the child's stay in care. Some of this new knowledge was so significant that it radically altered care plans, preventing the return of many children. But, equally important is information that would never have been discovered had the child not left home. This often has the effect of reducing social worker's confidence in parents' ability to care and engendering misgivings regarding return plans.

'I was quite happy about mother's competence and her ability to care for Tracey until I found out that as an unmarried teenager she had given birth to a child which she tried to keep but which had to be removed for protection and was ultimately adopted. This really threw me. It delayed Tracey's return for six months until I was sure the home was O.K. I know it's silly but I just lost my nerve. I couldn't take the risk and I'd done ten years in the mental health team.'

Tracey's mother, too, noticed the change:

'I always got on well with Mrs. Thomas (social worker) until one day I told her my own life history and how I didn't want Tracey to suffer the same things as me. She seemed to turn off and on the next visit when I asked 'will Tracey be home for Easter?', I got all sorts of excuses.'

A second problem results from the diminishing contacts between social workers and the natural family during the child's absence. Not only do links between family and absent child wither but when social workers have no contact and no means of re-establishing it, currency between social worker and family is devalued. Entry to reconstituted families poses particular problems when new arrivals take leadership roles.

In *Lost in Care*, we noted that contact between parents and absent children was maintained in several ways. There were visits, letters and phone calls; there were feelings of belonging to home and community; there was the currency of news and information, perhaps acquired through third parties; and there was children's awareness of their parents' power (if any) to act in their interests. If this currency is devalued and squandered, families have little to talk about.

Our interviews, which charted over time the perceptions of participants in the return process, all emphasise the importance of fantasy in maintaining contacts between separated people. By fantasy we mean an image that is visionary and fanciful, existing largely in the imagination and based on unfounded beliefs. It was often hard to distinguish fantasy from reality in the comments that parents and children made. For example, one 17 year old who had been completely rejected by his family but still hoped to return to live nearby told us that at week-ends when they did not telephone:

'I bet they're out finding me a nice flat'

A mother told us how she longed for her children's return and while waiting passed her time in the following way:

'I'm pretty hard up and often feel lonely, so about three times a week, I spend the evenings in town looking in the shops and gas and electric showrooms, imagining the things I will buy to make a nice home for the boys'.

Clearly, such perceptions serve to sustain relationships during the separation but can become so essential a coping strategy that they remain unmodified, even in the face of clear contrary evidence. Return becomes a moment of truth, a situation in which reality and fantasy meet. It is these gaps in perception and the fear of their exposure that makes return so difficult for all concerned.

The Child's View

Nowhere are these contrasting perceptions of return more poignantly demonstrated than in talking to children. Piaget (1954) suggested that children's thinking at primary school age is egocentric thus raising questions about interpreting their responses but his theory, with its emphasis on developmental stages and its scanting of affectivity, is now much questioned. Nevertheless, as Hobson's (1985) review of Piaget's contribution concludes, we still need to ask how children of all ages experience misfortune and loss.

It was difficult for us to gauge how far the children we interviewed could perceive alternatives to where they were and so have some understanding of what return would actually mean. Nonetheless, the children we interviewed all had a clear perception of 'home'. They knew who was in it and all but six of them wanted to be there. But it was a static view of a situation as they had once known it, a perception reinforced by the endless 'waiting' that seems such a feature of children's care experiences and which is so often exacerbated by chronic anxiety. Any subsequent change in the home situation, therefore, proved very difficult for children to comprehend. In addition, the young people displayed considerable anxiety that their home would disappear. Several explained vividly how they thought that their mother and siblings might simply go away and nothing would be left for them. Children seem to be aware of the fragility of the family home even if changes in its structure and membership are less easy to assimilate. We previously described Amanda, a 15 year old long in care. In this episode, she tearfully told us,

> 'I worry it will all disappear. I'll go back and there'll be nothing, just a big space.'

Such views may, of course, reflect the children's desperate attempts to make sense of what has happened to them. Indeed, many children felt extremely guilty that they had been or could be the cause of the family fragmentation they feared. This is exacerbated by the child's perception that something damaged can never be repaired. It was also clear that, in their anxiety to return, children pick up and distort information not intended for their ears.

Particularly affected by the static view of the natural family were children's views of other youngsters in the household. A likely effect of family dislocation and reconstitution is an increase in the number of siblings, whether natural, half or step, and of 'cousins' who can be numerous in large families. As Wedge and Mantle (1991) have shown, permutations of relationships within a family are greatly increased with the addition of a new child.

This difficulty in incorporating the changes taking place at home can lead to surprises when children re-encounter their siblings as a two year period produces considerable changes in children and adolescents. Teenagers, for example, quickly graduate from motor-bikes to the opposite sex or from romance magazines to the real thing. Thus, the time span of care careers is even more significant for sibling changes than it is for parents' situations.

It is difficult to conclude what precisely children in care can and cannot comprehend about future return to home and community. They can certainly remember people from their past and speak affectionately about them. They also have a clear perception of home, static as that view might be. Yet, under the stresses posed by an impending return, they clearly find it difficult to think logically or organise their feelings.

Important changes occur in the situations of the children away in care and their natural families. The problems posed by separation have to be tackled, family compositions alter, children move around and contact between social workers, children and families declines. These changes are not always apparent until return is considered. In addition, the new situation is compounded by the effects of new information that emerges from increased professional scrutiny and the difficulties social workers face in negotiating with reconstituted families. The diverging views of participants and the gaps between fantasy and reality also come into play, making it difficult for children to understand their situation.

From this more intensive look at children's care experience, we would suggest that the following factors are associated with children's favourable return outcomes.

1. No radically new information about family problems emerges during the separation.

2. Social workers find little difficulty in visiting the family or gaining accurate information.

3. Participants' perspectives of the return are realistic and there are no wide gaps between fantasy and reality in their perceptions.

Conclusions

Considerable research attention has focused on the deleterious effects of a child's separation from home but few investigations have explored the influence of the removal from home upon subsequent reunion. In this chapter, we have used the experience of the 31 children in the intensive study to address this issue.

The majority of children in care are reunited with parents or other relatives and social work planning can accommodate the draw home by an inclusive approach to the family. But entry to care can muddy even the clearest waters; parents can become mistrustful of social work efforts; children lose whatever security is afforded by their family life and expressive continuities which have given coherence to their existence are questioned; social workers find that their initial perspectives are complicated as new information on the family comes to light.

Very often, the tensions and anxieties associated with removal from home do not surface during the child's entry to care, but it is unlikely that they have evaporated. Indeed, as children and parents cope with the immediate problems of being apart, the causes and consequences of separation can be suppressed but they eventually surface in the days that follow reunion.

11. Return becomes an issue

At some moments in a separated child's career in care, the prospect of reunion becomes a strong possibility. For the majority of children, return becomes an issue early on in their care careers, for others many months may elapse before reunion is considered. We look here at the moment when social workers, children and families begin to face up to the challenges and realignments posed by reunion. Family roles will have to be re-learned and re-defined, cherished territories abandoned or shared. The episode of the first few days at home is also explored, highlighting the anxieties and false expectations engendered in many children and families as a welcome is extended.

There is a point in the child's career when return home becomes an issue. This is not to say that the child's rehabilitation has not previously been considered, indeed, for short-term care cases, return plans are probably initiated at the point of reception. But there comes a time when social workers bend their minds to returning the child.

For ten of the 31 children reunion had been part of social work plans on the day of separation, although for one young girl several previous attempts had failed to achieve restoration. For others, return plans began much later and, in five cases involving adolescents, it had begun two or more years after the entry to care. The reasons which stimulated plans for reunion varied with each child. In some cases home circumstances improved, in others, children's behaviour calmed down, while occasionally time and options simply ran out. Indeed, for ten children, return home was precipitated by events that were largely external and unexpected.

Episode Three: Return becomes an issue

Let us look at the effects of raising the prospect of return among parents and children. As reunion began to loom large it was clear that even the mention of return generated widespread anxiety among children and families, foster carers and social workers. We noted earlier as a general feature that return is universally stressful but even the thought of it seems to be frightening and occasionally disturbing, no matter how much people long for or expect it.

As one young person said:

'When Mrs.Dass said,'I think it's time we got you home', my stomach turned over, my heart beat fast, my hands sweated, I wanted to go to the toilet and I tried to change the subject. Yet, it's what I'd wanted her to say for ages.'

For parents, too, reunion means disruption, extra responsibility and additional expense. As a mother said:

'I know it's awful but we've got used to him being away and enjoy his coming home for short stays. The thought of having him back for good worried us, all the noise, washing, cost, getting him up for school. We couldn't sleep all night worrying about what to do and could we cope.'

Social workers also feared that return might signal a repetition of previous difficulties, especially in abuse situations.

'I wanted him home. I could see him getting institutionalised and the proper place for a child is with their family. But he had probably been physically abused and certainly he was neglected. Frankly, it's a risk to say that it won't happen again. I sometimes envisage a scenario of Blom-Cooper as the arresting officer and me as Martin Ruddock'.

The reasons for these fears are several. First, there is the fact that the fantasies which sustain the separation, described in the last episode, come under scrutiny. The idea of return questions their validity and raises suspicion about their shaky foundations. Indeed, several children we interviewed implied they had forgotten what living at home was really like, just as some parents said they could not remember how life was when the children were there. While fantasies may be functional for surviving a separation, there is certain to be a degree of 'let down' when return actually occurs. Naturally, the severity of the disappointment will vary according to the situation, the investment each has in the reunion and the extent to which reality accords with happy anticipation. Unfortunately, some aspects of reunion are not open to negotiation and fantasy reconciliation, such as a new baby or fresh neighbourhood; one simply has to get on with it.

Inklings about these future disappointments begin to nag as return becomes an issue. As Lord Macaulay wrote,

Dark and terrible was the day of their flight; far darker and far more terrible will be the day of their return.

As a mother described,

> 'When our social worker left (having discussed plans for reunion) I remember exactly how I felt. I've only ever felt like it once before. My father died one March when we were young and everyone was very kind. They said everything would be all right and we'd got the light nights to look forward to. But I remember after the funeral, everyone just went. Me and my sisters and my mother were left sitting there to face everything with no money or anything. That's what it was like when I heard they wanted Christopher to come home; I was suddenly frightened and felt I'm on my own.'

Secondly, fears of return are aroused because, as we have seen, roles often change when people live apart. Yet, we also observed contrasting strategies to maintain continuity. Children and families learn new roles and assume them whole-heartedly; they create new routines in a way that seems to deny and shut out the past. Indeed, so great can be the attachment to new situations that there is a vested interest in maintaining the separation. Thus, return is seen as a threat to the *status quo* and so creates anxiety.

A different coping strategy is oblivion, where children and families appear to forget the fact that they are separated and carry on as if nothing had happened. The pain of separation is denied and preoccupation with the trivial and immediate blocks out any regret. This response is sometimes interpreted by social workers as indifference. Children and families fail to involve themselves and are happy to drift along, they seem unaware of the damage done to their situation by separation. Both these adaptations strive to maintain continuity in shattered lives; but, as we shall see, each has different implications for the fulfilment of return plans.

While the thought of return is universally stressful, the preparation for the event is equally difficult. Nevertheless, there will usually be clear social work strategies, such as encouraging frequent access between relatives and absent children and regular weekend visits with over-night stays. But while *Lost in Care* showed that these are essential conditions for re-unification, they provide insecure foundations for reunion, particularly when relationships between children and families are poor.

Week-end contact is, of course, easy to arrange. It has the added advantage that it can be convenient to carers and is generally perceived by all as a good idea. Students, lovers and families the world over reserve week-ends as a time for the deeper things in life. In practice, however, both children in care and their families told us that they find such arrangements quite difficult to handle. The amount of access between parents and absent children gives little indication of the problems likely to arise on return.

In managing return, social workers usually focus on organisational issues such as facilitating access, arranging suitable accommodation and, wherever possible, meeting the wishes of families and children. Issues important to families facing the return of their child, however, are much more likely to be concerned with affective, emotional and even spiritual matters. Relatives will be thinking about how the returning child is perceived and asking whether he or she is really loved.

The evidence would suggest, therefore, that weekend visits are an appropriate preparation for return provided they do not become routinised or used as a reward. As our previous studies on children's family links have shown, contact between children and families has many functions. When return becomes an issue, there is a need to distinguish between access as a means of securing reunion and access for its intrinsic worth, for example, to maintain continuity in the child's life.

Working for return has to be seen as a negotiation of a set of roles, both instrumental and expressive, rather than simply regaining everything that was lost. This is why seemingly trivial things can become the focus of return hopes and negotiations. As one adolescent recalled:

> 'I remember when I was away in care last time, I kept thinking of my things at home. I lay in bed and I was thinking about my old records and one in particular. I felt if I could get back and play it everything would be alright. Funnily enough, when I got home, I don't think I ever put it on.'

In this context, weekend contacts and other access arrangements merely serve to facilitate the child's return. The danger is that they may not provide sufficient time to clarify or practise the new roles required. Short visits can be honeymoons and regular access is not a normal style of contact between children and parents. Both may give insufficient time to prepare everyone for establishing the *modus vivendi* that must follow the return.

While all but a few children experience return, the contexts in which it takes place are varied indeed. There are different levels and patterns of return and different grades of 'fixedness'. When we first looked at the 31 cases at the point when return for them became an issue, several major dimensions in which return contexts differed were identified. Each suggests questions that need to be answered when considering the way a child's return takes place.

Have there been previous separations and reunions?

Who initiated the return process?

Does the child's situation carry stigma?

Are the child's or parents' expectations of return unduly high?

What rights, formal and informal, does the child have to return?

Have either the parents or child used delaying tactics?

Has the memory of the absent child been kept alive in the home?

Do parents and child feel that past problems have been resolved?

Is there a refuge for the child if things go wrong?

When return becomes an issue, family, child and social workers begin to reap what was sown at the time of separation. Anxieties are aroused and conflicting attitudes and perceptions will be stringently tested as return plans proceed.

Indeed, when we studied the situation of the 31 children at the point at which social workers informed us that their return was under active consideration, it was clear that many families and children were still depressed socially, psychologically and economically even though reunion was imminent. Admission to care often eased situations by reducing the demands on parents and children but it was equally clear that to facilitate return, people's resilience and resolve have to be built up. This requires several strategies from social workers. There are relatively straightforward matters of housing and finance: incidentally, a constant concern of parents was the need to get child allowance paid quickly after the young person's return. But, equally important, are the conditions just described and the need to boost participants' self-esteem, clarify outstanding issues and give people confidence that things will work out.

Planning for return once more stirs the waters first clouded by the entry to care. Parents', children's and social workers' anxieties heighten. Even if an inclusive social work approach has been adopted, participants' perceptions have been realistic and the entry to care has resolved some of the problems which led the family to social services' door, when return becomes an issue, new complications will arise.

We have highlighted some strategies social workers might adopt to calm participants' anxieties but are there any factors we can propose to be associated with return outcomes? From the intensive data on 31 children, three indicators in this episode appear to be related to whether or not a child absent in care will go back to live with parents or other relatives. These are:

1. Participants absorb and identify with the roles generated by the child's return.

2. The child and family see the care situation as negotiable.

3. The problems necessitating the original separation are perceived as having been partially resolved at the point at which return becomes an issue.

Episode Four: The first days at home

Despite social workers' belief that the return of the child was under urgent consideration, and in some cases was imminent, not all 31 children went back home. Indeed, the anxiety aroused in everybody by raising the possibility of reunion foiled return in many cases.

Thus, only 20 of the 31 children under scrutiny actually went home to live in the 18 months we studied them. Some went back soon after separation, others were reunited with new relatives after prolonged periods apart from their family but in many reunions it was difficult to isolate the actual moment of return. Even for the 12 children whose restoration was planned by social workers, it was difficult to say when reunion was complete. In four cases, the child drifted back home and another four children, voting with their feet, ran back to their parents not knowing if they would be able to stay.

Although social workers and relatives, sometimes independently, made quite elaborate plans for children's restoration, aims and objectives seldom came fully to fruition. Even when social work plans seemed to be working especially well, a family's anxiety to hurry things along to a successful conclusion often encouraged parents to circumvent arrangements and, once begun, some returns assumed a momentum of their own. For example, one mother explained:

'Well, everybody at social services was very happy but not much seemed to be happening. So we kept making arrangements with the foster parents to keep Chris for a bit longer and then a bit longer and so, although she's not due back now until (three weeks time), as you can see she's here with me. I don't think everybody's happy but on the other hand they are leaving well alone.'

Clearly, it is difficult for social workers to delay reunion in order to allow family members to overcome possible obstacles. So, even in planned returns, it was difficult to isolate the moment of reunion. This speeding up of events does not appear to be detrimental to the eventual success of the return, although it was clear from many of our interviews that parents missed the opportunity to mark the event in a formal manner. This is illustrated by a mother who said to us:

'He was back before he should have been, as you know. And that was what we wanted, but we missed the chance to make a bit of a fuss. My first husband had been in the Navy and the days he came back were sheer joy. Most of the time we hated each other, but I loved those days and I wanted the same for Dan. They made a big fuss when he had to go away and it would have been nice to say "great to have you back".'

For those children who drifted back to parents, the day of return was even more unclear. Visits turn into overnight stays which become a week at home, only to be punctuated by a trip with the foster family. However, parents and children often retrospectively impose a point of reunion on complicated situations. So John, a 12 year old boy separated from his mother at the same time she left his father, was able to comment:

'I was sitting at home on Sunday having tea. I'd been out all day with people 'round here, Granny was here, Phil (the new step-father) was back from the pub and we were watching Bullseye on the telly. I didn't say much I suppose, but it was a really nice day. And then Mum asked me about going back and I said 'I'm not going'. And she didn't say anything so I suppose it was alright and I've been here since really.'

Parents similarly marked the point of reunion with the benefit of hindsight and this moment often occurred before the child came home to stay. A revitalised sense of belonging, triggered by a shared moment remembered, was often cited as the point at which parents felt their child was back.

For the remaining children who ran back to their parents, the point of reunion was, in one sense, clearly identifiable and memorable. However, the anxiety which followed seldom made for clarity of purpose or perception. Children were seldom sure their parents wanted them home, relatives felt concerned that social workers would object to a precipitate reunion and, indeed, social workers were always uneasy in such situations. So once again, the point of return was not always clear; was it the day the child ran home; the day the parents decided the child's return was a good idea; or when the social workers acquiesced in the train of events?

The evidence from the intensive study has led us to conclude that the moment of return occurs when sufficient family members feel that the child has come home to live. It is rare for all participants in a reunion to see the event in a positive light and, indeed, most will harbour lingering doubts. Relatives' and children's views on reunion will be coloured by their experience of separation and they are seldom entirely confident of the future. Nevertheless, their judgements of progress were usually reliable, even in apparently cursory remarks, such as 'I'm home to stay now' or 'It's not quite right, yet'.

Expectations and emotional upheaval

We have seen that, in comparison with the first episode in the return process, there are few rites of passage to mark a child's restoration. The clandestine way in which parents short-circuit social work plans or the slow drift home which characterises other reunions make it difficult for the family to celebrate. This may be an area in which social workers can help, making return something of a celebration. One should remember that the 'leaving prize' or retirement gold watch not only signifies the end of a long experience and the start of something new but, for the recipient, such moments mean that previous roles and territories cannot be resumed. Whilst there cannot be a general prescription appropriate to all cases, providing families with a date and means to commemorate formally a homecoming, would be welcomed in many of the cases we studied.

It is clear that it is difficult for social workers to plan a child's return and, if the family takes increasing responsibility, the outsider's role in the home can be less than straightforward. However, the evidence would suggest that once a decision has been taken that the child's best interests would be served if he or she were at home, the subsequent plans for reunion do not necessarily hold the key to success. More important are the participants' perspectives and their feelings that events are going at the right pace.

Several factors appear to influence participants' experience of the reunion. Initially, family members, especially the adults, are guided by cultural expectations, that is what they feel they are supposed to do. Memories of past separations and reunions also play their part and contribute to the reunion's being emotionally charged. However, with no rites of passage into which these emotions can be channelled, anxieties linger and, as we shall see, are neutralised in a short honeymoon period during which everybody is on their best behaviour. However, some family members are not fully involved in the reunion. Step-parents, for example, who have moved into the home during the child's separation from mother or father watch the return with suspicion and they too help to shape the way in which other family members view the event. Let us look at these features in more detail.

Family members often sensed that they were under scrutiny, that they were being assessed, especially during the days that surrounded the return. To an extent their apprehension was correct, for many social workers did notice a change in behaviour and expressive roles as the final restoration of child to family neared. One social worker commented:

> 'They're suddenly hugging for the first time ever. He walks in the door and Joan (the mother) gives him a big hug. I've been taking him on home leaves for two years and normally he walks in the door and nobody bats an eyelid.'

There is a contrast between those aspects of the return which are conducted in public and those which are private, involving only the family. For instance, neighbours may provide an audience for reunion and parents also put on an overt display of affection. However, when the family is alone, displays of affection can lose their function and the reunion becomes a disappointing, low-key affair, especially when parents contrast the event with cultural expectations. One mother illustrated this when she said:

> 'I had this idea it would be like something out of the movies with violins and everybody happy and we wanted to make a fuss but it wasn't really like that. It was all a bit empty really, I can't explain it to you.'

In the few cases where the final return was more clearly marked, the participants' satisfactions with the event were much greater. Mrs. Abbot who went with the social worker to collect her child John and his possessions from the foster parent's house obviously felt everything had gone well:

> 'We got everything ready and said our farewells to Brian and Sylvia (the foster parents) and I thought, I know this doesn't sound nice, but I thought you're not needed any more. I thought from that moment that I was back in control. Then we (mother and child) chatted in the back of the car on the way back, got rid of the neighbours and Steph (the social worker) and had a little party just ourselves. It was quiet, but it was just what we needed.'

Often participants' memories of previous separations and reunions were suddenly evoked, particularly for those parents who were in care themselves. Several parents broke down as they tried to recount their experiences at the moment of return:

> 'It all came flooding back to me. I didn't know what set me off. I was nervous and I opened the door and he was standing there in his school uniform looking all smart and I thought "I should never have let him go, what was I thinking of, letting him go" and I thought "never again, you're never going to leave me again". And I was crying my heart out and holding him tight, I don't think he knew what was happening but he was a bit tearful too. It was supposed to be a happy moment and it was really, but I was in a terrible state.'

Clearly, people have high hopes of return, expectations which cannot always be met in reality. In addition, participants are fearful about the reunion itself and the days following. When combined with the sense of guilt and all the other problems of separation, the reunion becomes emotional. Unfortunately, in none of the returns we scrutinised, did parents express their fears and feelings to social workers or, for that matter, to anybody else providing support. As such, the restoration often had the effect of breaking down defences carefully erected during the child's absence; indeed, the strength of emotions released took many by surprise.

As on any occasion when emotions are running high, mistakes occur during the reunion and participants display behaviour which might be misconstrued as petulant or selfish. A mother contrasted her obvious delight at her eldest's return with her somewhat un-welcoming behaviour:

'I felt all this love brimming up, but I couldn't say anything. I had a list of things I wanted to say about how it was partly me that had done wrong in the past and how I was going to make a fresh start, but when he came in I was sort of speechless. And he didn't seem to notice me at all and after ten minutes I lost my temper and told him off because he hadn't wiped his feet and he'd walked muck all over.'

The moment of return may be emotional but not all participants are ecstatic. We have seen that the social workers become very much onlookers. For example, one aunt said to us,

'I've never seen such a performance, all that hugging and kissing. Before they hated each other, they still do in fact.'

In this episode, however, the most difficult role is reserved for the step-parents, or others, such as step or half siblings, who have joined the family during the child's absence. They are required to display a welcoming attitude when they often feel deeply ambivalent. The limelight during the actual return falls upon the one coming home. The event is not viewed as the creation of a new family in which other recent arrivals are also going to play a part. As such, although pleased to see mother and child back together, many step-parents were far from enthusiastic:

'It was all very nice and I tried to be as nice as I could. But if I'm really honest with you I'd have to say really I felt a bit pushed out. You see, before it was our house, me and the wife, but suddenly on that day I felt I was in somebody else's home again.'

The evidence from the intensive study clearly shows that the participants' experience of return is shaped by a range of factors. Cultural expectations are important as are previous experiences of separation and restoration and simple self-interest. However, the features which contribute to a return pull the participants in different directions, with parents in particular finding it difficult to reconcile the need to put on a show for the social worker and neighbours with the attempt to accommodate guilt and anxiety resulting from the separation and make sure the child is happy. Not surprisingly, therefore, emotions run high and more tears are shed at reunion than at separation. As these emotions are difficult to control or engineer, planning for a successful return is not easy.

We have noted that parents have high expectations of return and most have to cope alone with the elation, anxiety and disappointments associated with reunion. The actual return produces emotions which are difficult to understand, especially for those unused to examining their own feelings or to empathising with the anxieties and needs of others. It is easy to forget that these skills are learned over time in optimum family, school and other social settings. Many parents, through no fault of their own, simply do not possess these skills. Indeed, families may need their greatest support at the point at which the social worker feels withdrawal is the most appropriate strategy. Thus, it is not difficult to understand why eleven of the twenty children who returned swiftly experienced another separation.

Nonetheless, the moment of return is a happy one for most families, whatever the future may have in store, and we should not underestimate the sense of unity expressed by many. 'I felt we were a family again' was a sentiment we heard many times during the study. As such, the honeymoon period which immediately follows return is functional in that it neutralises the emotions previously discussed and allows some recovery. We shall discuss this further below but first let us consider the changes which occur in the family home as soon as the child is back.

Change crystallised by return

Throughout the study we have stressed the continuities which bind together the participants to the restoration. However, at the moment of return certain aspects of their lives change and these can threaten the success of the reunion. Initially, we found that return means that participants separate from a lifestyle to which they may have become emotionally attached or at least have got used to. Secondly, the return leads family members to review each other and the home, to think again about what has happened. Indeed, as we shall see, a returning child can change the relationship between all family members.

Earlier, we discussed the case of Mrs. Abbot and her sense of triumph when she collected her son John from foster parents. In our interviews with John immediately following the return, he found it difficult to disguise his sense of loss of the foster parents. He was very sad to leave them behind, but his greatest anxiety was that his mother would discover his thoughts wandering back to the substitute family. He said to us,

'I don't like to talk about Brian and Sylvia (the foster parents) in case it do upset her (mother)'.

Consequently, John found himself back at home with little to talk about, a silence which added to the growing anxiety in the house.

Many returning children expressed this sense of loss of their previous placement and the people associated with it. For older children, this included boyfriends and girlfriends, some of whom were unknown to the natural family. Foster parent, too, felt the wrench and wanted to keep in touch. This aspect of return highlights conflicts between the instrumental and expressive functions of child-care placements; putting down roots complicates return. For the host family the return meant separation from a previous lifestyle, an existence often made easier by the absence of the child. Parents got used to being by themselves and enjoyed the reduced responsibilities. Even parents receiving children after a short separation were surprised at the change and some mothers compared the reunion to the birth of a new child. For example:

> 'It's like the birth, it's marvellous when it's over and in the hospital but when you're home and it's feeding and changing nappies all day and all night it suddenly hits you.'

The intensive study also revealed that a child's return has the effect of instituting a review of the new family order and the reverberations can be felt in all aspects of family life. For children this review was particularly important and extended to the physical qualities of the home. For five of the twenty returning children the reunion with relatives took place in a completely new home and 13 children had new adults to get to know.

For children, the smallest changes can have a marked effect and apparently insignificant aspects of the home become symbols of inner anxiety. For example, one adolescent comparing his own home with the foster home he had left, commented:

> 'I'd only been home five minutes and I went to the loo and I looked at the bath. It had brown stains all below the taps and it was all old fashioned and dingy. At (the foster home) it was all pine and they had a shower. I suppose it was then, really, I was just thinking how hard it was really going to be.'

Noticing change is not confined to young people. Very small children become upset because of small changes, even new wallpaper. Indeed, the re-decorating of one child's bedroom as a treat to mark the return nearly led to another separation. It is noteworthy that child psycho-therapists emphasise that the treatment room must remain identically organised for each session.

The review instituted by the return often involved all family members and, in many cases, was positive. Marriages improved and in four families, parents felt their sexual relationships had changed for the better following the child's return. Relatives absent while the child was in care suddenly re-appeared and suspicious neighbours became more friendly. Return can have the most unexpected effects.

Return involves separation; for the child there is a divorce with substitute carers and for the host family there is a break with a previous way of life. These changes in participants' lives may have positive as well as negative effects. It is difficult to take such changes into account when planning return but it is important to acknowledge them, especially in the case of young children unable to express the source of their anxiety. Once again we see the uncertainty surrounding return and the need for a honeymoon period, which makes up the next episode in the process.

Conclusions

In this episode, we have focused on the point at which return has occurred. The themes which run through each of the episodes have been apparent here. Return is a process not a single event and we found it difficult to decide in many cases the point at which the child could be said to be home. We defined the moment of return as the time when sufficient, that is to say not all, family members perceive that the child has come home to live. The families we interviewed were always clear about the point at which this happened, indeed it was apparent in the throw-away remarks they used to describe the event.

The expressive continuities which bind the family together have underpinned many of the themes apparent in this episode, for example the emotional aspects of the reunion. Likewise, we have viewed the importance of role and, as we shall see, participants have the ability to suspend accepted roles during the forthcoming honeymoon period. Territory, however, is less important during the moment of return and its immediate aftermath, as family members prefer to place great stress on the value of neutral ground.

We have also seen the emergence of new themes. In contrast to the separation we found fewer rites of passage marked the reunion, although making the episode a more public event may have the effect of safely channelling the wave of emotion which return washes up. Indeed, it is noticeable that parents in particular do respond to cultural expectations of reunion, embracing their children for the benefit of external observers as well as to express heartfelt feelings.

We have seen that return involves a separation from something to which participants are emotionally attached; children lose their substitute carers, families a life without the absent child. In addition, we have laid bare the emotional and spiritual aspects of return as past separations and reunions are brought to mind. Yet the sense of loss for the lifestyle prior to reunion and the affective dimensions produced by the actual return are seldom addressed by participants in this episode and a cauldron of unresolved and little-discussed issues slowly comes to the boil.

Despite this simmering discontent and potential for discord, the social work inputs which have featured strongly in previous episodes pale during the actual return and the days immediately afterwards. The social worker can find him or herself overtaken by events during the return and it is difficult to sustain a role once the child is back. However, this might very well be the time when the family most needs help. Clearly, this is not an easy situation for professionals and the implicit messages of withdrawal have to be assessed in the context of telling parents that return will be very difficult. Financial support and advice would also be welcomed by most of the families we looked at, most were finding it difficult with another mouth to feed.

Once again, the analysis of family experiences in this episode has suggested factors which appear to be associated with return outcomes. Given the discussion in the previous pages and a detailed study of children's progress at this stage in the reunion, we would suggest that the following factors appear to be associated with a positive outcome in return cases.

1. Participants have a clear perception of when return has occurred.

2. Social work return plans are tailored to meet the time-scales of family members.

3. Once the child is at home, the family perceives the social worker as willing to help if and when needed.

So much for the first days of the child's reunion. Let us now consider the further stages in the return process as we witness the negotiations and disputes that inevitably follow.

12. The child back at home

As parents and children and the wider family strive to make the reunion a success, tensions and anxieties are suppressed in a make-believe world of bonhomie and unity. But the charade cannot be maintained, pressures mount, expectations are disappointed, the cosy fantasies that helped all to survive the separation are exposed to kitchen sink reality. New roles are onerous and old territories are jealously guarded. Particularly anxious during reunion are new family members, step-parents and siblings, cohabitees and friends who feel elbowed aside by the returning child. The honeymoon period ends with a domestic row in which home truths, recriminations and the pent-up resentments of separation are aired. But the majority of families survive this convulsion and the clearing of the air after the storm helps parents and offspring to accommodate to the past, to fashion continuity and meaning from the experience of separation and to settle down.

Episode Five: The honeymoon

In each of the families which experienced a child's return there was a 'honeymoon period' in the days which followed. It was a period in which everyone was on their best behaviour struggling to make the reunion a success. In fact none of these reunions ended swiftly; the earliest breakdown occurred after three weeks, so family tolerance was considerable. We looked carefully at each case in an attempt to understand the components of the honeymoon and we concluded that there were four contributory factors to its existence. Initially, participants needed time to get to know one another again. Secondly, we found that poor behaviour, particularly children's, was viewed sympathetically. Thirdly, participants were happy to assume new roles and give up existing ones. Finally, family members were happy to abandon their independence, albeit temporarily. These behaviours characterised the honeymoon period.

It is clear that the days immediately following the return involve the participants getting to know one another. For most, for example mother and child, this is a re-acquaintance but for others, such as step-parents and child, it can be the first time they have lived together. As in a formal gathering at which guests do not know one another, everybody tends to be on their best behaviour immediately following return and even sibling rivalries and jealousies are repressed. Thus, one step-parent who felt frozen out of the family on the day the child came back was more optimistic when we visited three days later:

'I wasn't sure at first, I'll admit that. But I thought "I'll give it a go". And it's been good. Things between me and Susan (his wife) have picked up again, in fact never better really. And Susan and Tracey (his step-child) are going OK so I've been making an effort too. And so far so good.'

As in any family, certain repetitive behaviours cause irritation and children are by nature liable to upset their parents. However, in the days which followed reunion we found that tensions were avoided and misbehaviour dealt with lightly. Indeed, several children noted a complete *volte-face* by their parents which they found remarkable and seemed to symbolise the days following reunion. For example, an older adolescent boy explained:

'Before I went away I used to like sitting by myself and reading, not bothering nobody. And this used to drive her (his mother) mad, she couldn't stand it. Then this week, same again, I'm reading and she's sitting across the room and she says "You've got so much patience". It was embarrassing really but I was amazed; it was the first time she'd said anything nice to me.'

As we shall see in the following episode, this constant striving for neutral ground eventually palls and can become the source of tension. There is a limit to the period of time which can pass before participants mention the problems that led to the initial separation. Indeed, it is characteristic of the days following reunion for participants to comment 'it doesn't seem real'.

Part of this honeymoon period is the sharing of roles and the allocation of tasks for children. Previously work-shy children suddenly become eager to help with Sunday lunch or help with Grandad's allotment. Other roles are allocated on a strictly experimental basis, for instance trusting a delinquent daughter to go to the shops with mother's purse. For the adolescents, the days following return allowed them insights into their parent's social lives, joining Mum on trips to Bingo or the discotheque or Dad to the public house.

The honeymoon period was characterised by the individuals abandoning their independence and the family operating as a single, apparently cohesive, unit. As with all situations where roles are displaced or threatened, tensions eventually come to the surface. The battles for power within the family and the problems which led to the child's removal from home soon loom large, leading several of those we interviewed to comment, 'I'll be glad when it's all back to normal'.

Episode Six: The row

But the tensions of keeping going mean that this false consensus has to disintegrate. Usually the family is convulsed by a row, triggered off by something quite minor. The row and its aftermath can be a healthy reprieve from the stresses of return and from the strain of maintaining the pretence that nothing has happened. Admittedly, this relief might be somewhat modified by the 'home truths' freely scattered on such occasions.

So, for a while, the family pot simmers gently, occasionally it spits hot water, but for the return families we studied, it eventually boils over into a row. Most participants felt the tension slowly building up and, in retrospect, were able to pin-point the source of contention. Superficially, the tension concerned role or territory but, beneath this veneer, there hovered deeper unresolved questions such as the pain of separation.

The row can occur at any time during the weeks which follow reunion. In a few cases it came after a matter of hours and, in contrast, one family dragged the honeymoon out for three months. Commonly, the dispute is between mother and child but, where the offspring is a baby, the row can involve adults and others. Step-parents, noticeably absent in the previous episode, also find themselves drawn into the *contretemps*.

The catalyst for the row was usually a dispute over family roles. Parents and children argued about who should do the washing-up, parents fought among themselves about who should stay in and look after the baby and mothers chastised their daughters about the inadequacy of grand-daughter's upbringing. Territorial disputes were also common, especially between siblings over bedrooms and toys, but also between mothers and teenage daughters over where each could store property and occupy territory.

Financial rows also feature in this episode. Children were returned to parents who had grown used to managing a reduced food bill and it could be some weeks before social security caught up with the change in family circumstances. As we might expect, parental discipline was an enduring source of conflict and many rows occurred on a teenager's late return from a night out or following a toddler's refusal to do as he or she was told.

Of course, such disputes are common within all families but among return families the row encapsulates a range of deeper tensions. One mother talked about a 'slanging match' she had with her recently reunited teenage daughter and illustrated how minor conflict rapidly leads to more hurtful issues.

> 'Well it started with Karen wanting to come with me to the disco, she'd been with me three times since she was back and I was beginning to hope I could go by myself for a change. We had a bit of a to-do about it then I says she can please herself. Then she said she wasn't coming 'cos I showed her up, calling me a slag trying to get off with men at the disco. And next thing I'm telling her she's a fucking bitch for making that accusation against her dad and she's saying 'you should have believed me..... why did you let me go?' and before you know we are throwing things at each other and she buggers off. I didn't see her for two days, God knows where she got to.'

What is at the root of these deeper conflicts? Largely, it can be explained as part of the difficulty of closing the gap between reality and the fantasy of the perfect reunion. The emotions bubbling when somebody says 'I cannot wait to be home' are difficult to recapture several weeks after reunion. The reality of being home is facing up to many of the same problems which led to the initial separation. A parent may not have made a full recovery from illness, the spectre of neglect and abuse may hover long after reunion and delinquent boys are unlikely to become saints after a sojourn in care. Thus, suspicions lurk in everyone's mind that the past is neither dead nor buried. But there are other difficulties which occur as a direct result of the separation.

For six of the 20 families which enjoyed reunion, there was a lack of common currency of conversation, although participants had been expecting to 'never stop talking'. There were other barriers such as inadequacies in the host's competence to care, deficiencies which brought back painful memories and censure from the wider family audience. As a consequence, rather than being excited as they had been at the moment of return, many parents and children complained of disappointment and boredom as time passed. All of the family members we talked to were unprepared for these gaps between expectations and the reality of reunion.

Indeed, for many, the disappointment came as a shock and unguarded reactions to the uncertainty contributed towards the row.

But the void was wider in some situations than in others. Of the three returning groups of children described in Chapter Six, many of those children who drifted back home experienced the least difficulties in settling down, provided their return was perceived as structured and progressive. Surprisingly the gap between reality and expectation was widest for the planned returns and, less remarkable, for those children who ran home precipitately. Most of the early returners found the period of separation was insufficiently long for an emotional gap between parents and children to develop and they settled back easily. However, in one case, despite a very close bond between mother and child and although the separation was short due to mother's chronic illness. neither she nor the boy could cope with the reality of return. Thus, the child quickly had to return to care and after two more attempts at reunion seemed destined to hover in uncertainty.

For all of our returning families, the honeymoon ended with a row, indeed in two cases the dispute was so acrimonious and hard hitting that the children were removed from home once more. We have suggested the catalyst for these disputes revolved around role, territory and financial stringency. But the row often rakes over long dead embers which surprisingly flare up to fuel further trouble. Discussions are often bitter and brim with home truths. We have explained the row as a response to the anxiety which occurs when there is a wide gap between participants' expectations of the reunion and the reality of living together in the days following. It reflects the tensions and reluctance of family members to abandon old roles and to learn new ones, to share territories and to accept the increased responsibility of making return a success.

But, successfully handled, the row had considerable benefits; information which all were reluctant to share prior to the reunion was aired in discussion. The reasons for and the pains of separation had to be faced and families which made progress in these areas seemed to enjoy more successful reunions than those which did not.

Parental guilt about letting their children enter care and the pain experienced by children while away had to be aired. Parents and children were together for long periods and information each had previously shielded from the other inevitably came to the fore. Returning children swiftly learned much of what went on in their absence and, if parents were reluctant to tell, the wider family readily provided others who were anxious to spill the beans. Children, likewise, hide information from their parents often because they feel their parents are unable to help but, during the aftermath of a row, they, too, volunteer comments on the pains of separation. Indeed, children sharing unhappy experiences with relatives often compounded feelings of parental guilt which were expressed in statements such as 'I should have been there ... I could have helped' or 'Why did I let them take him away?'

Episode Seven: A new modus vivendi

The sentimentalised family reunion conjured up in *The Railway Children* certainly did not apply in these cases. Reconciliation in the families we studied was private, gradual and fragmented. Far from resolving the tensions of generations in three gin-soaked confrontations packed into one evening, in many families the reunion took several months to complete. As one parent said,

> 'You cannot go back. You cannot turn the clock back. When I look back and see what I allowed to happen I still wince, I think 'Oh no'. But it's done and over the last six months (since the reunion) we've got over some of the problems. .... No, I wouldn't say we've talked properly but it's (the separation) come up now and then, I tell him about how things got too much for me and he tells me about how he loved the children's home or hated the foster home. It's not a cure but it certainly helps.'

But re-establishing the reciprocity and warmth of a relationship after a convulsive row does not merely rely on tea and sympathy. There are family norms to re-establish. As we saw during the period of separation, children and relatives were relieved of burdensome decisions regarding one another. They enjoyed a new-found freedom. But after the reunion and especially after the honeymoon, the routine of family life becomes apparent to the participants. Relationships exact a price. Family members become aware of changes in each other. Children notice physical alterations in their parents who are greyer, fatter and slower. Parents who are concerned with children's intellectual and affective development, often find their offspring wanting. Hopefully, the anticipated silk purse does not swiftly become a 'sow's ear' but reality has to be faced.

For the mother of young children this means changing the nappy and feeding the baby. For older children there will be disputes about pocket-money, which is frequently less than that paid in the substitute care placement and far less reliable. For the adolescents, there are rules regarding dress, sexual behaviour and the time the young person must be in at night. Frequently there is a gap between what is expected of children while in care and what parents will tolerate once they have returned home. Accommodation and compromise have to be hammered out.

Step-parents, who melted into the background during the separation can become important as the child settles back home. If the reunion is to succeed, their role, status and rights need to be recognised. Demands on step-parents may be considerable, including sharing their partner's time with the returning child. As we have seen, siblings can relate well to each other in the early stages, indeed, almost uncritically in some cases, but, in the longer term, they too have to make considerable accommodations if the family is going to see itself as a unit.

Noticeably absent, however, at this stage in the return process is the social worker. Mindful of the stigma associated with the child's entry to care, the negotiations just described are viewed as a private affair and parents go to some length to hide the disputes and realignments from outsiders. From a distance and often ill-informed, the social worker has to encourage the family to maintain the impetus towards reunion while often, at the same time, he or she is not fully conversant with the problems the families have to face. Indeed, some parents and older adolescents felt that social workers exercised informal coercion to make the reunion last and played down the difficulties they were experiencing. This sense of 'take it or leave it' in the attitude of social workers was expressed by eight of the 20 families enjoying restoration.

Conclusions

In these final episodes of the return process, we have described the honeymoon and row which are important elements in the return process. Following such *dénouements*, either the return breaks down or the participants begin to feel that 'things are getting back to normal'. Yet, 'normal' may not be very satisfactory; it may be little different from the situation prior to separation and is very likely to be in marked contrast to the fantasy fashioned in the days leading up to reunion. Nonetheless, clearing the air comes as a great relief to all concerned and it begins a protracted period of negotiations during which deep-seated issues come to the fore.

Families seek a revised *modus vivendi* and discussions explore the reasons for the initial separation and the meaning of the experience for the family. The anger engendered in parents and children by their failures to live up to their own expectations has to be expressed. Parents and children have to find a new role in the family and to accept, even forgive, the role taken by others. Territories have to be established and adaptations must be made to the new set of circumstances. In addition, completely new social networks may need to be constructed, for instance at work and in school.

The new arrangement usually also involves some agreement about the issues we have discussed in previous episodes: the hurt of separation, the feelings of loss and despair in the days that follow, the hopes and expectations prior to reunion are all explored. Such exploration does not solve much, except to evaporate some of the confusion in children's minds over the initial crisis. Often sensitive issues are still concealed within the family but such catharsis does provide an opportunity for good counselling skills and work on reconciliation, a chance which sadly often passes unrecognised by professionals.

What are the elements of success for families who managed to stay together after reunion and were happy to be together? Two of the 20 families welcomed home babes in arms and negotiations were relatively simple, involving only the parents, step-parents or wider family members. Other families welcomed home older children and we witnessed them letting go of each other, giving each other freedom to pursue their own lives whilst at the same time making some efforts to gain *rapprochement* and repair the damage.

However stressful the reunion, the majority of families came to see themselves as 'a family' and this shared perspective helped the returner belong and settle back. Unfortunately, when older children have developed an identity based upon life outside the home then difficulties follow.

Finally, we have been reminded again in this episode of the importance of continuities in understanding return. Several months after relatives and child first parted, the conflicts, anxieties and problems within the family remain alive. The need to give meaning to the upheaval remains pressing for children and parents alike.

Can we, in conclusion, identify fresh factors which may be associated with a positive outcome for children who are returned to their relatives?

Naturally, we have chosen indicators which appear from the analysis of the intensive data to be the most important at this stage in the return process. They, along with the other indices suggest that a successful reunion is more likely when:

1. The family is prepared for the anxiety generated by return and the disputes which are likely to occur.

2. Family members are prepared to discuss with each other the pains of separation and their role in the rift.

13. Children's return to contexts outside the family

Pre-occupation with return to the family should not encourage us to ignore the wider context of return. Many children rejoining their families have to enter new schools, older adolescents will seek employment or join training schemes and all have to fashion friendships and social relationships in the local community. Sometimes, the stigma and insecurities of the past make these negotiations difficult for the young person, particularly if compounded by unease and tensions within the family.

Our focus so far has been the return of children in care to their families and home communities. We have looked at the many and various adaptations that they have made and seen how different aspects of return, such as the negotiations over role and territory, influence outcomes. We shall now explore children's re-integration into contexts outside the family and see whether these affect the success of any reunion. Returns have to be made to several contexts; to school, and for older children to employment or to vocational training. In addition, young people have to rebuild their social and leisure networks. Unfortunately, some of these areas such as entry to employment or re-negotiating school networks deserve study in their own right and the difficulties can only be glimpsed occasionally from what children and adults say.

Children's return from care to school

A particularly important experience for many children is return to school. For both short and long-term care cases, school can provide one element of stability, continuity and belonging in an otherwise disrupted life. It is also clear that the way schools are organised can militate against a child's easy and successful return home. There are a number of ways in which schools can assist a child who returns after a considerable absence. For example, it is helpful if the child is prepared for entry. Although the child's situation may already be known to teachers, peers will be inquisitive and their teasing may be distressing. As an adolescent commented:

'Everyone just asked questions. Because you'd been in a children's home they thought you were criminal, they asked "what did you do?", "how much did you nick?", "did you try to kill someone?"'

The recognition of the problems facing such children and the benefits of an induction programme have been highlighted by Fleeman (1984) and Pickup (1987). They emphasise the need for a particular teacher to be available for informal counselling and for senior staff to work in close liaison with social services. They also stress the benefits of close contact between the school and the pupils' families whenever possible.

Of the 450 children included in the *Lost in Care* study, we noted that 349 returned home within five years. Of these, nearly half were of compulsory school age, half of them young enough for primary education and the remainder needing secondary schooling. In the younger age group, two-thirds of the children left care quickly, that is within six weeks, and only a tiny minority stayed away from home for more than a year. Most of these children fell into the category we shall later call *organised* leavers. They had usually entered care because their parent had been admitted to hospital or was unable to look after them. For such children, there should be no detrimental effects on the child, provided the return from care and entry to school are properly organised. The older children, in contrast, face more complex problems for, while there were some short stay cases, the majority had been away from home for at least a year.

This emphasis on the importance of school for children in care had not, until recently, received much attention in social work literature. Parker (1966) found that foster home transfers were less successful when they were accompanied by changes of school. Kahan's (1979) exploration of ten children growing up in care showed clearly how their attitude to school reflected their living situations and that few realised how important education would be to their future life chances.

These studies were among a handful which drew attention to the significance of the school experiences of children in care. More recently, however, possibly following the emphasis placed on the issue by the Short Committee, more has become known. Jackson (1987), Heath, Colton and Aldgate (1989) and Fletcher-Campbell and Hall (1991) have since undertaken specific studies of the educational experiences of children in care.

However, in social work planning, return to school still has a low profile. Robbins (1990) noted that 'the educational needs of children in care are tackled relatively rarely' and Berridge's (1985) example of the girl who missed her GCE exam because she was not woken by residential staff highlights the indifference that some social workers can display towards the school experience of children in care. In our intensive study of families and children experiencing reunion, we found that return to school rarely coincided with the beginning of term and some older adolescents seemed to be left virtually to themselves to negotiate re-entry to the education system.

Certainly, a number of the social work reports did consider the child's educational welfare and in five cases care placements had been chosen for their proximity to the child's school, so facilitating a stable educational career. This strategy was particularly common for children attending special day schools. In addition, a number of the older children remained away in care until they had taken their exams. These efforts to help children attain and gain more from school seem sensible but, despite their significance for children's welfare, when reunion became an issue, few social workers looked beyond the child's family for factors which might influence the adjustment of the returning child. Yet, we know from our interviews that for adolescents, peer relations are a major preoccupation and one would hypothesize that feeling settled at school would be a contributory factor to a child's successful return.

Younger children find return to school easier than adolescents. Primary schools are more child-centred than secondary schools, in that one teacher is responsible for most of the day's activities and learning. There is less streaming by ability, more expressive and group activities, more play, music and drama, all of which encourage in children a sense of membership and group participation. The teaching and nurturing of children is largely the responsibility of one adult, thus the child who is not fitting in, is isolated or is having difficulty stands out much more. In urban areas the schools are more local in intake and likely to be more sensitive to the deprivations and difficulties that accompany childhood in their catchment area. Teachers will be familiar with the child protection register, with the clothing problems and poor nutrition of young children, they will know whose meals are subsidised and so on. The peer group which the child joins on return is less worldly wise and those coming back to school from foster homes or residential care are less likely to be considered delinquent or deviant. In the same way, the prodigal and his or her family situation and wider social structures are likely to be less of a pre-occupation with young children than with adolescents.

But return to the secondary school is more difficult. In organisation the school is subject centred rather than child-centred and, although some teachers have responsibility for age groups and others are delegated to pastoral or special needs responsibilities, the child's experience is not one of closeness to a particular adult but of numerous contacts with a wide variety of teachers. However, children's ability to seek out supportive and sympathetic adults should not be underestimated. As a boy commented,

> 'I hated the place, the big kids bullied you, they pinched everything you'd got and the teachers didn't care much about you at all, except Mrs. Johnson, she taught geography and made it interesting with videos and letters from kids abroad, I really liked it, you could talk to her about anything. She wasn't like a teacher at all. She seemed really pleased to see you when you came through the door.'

Indeed, with regard to the issue of settling back, the contribution made to the returning child by some sympathetic person within the school cannot be overestimated. As recent studies have shown, a teacher or even older pupils, aspiring apprentices for the caring professions, can ease the adjustment of new arrivals. Surely it is not beyond the wit of social workers or schools to organise such ways of easing return.

The school's experience of returning children

The educational disadvantage of children in or on the margins of care have been commented on by many. For example, Aldgate, Colton and Heath (1991) found that as many as 91% of foster children obtained a standardised score below average for one or more of the three measures of attainment used, although the performance of another group of 'at risk' children known to social services was equally low. The authors also found a strong relationship between permanence in foster home placements and in children's attainments; the longer the duration of the placement, the better children seemed to perform at school. They comment:

> The strength of the relationship between educational attainment and permanence deserves emphasis. It suggests that a sense of stability may be an important facilitating factor in allowing children to make progress

at school and the longer this stability exists, the more it reinforces chances of success.

Unfortunately, we know that for many children in care, stability and permanence in a placement are rare experiences. As we have seen, of children who stayed in care two years or more, 84% move placement at least once and 56% move two or more times. Many of these changes also involved transfer to another school, a feature also noted in the studies of children returning home on trial. Thus, the chances of school disruption for children in care are considerable and the attainments of those who move are likely to be further depressed. However, the picture is not overwhelmingly gloomy and social workers are making efforts to improve the situation. Fletcher-Campbell and Hall (1991), for example, found that a third of children in care experienced a stable school life.

The effects of movement are not only on school progress. Berridge and Cleaver (1987) showed that children in foster homes, whether short or long-term, who also changed school were twice as likely to experience a placement breakdown. On the other hand, Farmer and Parker (1991) found that children attending special day schools did better in their home placements than those receiving ordinary education.

In this study, we were able to look at the ways in which schools cope with those pupils who return after a considerable absence. Children coming back from care are only one group of mobile children needing help. Schools find returning children fall into three main categories. For the first group, both departure and return are more predictable. These are children who have to spend time in hospital, including those who experience several disruptions because of their treatment. In these cases, staff and friends from school are encouraged to visit and frequently do, parents and hospital are given a school work plan and the child's eventual re-entry is carefully organised. Once back, such children usually find school tiring but their absence need not have a detrimental effect on their work. In a school of 1,600 pupils visited during the study, in the space of a year only two such children returned after a prolonged illness. We can see, therefore, that this category of returners is small and that, because the absence is usually well managed and the children quickly re-adjust, the return poses relatively few problems.

The second category of returners common in schools involves pregnant girls. They have greater problems of re-adjustment to school life and the younger they are the more difficult the return. This is because girls' peer groups can be censorious in such situations and the child sometimes enjoys considerable notoriety. As one deputy head told us,

'The girl can become an outcast. However sympathetic we try to be, children can be cruel to one another and, once the girl returns to school, her friends can ostracise her sometimes with disastrous effects on her academic attainment'.

However, it should be emphasised that even in this inner city comprehensive, few girls actually returned after a pregnancy but, as with any exceptional child, whether those with disabilities, severe family problems or even those with unusual gifts, schools find it difficult to accommodate their needs.

The final group of children who return to school encounter far greater difficulties. This group can be described as highly mobile cases. They usually disappear due to sudden change in family situations, divorce or moonlight flits to avoid debt and other aggravations. They frequently move to live with another member of their family or enter the care of social services. Children who disappear in this way have usually been irregular attenders and have often been ostracised by peers beforehand, being seen as odd, sad, dirty or poorly dressed. Their academic performance is usually lack-lustre and they are often disruptive or withdrawn in class. Other children shrink from them and their departure can be a relief to all concerned.

Thus, the return of these highly mobile children to school presents problems all round. They come back, often unannounced and try to slot into routines without much preparation. They are made to feel unwelcome, acute problems of re-adjustment can arise and they can soon become disruptive. Their meagre attainments sink rapidly. However, it is interesting to discover that the number of children leaving and returning in this way was still low, about ten per year in the largest of the inner city schools we visited.

Unfortunately, children who have been in care for over a year fall mostly into this last group of highly mobile cases. Parents often felt they could not care for the child or cope with his or her behaviour and children's school attendance and attainments were poor. Offending and abuse were often additional complications. Thus, home and school problems, more often than not, were mutually reinforcing. Yet, when we scrutinised the return plans for these children, we found that, in nearly every case, return to school was not a considered part of the return strategy and, when included, was only a minor item.

The organisation of schools

The organisation of schools also has a role to play in helping vulnerable young people transfer successfully. A variety of approaches to the problem are possible, either within a particular school or among a group of schools, including further education, within a particular geographical area.

Naturally, one issue of school organisation has long haunted the welfare of children, namely the gulf that exists at all levels between education and social services. While both have the welfare of the child at heart, each tends to view those that return from different perspectives, with consequent problems of communication and lack of understanding.

We were surprised while talking to children's teachers that they find it difficult to conceptualise return to school as an issue. Often there is little notion of the child having a 'social' career or that problems in one area could compound problems in another. For instance, following one boy's return to school, we discovered, integration was seen as best promoted by a psychometric assessment of the child's ability and allocation to appropriate sets; the child's social network remained unconsidered and movement within the school aggravated his settlement problems.

Similarly, few attempts were made to build on the child's experiences while away in care. Thus, not only were subject choices dealt with perfunctorily but achievements in sport and art, which had often been used to boost the child's self-confidence while away, were also ignored and, overall, little attempt at continuity was made. One of the children in our intensive study had to cope with a move from one school where he was a 'star' athlete to another where sports were not seriously pursued. Indeed, the decline in significance of many non-core subjects in schools, the diminishing of extra-mural activities and sport have disadvantaged many children, not only those who return. Those who seek a role outside the classroom find that the spotlights have been turned off and the stage has gone.

Further limitations on the way schools approach the issue of return to school arise from recent educational changes. As many schools now control their own budgets, governors and senior staff have more power in deciding which pupils to accept and what resources should be allocated to special needs. Policies, therefore, now vary considerably between schools as well as among education authorities. For example, in a school of 1,200 pupils, there was a large special needs unit with nine staff, all of whom were also subject teachers. The school is a model in its approach to children with learning and social difficulties, among whom cluster several children on supervision and some recently returned from care. However, there now exists considerable insecurity because the cost of this provision is considerable and there is parental pressure to allocate money elsewhere and to ensure that the school comes out well on published assessments. Understandably, the parents of children 'in need' do not form a vociferous or influential group within the school.

The LMS (local management of schools) also has implications for the social careers of children who have to spend time away in care. LMS means that the suspension of children is the governors' decision and can only be rescinded after negotiation with parents. Children from deprived families are again at a disadvantage in such situations as they have limited legal power, few people pursuing their cause, parents who are poor negotiators and are likely to have had minimal home tuition.

An added problem for children who change schools arises from the introduction of the National Curriculum. In secondary schools there are now two key stages of return, at 11 and 14 years of age. From 11 to 14, and from 14 to 16, the National Curriculum runs in blocks. Although the same subject areas are covered in every school, the stages reached in each subject could differ and the content may vary locally creating problems when compulsory testing occurs.

It is easier, therefore, for a child to enter a new secondary school at the beginning of either the first or the fourth year. As one head teacher said,

'Recent changes have reduced our flexibility. I used to be able to tuck these children under the wing of Mr. Jameson in design and technology. He was marvellous with them but now he's not only too tied up to bother but also worried about the effects of such kids on his appraisal'.

Unfortunately, the moment of return from a separation in care is seldom influenced by these considerations.

At the level of immediate responsibility for the child, the contact between teachers and carers can most charitably be described as variable. Indeed, teachers and social workers can hold quite contrasting views on the importance of education for children in care. As children are likely to move around while away in care, teachers tend to emphasise the stability offered by schooling while social workers feel that other issues, such as who should care for the child, are more important.

Generally, whatever their professional ideologies, both teachers and social workers have low academic expectations of children in care. It is believed that such children will attain little and, as young adults, experience unemployment or, at best, take unskilled jobs. Some of the social workers we interviewed happily viewed regular school attendance as sufficient and communications with teachers more often than not concerned children's behaviour rather than their educational progress or vocational preferences. Aldgate, Heath and Colton comment,

> Recent educational research has emphasised the importance of parents' and teachers' expectations. Our results so far suggest a similar situation for children in care and we expect further analysis on social workers' and carers' expectations to add confirmation of fairly low expectations. The question remains as to whether higher aspirations and more remedial input could raise levels of attainment as Jackson (1987) has suggested. Hazel (1981) found that the combination of these factors had a distinct effect on the final educational attainment of adolescents placed in professional foster homes and compensated markedly for earlier educational disadvantage.

Yet we did encounter several conscious efforts to counteract the negative effects of being in care. Two of the residential units we studied had a policy of keeping the children at their original school whenever possible. This was partly a necessity due to the fact that local schools were reluctant to accept children from community homes but, nevertheless, the policy was costly as the minibus journey to schools took an hour. It was felt that the benefits of maintaining continuity in education outweighed the disadvantages of distance. It also provided some security and sense of belonging for children experiencing considerable upheaval at home.

Missing from our discussion so far is the child's experience of going back to school. In our intensive study of the 20 children who actually returned from care, 11 went to full-time schooling and we made a special study of their experiences. Initially, we would stress that most children found the transition easier than their previously expressed anxieties would suggest. Nevertheless, children were still terrified of 'getting it wrong'. We should remember that the smallest things worry children and not knowing what to do or feeling unable to trust others exacerbate these difficulties.

Indeed, our theoretical perspectives on return were brought down to earth when we interviewed children about their new schools. Children confirmed few of our wider anxieties over return but expressed surprise at things such as size, buildings, racial composition and unfamiliar routine. 'I didn't think we'd have to take our shoes off before going in the gym' was typical. But such worries should not be underestimated by teachers; they need to appreciate that these trivial anxieties are often the expression of wider and inexpressible unease. Indeed, the smallest fears can have considerable effects. One lad, for example, refused to eat school dinners simply because he was afraid that, in public view, he would not be able to operate the tap on the water urn correctly.

Many apparently routine things fill children with high anxiety when they are unaware of the required behaviours. Insecure children find the endless clatter, noise, and enforced bonhomie exhausting and disorienting. As a head-teacher told us 20 years ago,

> 'they trek along endless corridors, dropping precious pencils, to alien faces in distant rooms. Such an experience is even worse if you don't know which way the corridor leads and, as the last familiar companion disappears behind the sagging Nissen hut, you realise that you are not late but lost.'

The newcomer, as she or he enters the school gate is an object of considerable interest, something bright on an otherwise sepia landscape. Everything they do is public, scrutinised by an audience of peers anxious for a laugh, particularly at someone else's expense. There is competition and jostling for position besides which scholastic achievement takes second place. Thus, taking off one's clothes for gym, the chilly trip to the swimming bath, grabbing a seat at lunchtime, waiting for the bus, all anxiously loom in the child's mind long before the bell rings, like a morning on the Somme, a trill that signifies you are going over the top, alone and without a comforting swig of rum.

We noted earlier that any return involves negotiations over role and territory and that features which were once familiar to young people present new challenges. The successful establishment of a role takes time and diverts attention from anxiety but, once again, children returning to school from care face difficulties. Their return can follow a long sojourn in care and the questions of peers require a well-prepared story. Children who suddenly appear are objects of curiosity to classmates, mystery and fantasy will naturally abound. The problems of self presentation for children in care are considerable. Even factual misunderstandings can defeat the struggling returner. As one child said,

'I came home from Shrewsbury. It had been the centre of my life but no one had the remotest idea where it was.'

Several studies have stressed the importance of influential peer cultures in schools (Coleman, 1961; Hargreaves, 1967; Ball, 1981; Corrigan, 1979; and Willis, 1977). One of the problems we found was that even the most astute staff were not always familiar with the dynamics of the pupil world. The use of the wrong slang, for example, immediately indicates to others that the newcomer is 'different'. While being 'different' may not worry young adults, at least in some areas such as leisure and taste, it is very important for younger children and adolescents to feel part of the group and to be the same. Coming from a strange background, being a welfare case and struggling to find a niche in the leading crowd were all significant to the children we interviewed. The use of sympathetic peers to ease entry seems to be helpful and children seemed happier when there was a specific teacher in whom they could confide. Positive staff attitudes also seemed to help parents to overcome their depressed situation.

A child's return to school is only one of several transitions that have to be made when a child returns from care. Older children, in particular, have to fashion peer group relationships, find employment and cope with the vagaries of accommodation and social security. Let us look at some of these other contexts in greater detail.

Return to peer groups

On returning from care, young people head straight for familiar bits of their social network, usually to situations where they feel people have some obligation to them. These may involve family and friends and two very isolated children in our study found fulfilling relationships via their siblings' or parents' social life. However, children in care, who come mostly from poor working-class backgrounds, are at a disadvantage here because few such people are likely to exist and obligations may have been unmet in the past. Indeed, the Québec study previously discussed (Simard, Vachon and Moisan, 1991) stressed that difficulties in peer relations contribute significantly to young people's return difficulties.

But culture and class can also have benefits. For example, there was little of the middle-class guilt about not having kept in touch among the children we interviewed and instant peer interaction with few social skill demands seemed normal. Thus, children leaving care feel they have a right to behave in certain ways and need little preparation to help meet peers. When they do founder, however, it is because they are often unprepared for the changes that have occurred in their absence, namely the fact that familiar contemporaries have married, left the area or had children. Thus, the main defect in promoting peer relationships is the lack of 'currency' that arises during prolonged absences, a pattern we described earlier.

For the older adolescents in our study, there was frequently some oscillation between family and friends. When situations got difficult in the family home, the young people drifted to situations where people had some obligation to them but where they also perceived minimal control. This was particularly the case following rows with parents and siblings. Thus, as we found in our follow-up studies of Youth Treatment Centre leavers, there was a lot of to-ing and fro-ing from parents to other relatives and friends. Sometimes people such as distant aunts, scarcely known to the young people, were chosen simply because there was sufficient obligation to command entry to their home without the controls and detailed knowledge available to the immediate family. On some occasions, the young people went off to seek out friends they had known while away in care.

The situation of the young people in our study who found themselves homeless is also interesting in this respect. While we would not wish to underestimate the tragedy of their plight, we found that overnight they seemed able to find a peer group of similar people, suggesting that the same sense of obligation is shared among vulnerable people in times of greatest need. This was certainly functional in reducing the anxieties over accommodation that would riddle most of us. A similar situation arose with the young offenders in our group. As Little (1990) has found, while there was clearly considerable stigma in being a convict, the fact that everyone knew them, including the police, seemed to generate camaraderie and strengthen identity.

Achieving independence after return from care

When older teenagers return home from care, it is naturally hoped that they will successfully achieve independence, fulfilling their personal ambitions and playing a full part in society. For all young people, this transition is a complex process and independence is achieved at different rates in different areas. Indeed, emotionally we probably never become fully independent of our families. These changes require finding employment, being economically viable, getting accommodation and developing social and personal relationships. Again, these are inter-linked in that success in one transition can aid progress in others, findings echoed in the work of Stein and Carey (1986).

For older adolescents returning from care, these difficulties are often compounded. Youth training is theoretically available but offers little choice once key jobs are taken, normally in September and October. Leaving a job, even if it is unwanted, means a loss of benefit. Paid employment is not only hard to find but also difficult to keep and our finding from follow-up studies of very difficult adolescents that many leave jobs after a few days is borne out in our present study. As we have noted, withdrawal when things go wrong is a well developed strategy among deprived adolescents and when applied to difficulties in training and employment situations, it creates immense difficulties for the young person.

Similarly, accommodation is problematic for seventeen and eighteen year olds. They cannot sign on for social security and, at the time of our study, if they go to social services for help, they are usually sent to the 'council', that is the housing department, who send them back as they are not old enough to qualify for services. They usually end up clutching lists of homeless accommodation. Probation, of course, can sometimes help, but only for offenders.

We would conclude, therefore, that levels of homelessness among young people returning from care are higher than they might first appear. Homelessness does not, of course, necessarily mean wandering the streets without hope of improvement but it does suggest a large number of young people living on the goodwill of others and moving around a series of interim 'shack-ups'. Our follow-up would suggest that the number of homeless young people is far higher than those sheltered in cardboard suburbs. The negative implications of this for a young person's identity, whether of person or place, are obvious.

It is, naturally, hoped that the reforms introduced by the 1989 *Children Act* will improve these situations. The older adolescents leaving care in our study suddenly found themselves cut off from the support of social services and, even though they tried to maintain or resurrect relationships, found things difficult. One homeless 18 year old we interviewed described how he had revisited his old children's home. When we asked if he stayed there, he said ruefully, 'Oh no, children's homes are for children.'

While the new responsibilities for vulnerable young people up to the age of 21 are to be welcomed, we found that those who have stayed long in care generally have poor views of social services. While some of their dismissive attitudes may reflect the arrogance of youth, these unfavourable views must be considered when devising ways of attracting young adults to accept the new services envisaged. We need a clearer understanding of how difficulties in returns to contexts outside the network family affect young people's subsequent living situations. It is well established that in the period after leaving care, more boys than girls return to live with relations. These wider contexts may be influential in this, a relationship that would benefit from further research scrutiny.

Conclusions

In this chapter, we have explored children's returns from care to contexts outside the natural family. We have seen that the scope for helping children return successfully is considerable in all the areas we have discussed. In education, for example, it lies in administrative arrangements for schooling, in cooperation between teachers and social workers and in developing sensitivity to children's needs. While the education of children in care is important, for the reasons we have explained, it is still given little significance in social work planning, a situation which will hopefully change following recent legislation.

It is also the case that children in care are often cleverer and more capable than professionals like to think. They are seen as 'dim' or 'unreliable' and are rarely encouraged to apply themselves at school, in work or in the pursuit of personal relationships. As we wrote in *Locking Up Children*,

> because we cannot envisage the Sistine Chapel being nurtured in a secure unit, we must act accordingly.

But, innate intelligence apart, the experiences of children in care can be defeating because of the situations we put young people in. To return from a child-centred, supportive care placement to a large, structured day-school or unsupportive work situation and to expect children to cope without money, accommodation and friends all add up to a recipe for failure. The children will get things wrong and adapt accordingly, either by the well-tried strategy of withdrawal or by manipulating professionals, friends and relatives against one another.

We were surprised in our intensive studies at the low educational, employment and social expectations put on children returning from care and at the ways, many of them very subtle, that care experiences militated against academic and other achievements. One school report stated, 'the trouble is he's not educationally motivated.' True as this might be, the fact remained that without the sensitivity we have described, he was never going to become so.

This chapter re-affirms many of the points about continuities and transitions made throughout this study. A successful re-union reflects not only the child's reintegration within the family but also his or her ability to make progress in other settings, most notably school or, for older adolescents, work. In the light of this evidence, the following factor is helpful in understanding return:

> Once at home, the child establishes a role outside of the family which does not undermine his or her role within it.

Summary points

1. Children return from care to a variety of contexts. Apart from their families, children may have to adapt to school, peer groups, employment and moves to independence.

2. Entry to and departure from care and the placement changes experienced while away are likely to involve changes of school for the child. Provided the absence and return are properly organised, short-stay children suffer relatively little damage to their education. Long-stay cases, however, face more complex problems. Education often has low priority in their care plans and has to fit into other arrangements. Thus, educational continuities are difficult to maintain.

3. Return to primary and special schools is easier than to secondary schools because of the class-teacher structure and flexible curriculum. Recent changes in schools, such as Local Management, the National Curriculum and published assessments have exacerbated the difficulties of finding schools for children returning from care.

4. The success of children's return from care to school is further hindered by infrequent contacts between teachers and social workers and by conflicting professional ideologies about what constitutes the child's best interests. In addition, the timetable for care plans rarely matched school terms.

5. Entry to a new school is especially difficult for children returning from care. Children are uncertain and frightened by seemingly trivial things, classmates can be cruel and making friends is not easy. Teachers and social workers need to be aware of this.

6. Older children returning to peer groups, youth training, employment and moves to independence face especial difficulties and the provision in the 1989 *Children Act* to support 18-21 year olds is an important step in lessening the problems such young people face.

14. Long-term outcomes

Here we study what happened to the 31 children from 24 families in the intensive study. All had been expected to return home in the near future. We find that, in spite of social work optimism, a third of the children for whom return seemed imminent did not go back. We explore the reasons for these disappointments and, conversely, the outcomes for those who managed *rapprochement* with their families. Were their reunions crowned with success?

In this intensive study, we have charted the return situations of 31 children from 24 families. Social workers expected all of these children to go home, hence their inclusion in this part of our research. However, the predictive indicators obtained from the extensive survey suggested that some of the 31 children would not be returned easily or would face problems once home. In the event, 11 children failed to go home at all and 11 of the 20 who did return subsequently left, four of them in less than satisfactory circumstances.

In this chapter, we assess the situation of all 31 children at the end of our 18 month follow-up scrutiny. We look first at the 11 children whose returns never materialised as their failure to go back home tells us much about return processes. We shall then review the long-term outcomes of the 20 children who enjoyed reunion and see that the restoration process continues long after the child first comes home. Let us look first at the 11 children who were not reunited with relatives.

Children who did not return

Even though we designed the intensive study to include children who would experience return problems, we were surprised that, in the follow-up period, a third (35%) of the cases nominated by social workers as highly likely to return did not get back. Clearly, although considerable proportions of professionals' time are devoted to the reunion of children with their families, not all efforts are successful.

As our predictive criteria from the extensive study had suggested, hopes for a swift reunion for all 31 children had probably been over ambitious but in five of the non-returning cases, the social work plan was still for rehabilitation, 18 months after return had first become an issue.

Delays had been caused by difficulties of rehousing, the need for the child to complete an educational course and by vacillation among participants. In all five cases, the slowness of the reunion was not seen by social workers as detrimental and, thus, reunion remained the case plan.

Two cases typify the return problems of such families. In the first, an eleven year old girl and her mother continually changed their minds; when one wanted restoration the other chose prolonged separation and *vice versa*. Social workers accommodated the wishes of the family and so were also accused of dithering. In the second case, involving two teenage boys who had been in and out of care over several years, the older brother went home not to mother, as planned, but to his father. The younger child was not ready to make this adjustment but the father's renewed interest had the effect of reducing the mother's desire to have her son home. He, consequently, stayed with foster parents. Social workers maintained high levels of access between all family members and, at the time our scrutiny ceased, the aim was still towards eventual reunion.

For six children, however, the situation was different. Return was not only postponed but also abandoned. In one case, involving two children aged two and four, the physical and mental health of the children's mother deteriorated unexpectedly. Heavy drinking and possible substance abuse compounded her diabetes, leading to several emergency hospitalisations and generally poor health. She was persuaded that her daughters should stay in care until she fully recovered and frequent access between them was encouraged. However, the children's foster home was quickly changed to one that had long-term possibilities. Despite the inclusive nature of the social work plan, the mother realised her ability to parent was becoming increasingly impaired and, at the time our research was nearing completion, she was urging that her children be adopted.

In a second case, there was a similar unforeseen change, but this time in the home situation. It resulted from an acrimonious breakdown in a mother's marital relationship and from the financial and housing difficulties that swiftly ensued. As there was little prospect of any immediate improvement, the infant child, who had originally entered care because of a family crisis, was seen as likely to remain there because of the mother's continual ambivalence and disappearances back to Ireland to see her relatives. In addition, contact between mother and child, which had always been fitful, became very intermittent indeed, even when she came back to the child's immediate vicinity. Furthermore, the natural father shunned any parenting responsibility. Both parents showed no interest in the foster home and justified their coolness by maintaining that their child was better off away. Needless to say, all was not satisfactory in the placement; the foster parents were angry at being the victims of such whimsical behaviour and hardly encouraged shared care.

In a third case, it was a deterioration in the young person's behaviour that scuppered return plans. Leroy's aggression increased to such an extent that he had to be separated from his sister who was not in our study group. She remained happily in the foster home and went back to the natural family three months later. Leroy, aged nine, had been stopped from going home at weekends because his parents could not cope with his tantrums. They said he was 'impossible to satisfy'. Indeed, when he realised his sister was at home and he was not, his aggression increased. Soon, the foster parents could not cope either and he was moved to an assessment unit, a setting swiftly followed by a residential school 30 miles away. All this was done with the full consent of his parents. This pattern by which siblings are separated because of the increasingly disturbed behaviour of one of them has been noted in child-care literature. However, it is important to add that, for the child involved, it not only leads to a placement change but also to a delayed return, often in contrast to the experience of the other sibling.

In the final two cases, child-abuse came unexpectedly into the picture between the initiation and execution of return plans. In the first case, a 14 year old girl, who had entered care because of being 'at risk' in the community, was visiting her mother and sisters in preparation for return but less regularly than the social worker wished. There seemed to be some reluctance on the girl's part, with minor excuses and procrastinations; nevertheless, she was expected to be living back at home within six months.

However, plans took a complete *volte-face* when the mother formed a new friendship with a raffish, scheduled sex offender. As a result, access was carefully controlled and conditions concerning the cohabitee's presence in the family home were specified. When the mother allowed her boyfriend to move into her house, social services felt return was not foreseeable and plans for reunion were abandoned.

In the final instance, both social workers and researchers were taken by surprise. Here was a case which seemed to be progressing well and all the research indicators pointed to a speedy and successful return. The situation involved a seven year old boy in the care of a single father. His wife had walked out of the family home after a torrid affair with her brother-in-law. Voluntary arrangements to look after the child and support the father, who desperately wanted to resume parenting and engineer his son's return, were effected. Social services were very sympathetic to the father's needs and fostered the boy locally, encouraging access to Dad and grandparents at weekends and public holidays. However, social workers were uneasy at the lack of a female carer. Nevertheless, eventual reunion was planned and, after six months in care, going home was imminent.

This situation continued for longer than expected because of uncertainty about the parental relationship. On more than one occasion, the child's mother unexpectedly turned up to re-assume her position in the family home. Moreover, while father's continued unemployment gave him time to look after his son, his financial situation deteriorated. Steven lived in three different temporary foster homes during this period but this aroused little anxiety as his wishes were clearly to be back with dad and the father-son relationship seemed strong. Return was always the plan, even though it seldom seemed near to fruition.

Suddenly, the foster parents became aware that certain comments made by Steven could indicate abuse. They informed social services as a precaution. When questioned by social workers, Steven described consistent sexual abuse by his father on weekend visits. Father, too, admitted everything when challenged. Needless to say, there is now no access; Steven is still living in a temporary foster placement, is utterly bewildered and is reputedly becoming difficult. Father is on bail awaiting a Crown Court appearance. Social workers and researchers who had visited the father and son while at home together had never had an inkling of what was going on. All were understandably concerned that despite following procedures in the *Charge and Control Regulations*, they failed to protect the boy. Naturally, return plans have been abandoned and, even if ever revived, there is a probability that Steven will have nothing to return to. His mother is now missing completely and father's tenancy will almost certainly be surrendered when, as seems likely, he goes to prison.

The significance of non-returners for our study

How are these non-returning cases relevant to our study of children's return experiences? Initially, we would highlight the surprising findings that over a third (35%) of the children who were expected by social workers to return home failed to do so in the time expected and that for a sixth of them return plans were abandoned altogether. While, because of the nature of our sample, this figure cannot be generalised to the whole care population, it does indicate the difficulties that reunion poses for children and families and the complicating factors that can intervene.

These cases also highlight the cultural barriers and expectations associated with return home. For example, social workers were reluctant to return Steven to a lone father. Vicky, the adolescent girl, reluctantly went along with social work plans, pretending to enjoy her home visits when she was actually shattered by her mother's preference for a known sex offender. These two cases also show how the possibility of the child's return from care puts the child's family under extra scrutiny and the way that the new information this generates can block return plans. All of the children we interviewed were clearly confused by the failure of their returns to materialise and the tendency for plans to blow hot and cold. Social workers clearly have a skilled and daunting task in helping children understand why their hopes have been dashed, particularly if they are under the impression that their care placement is temporary.

It is equally clear from our evidence that return strategies must accommodate possible changes in children's family situations. An inflexible approach that relies totally on a stable family structure with predictable patterns of relationships is likely to be confounded. Steven's return, for example, was contingent upon his mother being off the scene while the restoration of the baby, whose mother disappeared, depended on her having a place to live. In neither case were these requirements met.

These conclusions suggest one answer to the important question posed by Farmer and Parker (1991) in their study of placements with parents. This used to be known as 'home on trial'. In noting that social workers have few sanctions, limited powers and little contact with the children, the authors asked, 'who is on trial?' Our study would suggest that it is the decision to return that is being tested just as much as the children or parents.

In the light of this evidence on children who did not return, we would add the following riders to the factors associated with the likelihood of a child's return from care.

1. After the point at which return becomes an issue, there are no unforeseen changes in parents' health, family relationships or household membership.

2. After return becomes an issue, intended return plans are not affected by new information emerging concerning risks to the child, eg. of child abuse.

This concludes our study of the children who did not return during the eighteen month follow-up. Let us turn to the 20 children who were reunited. What happened to them in the long-term? As we shall see, it takes some time before a satisfactory outcome is achieved and, in many cases, fluidity and change continue to be a prominent feature in the child's life. What do these long-term outcomes reveal about the return process?

The children who returned

During the preceding chapters, we have described the reunion of 20 children. One of the advantages of adopting an intensive scrutiny is that we have been able to make careful assessments of the success of each return and extend the evaluative criteria beyond those used in the extensive study, namely whether or not the placement endured. Of the 20 children going home during our 18 month follow-up, nine stayed throughout with relatives, while the remaining 11 moved on. Let us look first at the nine who, using the outcome measures of placement stability previously employed, would be judged as successful. How well did they actually fare?

In reviewing children's return situations, we looked at their situation from a variety of perspectives. These included not only those of social workers but also those of parents and the children themselves. We compared the child's situation after 18 months with that which existed at several key moments highlighted in the episodes; for example, the circumstances surrounding admission to care, the entry to care itself and the point at which return became an issue. We were also able to look at the child and family in much more detail than had been possible in the extensive study. This included information on family and social relationships, the child's social and anti-social behaviour, his or her physical and psychological health and, where appropriate, educational progress and employment.

When we applied these wider outcome criteria, we concluded that in five of the nine cases, the return had been a complete success. Three of these cases were *early returners* going home in a relatively uncomplicated fashion after the mother's recovery from illness. The fourth case involved an adolescent girl estranged from her Irish mother and Afro-Caribbean father but who settled well with paternal grandparents. The final successful reunion was a 17 year old boy who had been long in care. He settled well at home, began working with his step-father and got engaged to a local girl. Previous delinquent behaviour was not, to our knowledge, repeated.

For another three children who stayed at home after reunion, our scrutiny of the situation led us to have some reservations about the return situation. In two cases, one sibling had stayed at home while the other took a different course. The stability of the children, whether at home or being looked after, was adversely affected and the rows and negotiations described in the previous chapter were never resolved. In the third case, a 16 year old adolescent girl went back to live with her mother and step-father after a long separation. Unfortunately, the girl's accusation of emotional rejection, which had precipitated the original entry to care, continued to plague the relationship between mother and daughter and a breakdown always seemed imminent.

Finally, among the nine children who went home and remained there for the duration of the follow-up, there was one eight year old boy who we felt could have benefited from a further period of respite care. This boy had been a victim of physical abuse and had been able to return despite the criminal conviction and removal of his father. Our predictions suggested he would go home with relative ease to his mother but, once back, his behaviour became difficult and disturbed. While there was no suggestion of further abuse, it was clear that his mother was straining to cope. Nonetheless, neither she nor the social worker were prepared to let the child go back to foster parents and, anxious to escape close professional scrutiny, mother requested that the care order be discharged.

So much for the nine children who went home and stayed. What happened to the 11 children who were restored to relatives but subsequently moved to live elsewhere, either back in care, with friends or relatives or in their own accommodation? As we shall see, just as not all those staying at home are successful, not all those moving on after return can be deemed unsuccessful. Three children from the same family went back to foster parents two months after the reunion when their mother once again found herself unable to cope. However, on going home second time around, there were no such complications and so the children could be categorised as short-term breakdowns as described earlier.

Another boy, however, was less fortunate. He went home on three occasions during our follow-up without ever achieving success. He typified the circumstances of children who oscillate in and out of care. At the end of the intensive study, two days before his sixth birthday, this young boy was living in his fourth foster home and long-term plans about his future were far from clear.

Not all of those moving on were so unfortunate. Four adolescents continued to enjoy good relationships with their parents after departing the family home, although the circumstances surrounding their leaving were fraught. These cases all served to remind us of the continued problems which follow from persistent delinquency for all four left home after getting into further trouble with the police. Two other *long-term returners* went back without any problems, re-established healthy relationships with their parents and used this as a bed-rock to seek independence.

Finally, for one of the participating families, we felt unable to decide whether or not the outcome was satisfactory. Here, a 17 year old boy was restored to his Asian parents after a three year separation in a CHE for serious offending. Relationships at home were difficult in that there were language problems (the boy could not speak Urdu and his mother could not speak English) and parents were dismayed at the delinquent identity in which their son revelled. The reunion never seemed likely to endure. However, six months after reunion, there was a sudden change in events when the boy moved to relatives in India. Whether this was a voluntary decision for him to cast off his delinquent past and fully reintegrate into the cultural norms of the family or whether his parents had imposed their will was not clear. At the end of the study, this boy remained abroad.

This evidence on the 20 children who returned during our intensive study shows the variety of long-term outcomes which are possible in return cases. Even when we simplify the complex histories of the participating families, we still find eight alternative conclusions for the 20 children we studied. These are summarised in the following table.

Table 14.1: The long-term outcome for the 20 children who returned by the type of return case

	Type of case			
Outcome	Early return	Intermediate return	Long-term return	TOTAL
1) *Child returned & stayed at home*				
Outcome satisfactory	3	1	1	5
Concerns persist	-	2	1	3
Further separation needed	-	1	-	1
Sub-total	3	4	2	9
2) *Children returned and subsequently moved*				
Short-term breakdown	3	-	-	3
Oscillator	1	-	-	1
Satisfactory outcome but difficult move	2	1	1	4
Child seeks independence	-	-	2	2
Child moves to India	-	-	1	1
Sub-total	6	1	4	11
TOTAL	9	5	6	20

From this analysis of the progress made by the 20 children who returned from care to live with relatives, what general conclusions can we draw which are relevant to all return situations?

The process does not end

As we have seen throughout this study, the separation that accompanies entry to care does not cure family problems. The structural situation of children in care, their poverty, their vulnerability to abuse and neglect and their propensity to emotional and conduct disorders all endure. None of these problems can be made to vanish with the magic wand of a substitute care placement. Nor does a partial resolution of the emotional upheaval witnessed in previous pages reduce the likelihood of further difficulties.

Furthermore, even when the problems which led to the entry to care have subsided, new difficulties are likely to emerge. The five children who returned satisfactorily and stayed at home continued to cause anxiety on several fronts. The baby who was reunited with parents after a fortnight's separation subsequently developed medical problems which captured the attention of health agencies. The adolescents all had problems at school and tested their parent's patience with recalcitrant behaviour.

Of course, such difficulties can afflict all children but for those returning they can assume a special significance. Our study again emphasises the importance of positive continuities in children's lives. Where disconnection has occurred or where a sense of loss has not been resolved, the likelihood of post-return problems is increased. We can illustrate this with two contrasting quotations from mothers.

> 'I am at the end of my tether. If he does anything else I'll go mad. Every time you think you're getting on top of one thing another comes up. It's all since he went away, I don't know when we'll get sorted out.'

> 'He's been OK really. I haven't noticed that anything's the matter. We've just been getting on with things. I suppose I should pay more attention and keep an eye on things but it's hard really. Since he got back it's really up to him.'

Of these two cases, it was the first who returned successfully for, although the mother was at the end of her tether, she was concerned and was doing everything in her power to make things work. In the second case, satisfactory progress appears to have been made but this reflects the mother's ambivalence towards her son following his return home. On visiting this family, we were dismayed at the lack of attention paid to the child. Unfortunately, continuity cannot be imposed once it has been lost and, although they parted on reasonable terms, mother and child drifted apart during the child's absence.

In the previous chapters, we have charted the process of children returning from care. This begins with the separation for, even at this moment, participants are thinking of being back together. We have then followed events through to the physical restoration which usually follows. However, although the child is then at home, we cannot always say that she or he has been *returned*. For, in addition to the physical aspects of a reunion, there are also spiritual dimensions when parents, children, wider family members and professionals feel the child is 'at home'.

When does this happen? It took at least nine months for any of the nine families in which the child's reunion endured to be able to see the separation and return in the context of the new *modus vivendi*. Even for these families, not every tension reached its nemesis and certain stresses remained. Indeed, in three families the level of anxiety was so high even 18 months after the restoration that none of the participants felt the child was once more an integral part of the family.

How did we decide the moment at which the child was no longer returning and was 'returned'? Four aspects of the family situation are important. Firstly, the child must have a place in one of the homes of the family to which he or she has returned. The child may not live in this place; for example, one adolescent boy felt he had achieved a full reunion with home whilst living away with his girlfriend. Nonetheless, he had a room there and all the participants agreed that its occupancy was his right should he want it.

Secondly, there has to be the sense of belonging that we have referred to in previous chapters. Most important is for the family to consider that the child is home to stay and for each to feel secure in the knowledge that there will not be a rapid turn-about; such feelings can waver during the honeymoon, the row and the early negotiations.

The third dimension to the child's full return is the professionals' view of the situation. Social workers must feel confident that the child is properly placed at home and agree, at least in broad terms, with decisions made on the child's behalf. Where there is social work anxiety, nobody feels fully secure that further separation will not follow. Finally, the sense of family identity, which we referred to in the preceding chapter, is an important component in the child's full reunion. The family should perceive themselves as a single unit.

Arriving at this point can be long and painful. Yet, in retrospect, most family members in this situation could see the function and benefits of the difficult negotiations that had taken place. One mother summed the situation up thus,

'Well, I wouldn't like to go through all that again and it was hell at the time. I'd even go as far as saying it was worse than the day he went into care. You saw what was happening to us, all the rows and things. But, I can see that there was a point to it all. We cleared a lot of stuff out of the way, we know where we stand with each other and I know it will never be the same again but we know at least, and I think Mrs. Jarman (the social worker) agrees, that we all belong together, back here together.'

This mother's comment that the situation on return is not the same as that prior to the separation was mirrored by all of those participating in the study. As we have seen, during the return process there were many changes in family membership and even in the houses in which the child lived. Nonetheless, even for those returning to the *status quo ante,* there were affective changes in family relationships. In the past, this probably reflected the increased maturity of both adults and children common to all families but it is also consequent upon the lingering pain and guilt which follows separation and the sense of triumph over adversity experienced by those who had soldiered on to the end of the return path.

On the basis of the evidence just described, we would add two new factors which appear to be associated with reunion and its success. These are:

1.   The family perceives itself as a 'family'.

2.   Family members are able to see value in the tensions associated with return.

Conclusions

This concludes our review of evidence from the intensive study of 31 children from 24 families. In looking at the episodes that make up the child's return, we have charted the various steps in the process as well as the hiccoughs, false alarms and changes in plan which can occur. In this chapter, we have looked at the children's situation 18 months after return first became an issue, an analysis which re-emphasises the complexity of reunion and its many possible outcomes. We have also given a definition of when return can be said to have been achieved and, in so doing, have re-stated the importance of the spiritual aspects of the process.

In this chapter we have also added four new factors which, having carefully scrutinised the long-term outcomes for those participating in the intensive study, we feel are useful in predicting whether or not children going home will enjoy a successful homecoming. These can be added to the indicators evident from the extensive scrutiny of 875 children and those described in previous chapters. Let us now bring these all together as we draw the study to a close with check-lists useful to those making decisions about children's restorations.

15. Indicators of a child's successful return

In both extensive and intensive aspects of this study we have sought to select factors which are likely to be associated both with children's likelihood of return and their success once reunion has been achieved. In this chapter we lay out these factors in check-list form. The criteria differ depending on the alacrity with which the separated child achieves reunion or whether the child falls into a category of those at high risk of return problems.

In Chapter Eight, we used a statistical procedure to select factors predicting children's likelihood of return and its success. We then considered the intensive material and identified further indicators significant for understanding the reunion of child and family. We shall now combine these two groups of predictors to produce check-lists that social workers can use when making decisions about children's returns. We shall also re-examine the case studies described earlier to see how these, too, might work in practice.

We begin by looking at the factors produced by the intensive study and examining how they work in combination with the quantitative evidence. We shall see that this will lead us to abandon certain indicators.

Using the intensive factors to make return predictions

Using the methodology previously described, we have been able to assess the significance of factors highlighted in the intensive study as predicting a successful return. What does this exercise show? Initially, it was clear that not all of the factors we have identified as significant could be applied to all of the 31 children. Some were specific to those going home and others only applied to non-returners. Furthermore, in some cases we were unable to make an accurate judgement. For example, it was not possible to assess whether the younger children had realistically absorbed and identified with roles while away from home, a factor suggested as important by the analysis of participants' experience in the second episode. If we were to make comparisons between all 31 cases, therefore, it was necessary to produce a summary score for each case. This was calculated by expressing the factors that were present as a percentage of the total that applied to each individual child. A high score indicates a likely successful reunion while a low score suggests return difficulties.

We then compared the scores obtained with the actual outcome. The results of this exercise are as follows.

Table 15.1: The actual outcome for the 31 children participating in the intensive study compared with predicted outcome

1) Child returned & stayed at home	Range	Mean	N=
Outcome satisfactory	100-79	91	5
Concern persists	85-65	75	3
Further separation needed	60-60	60	1
Sub-total	100-60	82	9
2) Children returned & subsequently moved			
Short-term breakdown	85-85	85	3
Oscillator	47-47	47	1
Satisfactory outcome but difficult move	94-35	69	4
Child seeks independence	85-84	85	2
Child moves to India	50-50	50	1
Sub-total	94-35	72	11
3) Child did not return	77-15	40	11

High score indicates predicted positive outcome.

For each of the return outcomes described in the previous chapter, we have given the mean average and range of scores achieved by children in each category. Thus, the predicted outcome is compared with what actually happened. As table 15.1 illustrates, at a general level the factors do distinguish between the various return outcomes. It can be seen that children going home without complications score higher than those who experience difficulties. They also score far more indeed than those who fail to get back at all.

However, the table also reveals some anomalies. For example, one child who did not return home scored relatively well (77). In addition, the range for certain groups, for instance, those who enjoyed a satisfactory outcome but experienced a difficult move home, was wide (35 to 94).

Further analysis, therefore, led us to abandon two factors identified in the episodes. While important in assessing return, they seemed to duplicate other factors included in the predictive exercise. These were:

Participants absorb and identify with the roles generated by the child's return.

The child and family see the care situation as negotiable

In addition, we added two new factors highlighted as significant by this application of factors to cases. These reflect the importance of the placement prior to the child's restoration and his or her family situation on return. We found that in several cases, a particularly sensitive foster parent or residential worker made the difference between a child's successful and unsuccessful restoration, a finding supported by Goerge's (1990) research in the United States. Secondly, we also found that the child's return sometimes transformed relationships within the home and that this change altered social work strategies to support the family, considerably enhancing the chances of a child's successful reunion. The two factors added, therefore, were:

1. The placement prior to the child's return makes especial efforts to ease the transition home.

2. The return brings about a radical change for the better in family relationships.

It is also important to report that one indicator of reunion from the intensive stage, namely whether or not 'the family is prepared for the anxiety generated by return and the disputes which are likely to occur', has been kept in the model even though it did not apply to two-thirds of the returning children. We found that few families were prepared in this way and many found it hard to comprehend the rows which we saw as an integral part of a successful reunion. Nonetheless, as there may be much that social workers, foster parents and residential centres can do to prepare parents and children for the vicissitudes of reunion, we decided to retain this factor in the final list.

Predicting children's return experiences

Having clarified and checked the value of the intensive factors in predicting return outcomes, we can now combine them with the indicators obtained from our extensive study of 875 children in care. This produces, in all, 37 factors which are helpful in understanding different aspects of return although, obviously, not all are relevant to all return questions.

How can the indicators be used? While we are confident, on the evidence we have collected, that the predictive factors provide the best combination of independent indicators of children's return outcomes, we would stress that the following lists should not be the sole arbiter of whether or not we should let children go home. Nevertheless, we believe they can usefully be used by social workers to focus their return plans, for example, to accelerate the reunion of certain children or to increase the amount of support and information to host families.

The findings can be also applied in different care contexts. For children entering care, they indicate the likelihood of return within different time periods. For those already in care, the probability of reunion within specified time periods is suggested. For those children about to go home, the indicators show the chances of a successful outcome.

We begin with a check-list which can be used for all children who are looked after. It contains those factors which predict the likelihood of children going home to parents or other relatives within the following six months. We have distinguished indicators known at the point of separation from those which only become apparent at the point at which return becomes an issue.

CHECK-LIST A: Factors associated with a child's return within six months of separation

a) Variables known at the point of separation

That the child's separation is arranged on a voluntary basis.

Family and children perceive the problems necessitating the original separation to have been resolved or to have been much assisted by the child's admission to care.

Participants' perspectives of the return are realistic and there are no wide gaps between fantasy and reality in their perceptions.

There are relatively few stress factors within the family (in the context of children in care).

The family relationships as assessed (using the factors described in Appendix B) are of a relatively high quality.

b) Variables known at the point return becomes an issue

That the child had enjoyed regular contact with family members during his or her absence from home.

That the social worker encourages family links with the absent child.

The problems necessitating the original separation are perceived as having been partially resolved at the point at which return becomes an issue.

The family perceives itself as a 'family'.

There are continuities in the child's life (including family relationships, education, cultural identity and social networks).

The child retains a role within the family at each stage in the return process.

The child retains territory in the return home either by having a room, a bed or by the leaving of toys and other personal possessions or by the retention of keepsakes.

The social work plan is 'inclusive' (ie. that the family have maintained a caring role and have been involved in decisions).

All of these factors are 'protective' in that their presence is associated with a swift reunion. There are, however, 'risk' situations which can delay the return of children in care. These have to be balanced against the preceding indicators.

c)   *Risk factors which can delay a child's return*

There is a history of abuse and/or serious neglect at the time of the child's separation.

After return becomes an issue, intended return plans are affected by new information emerging concerning risks to the child, eg. of child abuse.

The second check-list can be applied to those children who have already been looked after for six months. The factors, which are divided into those known at the six months point and those on which information emerges once return becomes an issue, predict the likelihood of the child's return within the following 18 months, that is between six and 24 months after coming into care or being accommodated.

CHECK-LIST B: Children looked after at six months: Factors associated with the child's return in the following eighteen months

a)   *Variables known at six months after separation*

There is no history of abuse and/or serious neglect at the time of the child's separation.

The child has no siblings or, if there are siblings, they are separated from one another during the child's absence from home.

Relatives of the child (especially parents) participate in care decisions.

Family and children perceive the problems necessitating the original separation to have been resolved or to have been much assisted by the child's admission to care.

There are continuities in the child's life (including family relationships, education, cultural identity and social networks).

The child retains territory in the return home either by having a room, a bed or by the leaving of toys and other personal possessions or by the retention of keepsakes.

There are relatively few stress factors within the family (in the context of children in care).

The social work plan is 'inclusive' (ie. that the family have maintained a caring role and have been involved in decisions).

The family relationships as assessed (using the factors described in Appendix B) are of a relatively high quality.

b)   Variables known at the point return becomes an issue

After the point at which return becomes an issue, there are no unforeseen changes in parents' health, family relationships or household membership.

Social workers find little difficulty in visiting the family or gaining accurate information.

Participants' perspectives of the return are realistic and there are no wide gaps between fantasy and reality in their perceptions.

The problems necessitating the original separation are perceived as having been partially resolved at the point at which return becomes an issue.

The family perceives itself as a 'family'.

The child retains a role within the family at each stage in the return process.

The third check-list concerns long-stay cases, that is children who have been away for two years. If a child long in care or voluntary accommodation meets the criteria in the forthcoming list, the chances of his or her reunion with parents or relatives in the following three years, that is between 25 and 60 months after separation, are greatly increased.

CHECK-LIST C: Children away at two years: Factors associated with the child's return in the following three years

Mother is the main provider of the child's emotional support.

The child is a boy.

The family receives income support from the Department of Social Security.

Family and children perceive the problems necessitating the original separation to have been resolved or to have been much assisted by the child's admission to care.

No radically new information about family problems emerges during the separation.

Social workers find little difficulty in visiting the family or gaining accurate information.

Participants' perspectives of the return are realistic and there are no wide gaps between fantasy and reality in their perceptions.

The problems necessitating the original separation are perceived as having been partially resolved at the point at which return becomes an issue.

There are continuities in the child's life (including family relationships, education, cultural identity and social networks).

The child retains a role within the family at each stage in the return process.

The child retains territory in the return home either by having a room, a bed or by the leaving of toys and other personal possessions or by the retention of keepsakes.

There are relatively few stress factors within the family (in the context of children in care).

The social work plan is 'inclusive' (ie. that the family have maintained a caring role and have been involved in decisions).

The family relationships as assessed (using the factors described in Appendix B) are of a relatively high quality.

Finally, we present a fourth check-list which contains factors which best predict the success of a child's reunion. For these, we have separated indicators into those that are known at the point the child goes home and those which can only be known after he or she is back

CHECK LIST Factors associated with **the success of children's returns**

a)   Variables known at the point of return

There is evidence of highly competent social work (ie. that options are considered, a plan is created and social workers are highly committed to its implementation).

The child has never previously been returned after being looked after by social services.

The social worker is sufficiently confident about the situation to consider discharging the care order or is entirely satisfied with the voluntary arrangements.

Social work return plans are tailored to meet the time-scales of family members.

The family is prepared for the anxiety generated by return and the disputes which are likely to occur.

Family members are prepared to discuss with each other the pains of separation and their role in the rift.

Family members are able to see value in the tensions associated with return.

There are continuities in the child's life (including family relationships, education, cultural identity and social networks).

The child retains a role within the family at each stage in the return process.

The child retains territory in the return home either by having a room, a bed or by the leaving of toys and other personal possessions and by the retention of keepsakes.

The child is not an offender

The social work plan is 'inclusive' (ie. that the family have maintained a caring role and have been involved in decisions).

The family relationships as assessed (using the factors described in Appendix B) are of a relatively high quality.

b)   Variables known after return

The social worker does not experience difficulty in gaining access to the child or family.

Once the child is at home, the family perceives the social worker as willing to help if and when needed.

Once at home, the child establishes a role outside of the family which does not undermine his or her role within it.

Participants have a clear perception of when return has occurred.

In making assessments about the likely success of children's returns, we have to take into account special cases. For example, in both the extensive and intensive studies, we have found that persistent offenders seldom settle back at home, although their departure does not necessarily indicate an unsuccessful reunion. Deep-seated offending patterns are difficult to break and repeated court appearances and sojourns in custody frequently separate the persistent delinquent from his or her parents. This risk factor can overwhelm the protective indicators described above.

There are also some children who fail to match the criteria in check-list D but who nonetheless succeed back at home. As we explained, in exploring these situations, we discovered two protective factors which can make an apparently bleak scenario more optimistic. These are:

c)   Variables which can protect a child vulnerable to difficulties after return

The placement prior to the child's return makes especial efforts to ease the transition home.

The return brings about a radical change for the better in family relationships.

This concludes the four check-lists that social workers or other professionals can use in making decisions about the return of children in care. Further confirmatory studies have been mounted to refine the Check-lists and monitor their work in practice, but we are confident that they represent the best combination of factors obtainable from the evidence we have gathered. These discussions have still been general, focusing on groups of children in care rather than individual cases. Let us look, finally, at the individual children we have previously described to see how the predictive factors apply to their situations.

16. Applying factors to individual cases

As an illustration of their usefulness to social workers, in this chapter we apply the check-lists previously described to several case studies. We conclude the follow-up of children first studied in Chapter Eight and examine the case of Jasmine Beckford, who tragically died after return to parents.

In Chapter Eight, we described two families to illustrate how the factors suggested by the extensive research study worked in practice. The first case study involved Melanie and Michelle who, it will be recalled, unexpectedly returned to live with their father, and the second, Kelly, the toddler who became an *oscillator*. Both these examples were exceptions to the norm in that the return outcomes were the opposite of those predicted by the background factors. However, closer scrutiny revealed that the mismatch was explicable in terms of idiosyncratic and unpredictable factors, namely Gary's meeting the social worker and Madelaine's pregnancy. These altered the expected course of events with surprising consequences, thus these cases fell into the category of statistical *outliers*. By carefully examining such cases, we can understand further the interaction between factors and the neutralising effects of certain situations.

Let us now apply the check-lists of factors developed so far to these two cases. How accurate will they prove to be? First, we shall look at Melanie and Michelle.

The check-lists applied to the case studies

i) Melanie and Michelle

It will be recalled that Melanie and Michelle returned to live with their father, Gary, once more back on the road with his mobile chippy. The two sisters, aged nine and seven at the point of reunion had already lost touch with both their natural mother and step-mother and the return to father meant a further separation from their two half-sisters, Karen and Kim, who remained with foster parents. Nonetheless, wider family members had been supportive of the move and, although harbouring some doubts about the likely success of the children's return, the social worker made special efforts to make the restoration work. A family *aide* and volunteer were provided and a party to mark the girls' homecoming raised hopes of a positive outcome.

At the point return became an issue, Melanie and Michelle's social worker was faced with difficult decisions about the girls' future. If Check-list B had been applied, to indicate the likelihood of reunion in the coming 18 months, what would it have shown?

Check-list B: Applied to Melanie and Michelle after they had been looked after for six months to predict whether they would return in the following 18 months

a) Variables known at six months afterseparation.	
There is no history of abuse and/or serious neglect on separation.	**8**
The child has no siblings or, if there are siblings, they are separated from one another during the child's absence from home.	**8**
Relatives of the child (especially parents) participate in care decisions.	**8**
Family and children perceive the problems necessitating the original separation to have been much assisted by the child's admission to care.	**4**
There are continuities in the child's life (including family relationships, education, cultural identity and social networks).	**j**
The child retains territory in the return home either by having a room, bed or by the leaving of toys and other personal possessions or by the retention of keepsakes.	**4**
There are relatively few stress factors within the family.	**4**
The social work plan is 'inclusive'.	**4**
The family relationships as assessed (using the factors described in Appendix B) are of a relatively high quality.	**4**
b) Variables known at the point return becomes an issue.	
There are no unforeseen changes in parent's health, family relationships and household membership.	**4**
Social workers find little difficulty in visiting the family or gaining accurate information.	**4**
Participants' perspectives of the return are realistic and there are no wide gaps between fantasy and reality in their perceptions.	**4**
The problems necessitating the original separation are perceived as having been partially resolved at the point at which return becomes an issue.	**4**
The family perceives itself as a 'family'.	**4**
The child retains a role within the family at each stage in the return process.	**8**
j=NK	

Of the fifteen factors in check-list B, all of which indicate increased likelihood of a child going home, Melanie and Michelle failed on only four. Three of these factors were highlighted in the extensive study of 875 children while the fourth reflected the failure of the children to keep a role in the family at each stage in the return process. Despite regular access to their father and a social work strategy which was inclusive, there were periods of time during the separation when Melanie and Michelle played little, if any, part in the lives of their parents.

All but one of the other indicators suggested that Melanie and Michelle would go home within the next 18 months. The exception is the fifth factor in the list. We could not say assuredly that there was a continuity in the children's family relationships, education, cultural identity and social networks. There was, naturally, a spiritual continuity which bound the father to his daughters but there were also new temporal continuities in the girls' lives, for example, with the foster parents and at the primary school. There were also vicissitudes in the mental health of the father and the emotional well-being of the girls both of which seemed to be tied to the fortunes of the mobile fish and chip van. Under different circumstances these could have reduced the chances of their restoration.

Despite these reservations, the check-list demonstrates that the girls were highly likely to go home although there would be considerable obstacles on the way. What if we now apply Check-list D which offers an *aide-mémoire* when considering how well the children will fare once back with parents?

As we can see, the following check-list would suggest an optimistic outcome for Melanie and Michelle's return. Indeed, by preparing the father for the inevitable anxieties that were likely to arise after the children's restoration, the social worker could have further reduced the chances of the home placement breaking down.But, was this prognosis correct? Our follow-up reveals that the placement did endure for the remainder of our involvement. The family *aide* and volunteer who had supported the father in the care of his children were slowly withdrawn during the first year after return, indicating the growing social work satisfaction with the girls' progress. Later, Gary met Eva, a widow with long experience of coping with inadequate men. Eva and Gary were made for each other and under her capable tutelage, the family thrived. Eventually, the couple married and there was even a suggestion that the girl's two half-sisters, Karen and Kim, might also join the family; a plan which never came to fruition.

Check-list D: Applied to Melanie and Michelle to predict the likely success of their return

a) Variables known at the point of return	
There is evidence of highly competent social work.	4
The child has never previously been returned after being looked after.	4
The social worker is sufficiently confident about the situation to consider discharging the care order or is satisfied with the voluntary arrangements.	8
Social work return plans are tailored to meet the timescales of the family.	4
The family is prepared for the anxiety generated by return and the disputes which are likely to occur.	8
Family members are prepared to discuss with each other the pains of separation and their role in the rift.	4
Family members are able to see value in the tensions associated with return.	4
There are continuities in the child's life.	4
The child retains a role within the family at each stage in the return process.	8
The child retains territory in the return home either by having a room, bed or by the leaving of toys or the retention of keepsakes.	4
The child is not an offender.	4
The social work is 'inclusive'.	4
The family relationships are of a relatively high quality.	4
b) Variables known after return	
The social worker does not experience difficulty in gaining access to the child or family.	4
Once the child is at home, the family perceive the social worker as willing to help if and when needed.	4
Once at home, the child establishes a role outside of the family which does not undermine his or her role within it.	4
Participants have a clear perception of when return has occurred.	4
c) Special variables which may protect a child vulnerable to difficulties after return	
The placement prior to the child's return makes especial efforts to ease the transition home.	k
The return brings about a radical change for the better in family relationships.	4
k = NK	

The mobile fish and chip van was eventually traded in by Gary and his partner, Brian, for a pizza take-away business. This was hardly more profitable but was more reliable than the 'mobile'. There were clearly tensions attached to the new family arrangements but at least the food was good. Overall, the return could be said to be successful and the girls, no doubt buoyed up by good school performances, a strong network of friends outside the family, and, for once, an enduring, predictable maternal figure, were happy.We can see, therefore, that the check-lists seem to work well in the case of Melanie and Michelle, at least in the short-term. Not all aspects of the girls' situation point towards a successful homecoming and, indeed, problems persisted throughout and after the return. In the longer term, the weaknesses in the family which have caused difficulties in the past are still evident, thus emphasising the need for enduring supports.

ii) Kelly

What of our other exception? It will be recalled that Kelly was born to Madelaine, a teenager from a large, black family who found her life chances in her drab Midland town somewhat limited. Kelly was received into care while her mother decided what to do about her second pregnancy. While her daughter was sheltered with Afro-Caribbean foster parents, Maddie had an abortion. With considerable support from social services, Kelly was returned to Madelaine, a lone mother in a council flat. Although the situation was less than ideal, the factors obtained from our extensive scrutiny all pointed towards a successful reunion for Kelly and her mother. What happens when we apply all of the factors from both studies as listed in check-list D?

It suggests that Kelly would have problems back at home with her mother. Its application swiftly focused attention on the aspects of Madelaine's home situation which reduced the likelihood of a successful outcome. During her daughter's absence, Madelaine had resurrected her hedonistic lifestyle and was never really ready for Kelly's return. Once Kelly was back home, Madelaine began to miss appointments with her social worker and, when visits were insisted upon, the mother rightly perceived the relationship with social services to be one of control rather than support.

Check-list D: Applied to Kelly to predict the likely success of her return

a) Variables known at the point of return	
There is evidence of highly competent social work.	4
The child has never previously been returned after being looked after.	4
The social worker is sufficiently confident about the situation to consider discharging the care order or is satisfied with the voluntary arrangements.	4
Social work return plans are tailored to meet the timescales of the family.	8
The family is prepared for the anxiety generated by return and the disputes which are likely to occur.	8
Family members are prepared to discuss with each other the pains of separation and their role in the rift.	-
Family members are able to see value in the tensions associated with return.	8
There are continuities in the child's life.	8
The child retains a role within the family at each stage in the return process.	8
The child retains territory in the return home.	4
The child is not an offender.	4
The social work plan is 'inclusive'	**8**
The family relationships are of a relatively high quality	4
b) Variables known after return	
The social worker does not experience difficulty in gaining access to the child or family.	8
Once the child is at home, the family perceive the social worker as willing to help if and when needed.	8
Once at home, the child establishes a role outside of the family which does not undermine his or her role within it.	-
Participants have a clear perception of when return has occurred.	**8**
c) Special variables which may protect a child vulnerable to difficulties after return	
The placement prior to the child's return makes especial efforts to ease the transition home.	k
The return brings about a radical change for the better in family relationships.	8
k = NK ; - = NA	

Kelly was neglected during this period as her mother tried to combine the role of being a mother with that of an older adolescent in a vibrant West Indian community. When she became pregnant a third time, Madelaine looked for escape from her child-care responsibilities and, overwhelmed, was happy for Kelly to be accommodated once more by the local authority. This time Maddie decided to have her baby. However, when return once more became an issue, many of the positive features of the family had been lost and there was the additional complication of a new baby. Return the second time around was always likely to be difficult.

In fact, Kelly's second return was delayed for nearly two years. Madelaine initially asked for Kelly to be placed for adoption but social workers sought long-term foster parents as they tried, with intermittent success, to maintain links between Kelly and her mother. When the foster placement eventually broke down, Kelly was placed at home. If however, we apply Check-list D at this point in Kelly's care career, none of the factors have a tick beside them, and the prognosis seemed poor, an outcome borne out in reality. Kelly became an *oscillator*, as described in Chapter Seven, moving regularly between substitute care placements and, when all else failed, the parental home.

But, while we may take comfort in the successful application of our research findings to actual cases, hardened practitioners may still be sceptical. After all the most contentious of all return situations remains unexplored, namely child abuse situations. It is clear that such cases crystallise the inherent tensions between child rescue and rehabilitation and social workers attempting to plan for such children find themselves in a 'no win' situation. On the one hand, if re-abuse occurs, as has happened in several well-documented tragedies, they are castigated for being over-zealous in their return ambitions. If, on the other hand, the child drifts in care, they are lambasted for allowing family links to wither. Let us in closing, therefore, apply the check-lists we have developed to the most intensively studied child-care tragedy, the case of Jasmine Beckford.

The check-lists applied to the case of Jasmine Beckford

The case of Jasmine Beckford became a child-care *cause célèbre* in 1985 when a panel of inquiry chaired by Louis Blom-Cooper brought to a head more than 12 months of press speculation and recrimination. The recommendations of the report *A Child in Trust* were influential and led, in time, to the *Charge and Control Regulations* earlier described.

Jasmine Beckford was born in December 1979 and died at the hands of her step-father in 1984, five months short of her fifth birthday. Jasmine had been taken into care under emergency procedures in August 1981 when she was admitted to hospital with a broken femur. After a short stay, Jasmine joined her younger half-sister Louise in a foster home.

Very early on, social workers decided to return Jasmine and Louise to their mother, Beverly Norrington, and Morris Beckford, Louise's father. The report describes how:

> Every step in the process over the next two and three-quarter years was taken against the blackcloth of an ill-conceived programme of rehabilitation. Every step taken was part of the social work mosaic which bore the brand of inevitable disaster upon its face

While in care, the children enjoyed weekly access to their family and Beverly was taught how to respond to and communicate with her children. Ms. Norrington wanted to see her children more frequently. This request was not granted but, as the initial visits appeared to be successful, the children were allowed to go home for access visits.

In April 1982, eight months after entering care, Jasmine and Louise went home. The decision followed a case review in which there were no dissenting voices. The inquiry team were of the opinion that the decision was a rubber stamp of one hatched many months before. There was, however, a serious difference of opinion between the foster parents and social services, a dispute that went beyond whether or not the girls should be allowed home.

The day of the children's return, or 'handover' to use the inquiry team's phrase, was clearly very tense, although we get little idea of the full extent of participants' anxiety from the report. We can, however, say that social workers made impressive efforts to help and support the family once they were back together.

Clearly, professionals were under the impression that the family were making good progress. Three months following the restoration, Ms. Norrington became pregnant with her third child, Chantelle, and social workers applied to the court to have the care orders on the two other children revoked. The court refused but, from the day of the hearing, social workers acted as if no order was in force.

Social work activity declined and was 'barely existent' when, in the autumn of the following year, alarm bells were loudly ringing. At this time social workers were finding it difficult to visit the family and were stymied by a variety of excuses from Beverly Norrington.

On the 12th March 1984, the social worker saw Jasmine alive for the last time. She was in a room with her two sisters. Jasmine was almost certainly the victim of recent physical abuse but her mother carefully concealed any bruising from the social worker who, in any case, did not look too closely.

As the inquiry team found, the focus of social work activity fell predominantly on the parents and not on the children. The social worker or family *aide* never took the children out alone and most visits to the Beckford household were taken up with conversations with the parents. *A Child in Trust* re-states Sir Walter Monckton's phrase in his 1945 report on the death of Dennis O'Neill, that the relationship of the local authority to a child in care is a personal one, 'the duty must neither be evaded nor scamped'.

It is unlikely that professionals' relentless efforts to get the Beckford children home would ever have been deflected by one of our check-lists. Nor are these check-lists designed to pick out the most vulnerable children like Jasmine and her sisters who are at very grave risks from their parents. However, it is interesting that the inquiry team did recommend that a team of medical sociologists 'refine the techniques for predicting accurately those children who will continue to be at risk'. Naturally, our research brief has been much wider and, while we have been able to highlight children who are likely to experience return problems, the identification of high-risk abuse cases is a different matter. Nonetheless, by applying the check-lists to Jasmine at different points in her short life, we are able to reveal more strengths and weaknesses in the approach we have adopted in this study.

Using the check-lists on the Beckford case has not been without problems. We have had to look retrospectively at information contained in the inquiry team's report and those more familiar with the events may disagree with our judgements. Nevertheless, the unequivocal fact is that not only is the outcome known, but it is indisputably bad.

As we can see from the following tables, there were two items on the check-list where the information to make a satisfactory judgement was insufficient. However, of the remaining thirteen factors, only two were answered in such a way which would suggest that reunion was likely. These both concerned social work activity which, as we know, was almost solely concerned with rehabilitation. If this check-list had been applied, it would have been clear that a closer scrutiny of the family and the children's role would be required if the children's prospects of restoration were to improve.

We began with check-list B which is used for children in care at six months to predict the likelihood of return to parents and/or guardians in the following 18 months. The results of the application are as follows:

Check-list B: Applied to Jasmine Beckford after she had been in care for six months to predict whether she would return in the following 18 months

a) Variables known at six months after entry to care	
There is no history of abuse and/or serious neglect at the time of the child's separation.	8
The child has no siblings or, if there are siblings, they are separated from one another during the child's absence from home.	8
Relatives of the child (especially parents) participate in care decisions.	8
Family and children perceive the problems necessitating the original separation to have been resolved by the child's admission to care.	8
There are continuities in the child's life (including family relationships, education, cultural identity and social networks).	k
The child retains territory in the return home either by having a room, bed or by the leaving of toys and other personal possessions or by the retention of keepsakes.	8
There are relatively few stress factors within the family.	8
The social work plan is 'inclusive'.	4
The family relationships as assessed (using the factors described in Appendix B) are of a relatively high quality.	8
b) Variables known at the point return becomes an issue	
There are no unforeseen changes in parent's health, family relationships or household membership.	8
Social workers find little difficulty in visiting the family or gaining accurate information.	4
Participants' perspectives of the return are realistic and there are no wide gaps between fantasy and reality in their perceptions.	8
The problems necessitating the original separation are perceived as having been partially resolved at the point at which return becomes an issue.	8
The family perceives itself as a 'family'.	k
The child retains a role within the family at each stage in the return process.	8
k=There is not sufficient information to make a judgement	

But the children went home. What happens if we apply Check-list D which indicates the likely success of reunions?

Check-list D: Applied to Jasmine Beckford to predict the likely success of her return

a) Variables known at the point of return	
There is evidence of highly competent social work.	8
The child has never previously been returned after being looked after.	4
The social worker is sufficiently confident about the situation to consider discharging the care order or is entirely satisfied with the voluntary arrangements.	4
Social work return plans are tailored to meet the timescales of the family.	k
The family is prepared for the anxiety generated by return and the disputes which are likely to occur.	8
Family members are prepared to discuss with each other the pains of separation.	8
Family members are able to see value in the tensions associated with return.	8
There are continuities in the child's life.	k
The child retains a role within the family at each stage in the return process.	8
The child is not an offender.	4
The social work plan is 'inclusive'.	8
The family relationships are of a relatively high quality.	8
b) Variables known after return	
The social worker does not experience difficulty in gaining access to the child or family.	8
Once the child is at home, the family perceive the social worker as willing to help if and when needed.	4
Once at home, the child establishes a role outside of the family which does not undermine his or her role within it.	8
Participants have a clear perception of when return has occurred.	8
c) Special variables which may protect a child vulnerable to difficulties after return	
The placement prior to the child's return makes especial efforts to ease the transition home.	8
The return brings about a radical change for the better in family relationships.	8
k = There is not sufficient information to make a judgement	

Once again, we can see from the above table there are gaps in our knowledge which make it difficult fully to complete the check-list. But, even so, there are only three positive answers to the questions posed. Firstly, the children had never previously been separated and returned. Secondly, the social workers had not only considered the discharge of the care order but had also applied for its revocation - although this was, in retrospect, clearly an ill-conceived plan. Thirdly, the family perceived the social worker as ready to help which, in fact, she was. However, so eager were the professionals to make the rehabilitation work, the report suggests, that the parents were able to mislead them.

So, even if we ignore the special feature of this case, the gross abuse which Morris Beckford inflicted upon his step-child, our check-list would suggest that the likelihood of the home-on-trial placement working was never very high.

By presenting the check-lists in this way we have exposed other *lacunae* in our approach. It may be that social workers completing such forms will be alerted to the dangers of rushing headlong into the restoration of abused children to abusing parents but, frankly, this is unlikely. However, even if it were 100% accurate, there would still be a danger of using the check-list as a 'one-off' *aide*. Our focus on return as a process emphasises that decisions have to be followed up and double-checked and, as families change, new assessments have to be made. As the Beckford inquiry team state,

> Children, while living with their parents at home on trial, must *remain* in trust to the local authority.

Conclusions

The check-lists described and employed in this chapter bring together the results of the extensive and intensive studies. While the factors need further testing in prospective studies, when applied to the two case studies and to Jasmine Beckford, they can be seen as a useful adjunct to existing procedures for making return decisions about children in care and should be of practical use to social workers. While these check-lists cannot be used as the sole arbiter of whether or not a child should go back, they will highlight deficiencies in the social work strategies for children's returns and indicate weaknesses in the host family. In the end, professional judgement has to prevail, but we have produced an instrument which is applicable to the majority of children in care and which should, with time, ease the pain and anxiety which we have found so often to accompany their return home.

17. Conclusions

Recent years have seen much questioning of the ability of the state to provide substitute parenting for children. We have moved away from ideas of child rescue and have begun to give natural parents and the wider family an increasing role in the care of children that have to be separated. Stimulating the contribution of parents has been a gathering pre-occupation well outside the concerns of social services, for example, parents are being increasingly encouraged to participate in concerns of health, education and vocational training of the young.

The 19th Century and early years of this century were haunted by attempts to disrupt a supposed cycle of deprivation and to rescue children from parents unable or unwilling to rear them satisfactorily. It was firmly believed that such young people needed a new start away from contaminating neighbourhoods and families in which the young eked out a precarious existence. We have also noted that these beliefs in rescue were not entirely compassionate or altruistic and even religious fervour could be sectarian and partisan in motivating attempts to succour destitute children.

Such beliefs have increasingly been questioned, a process stimulated by the failure of care alternatives to meet the needs of children or of reformatory settings to check delinquency. Considerable doubts were being expressed over the adequacy of provision for children made by the state and by private philanthropy even before the upheavals of the Second World War. But in 1939 and 1940 the evacuation of a large number of children from our inner cities highlighted both the poverty of many families and the inadequacy of much child health and welfare provision. Residential care was particularly criticised. As we have observed, the recent 1989 *Children Act* represents yet another scene in a domestic drama that was initiated by the *Curtis Report* of 1946. Reform was also stimulated by a variety of professional voices bewailing the effects of separation and the wrenching apart of family bonds.

In more recent years, accumulating research has questioned the efficacy of state care and the ability of professionals to provide adequate nurture for separated children. Too often isolation, drift and anomie have been identified as the experience of children taken into state care and studies of leaving care have highlighted the poor social and vocational skills, the inadequate educational attainments of those who linger long away from home. While the separated children may be no more deficient in skills than deprived children who remain at home, the care experience hardly seems to enhance life chances.

This study has reminded us that the majority of children and adolescents who are separated return to parents or the wider family once they leave care. The majority of these reunions occur in spite of the reasons for entering care or the length of time away. Even young adults, some convicted of grave offences, long separated from home, periodically rest in the bosom of their families once professionals have ceased their ministrations. As we abandon the task, it is usually the family, frequently identified as damaging or deficient, which takes up the role of main supporter of children and young adolescents. Young people may not stay long at home, they may use the family as a springboard or bolt-hole from outside excitements, they may return home swiftly because all else fails or because they exhaust the tolerance of other benefactors. But, parents and the wider family, probably deficient on many criteria, are a resource which could be enhanced by social work support and encouragement. Involving parents and sharing care with the family is now recognised as good social work practice.

This study has addressed specifically the problems surrounding reunion because literature and research evidence concerning separation rarely looks at children's experiences as they go home. In most studies, glances at reunion are incidental to other concerns. Nevertheless, much evidence suggests that return is as fraught and as stressful an experience as separation, that the management of reunion is far from simple and that, while the majority of reconciliations are successful, those that fail can carry with them serious long-term implications for the rejected child.

Not only do most children go home, the majority enjoy a very swift reunion with parents. We have seen that 87% of the children who are looked after by a local authority away from home return there within five years. Indeed, nearly three-fifths of all possible returners are home before six months have elapsed and almost a fifth of these go back in the first week. Moreover, 4% of the children, although legally in care, were never removed from home during that period. The swift return of the majority of separated children, 16,500 every year, is a largely unsung social work contribution to family welfare.

This success story should not, however, obscure the problems of those few who linger. Indeed, the problems of reunion for those long-separated from home, usually adolescents, have excited particular concern. Nevertheless, our evidence would suggest that even adolescents who stayed long in care and were particularly difficult, maintained high chances of reunion. Naturally, some groups of children have more favourable prospects than others. For example, some older children do not necessarily stay long at home after reunion and a small number are prone to precipitate breakdown in family relationships.

In looking at return, we have found it helpful to distinguish between children according to the lengths of time they are looked after. Not only did duration in care distinguish children with different characteristics and family structures but length of separation also highlighted differences in children's chances of an enduring, successful reunion.

We have seen that *early returners* are usually children whose families have been temporarily unable to cope, disabled by illness, by marital disputes and/or by problems of accommodation. Families have had to surrender their children to social services. Thus, *early returners* form the majority of children leaving care and less than a quarter have been in care before, a far lower proportion than among those whose stay in care lasts longer than six months. Infants and those of junior school age form the majority of those enjoying a swift return; while the families to which they return are not as turbulent as those of long-stay children, nevertheless, they remain vulnerable. Households are poor and anxieties considerable. For example, nearly half of the children are from single-parent families and three-quarters of their fragile households are dependent on social security.

These *early returners* contrast markedly with those who go home later, *intermediate returners*. After six months had elapsed, 189 of the 450 in the original study group were still separated and only two-fifths of them were reunited in the following 18 months. These were predominantly adolescents removed from home for behavioural difficulties or family problems to which the child made a considerable contribution. Nearly half of the children came into care via court orders and the majority, three-fifths, were boys.

While less oppressed by poverty and insecurity than the families of *early returners,* this *intermediate* group of children going home between seven months and two years after entry to care faced ambivalent and rejecting families. More than a third of the parents failed to participate in any way in the care of their separated children, links between these children and their families were fitful and tenuous, indeed, in more than one-third of cases there were restrictions on access. For these children, many in residential care and prone to movement while separated from home, social workers entertained little optimism for eventual reunion with their families. One-third were viewed as likely to remain away from home for the foreseeable future.

Those children who stayed long in care or accommodation, that is more than two years, shared many characteristics with the *intermediate returners* just described. *Long-term returners* were older on entry than the majority of children looked after; for example, two-thirds were over the age of 12. One-third of the children had been in care or accommodated before and in nearly half of the cases the child's behaviour was a strong contributory cause of their entry. Naturally this will complicate the management of any return strategy.

Nevertheless, social workers remained quite optimistic about return in the majority of cases. They estimated that three-quarters of long-stay cases would eventually return home and family links were greatly encouraged in the majority of situations. Unlike those children whose stays in care are short and where social workers negotiate almost all aspects of the reunion, in long-stay cases return is frequently informally negotiated between relatives and offspring. Sometimes these negotiations were in defiance of social work decisions and some adolescents actually voted with their feet. There were high levels of family change during the children's separation from home. Nearly half of them returned to families with different key family members.

But the passage of time is not entirely detrimental, it allows for reflection and self-examination. Some adolescents repaired long-damaged relationships, became more tolerant of home circumstances and more sympathetic to hard-pressed parents. In addition, many parents were more benign about the antics of their offspring and welcomed the prospect of their having a job and eventually achieving some independence.

How successful were these reunions and what were the consequences for children and families of a stressful return that finally ended in breakdown? As we have seen, the outcomes of reunion are difficult to assess. Even if a child lingers under the parental roof, there is no guarantee that happiness and fulfilment attend the stay. We have seen that the need to re-negotiate family roles, to compromise and to share territories, often with new adults and rival children, made return stressful for some young people. The passage of time, however, encourages many to settle.

It is encouraging to note that the majority of children who go home stay put and that social workers' assessments of the reunion suggest it is tranquil and unremarkable. For example, some 70% of those who went home stayed, apparently in satisfactory circumstances. As might be expected, those whose separations were short tended to settle more readily than those who were long looked after, particularly if they stayed longer than two years away from home. On return, adolescents were more footloose than younger children but many, even those in their late teens, achieved a *modus vivendi* with their families. Naturally, the older the young person, the more movement around the family occurred and the more common were forays into independent living followed by retreats to the asylum offered by home. However, it is important to note that a considerable proportion of our long-stay children go home and remain with their families without any noticeable disadvantage.

Nevertheless, this study has identified groups of children who are particularly vulnerable to return problems. A number of children whose separations are short fail to settle on their return home and about a quarter of those going back within six months return once more to substitute care. While the majority of these children are rehabilitated at the next attempt at reunion, a small number continue to oscillate in and out of care for a considerable period. Some adolescents cause similar problems on return; as we have seen, the majority settle back at home but a small number of skill-less adolescents drift rapidly into the ranks of the homeless. Unremarkable other than by their poor care experience and withering links with home, these casualties of the care system are difficult to spot early on. This makes special strategies of reunion for these children particularly difficult to mount.

This study has also demonstrated that a number of variables are associated with return outcomes. Using multi-variate analysis, we have highlighted those factors which predict how swiftly children who enter care and are separated from their families will go home. These variables have been produced as a check-list, appropriate for the different groups of children being looked after, which social workers can easily apply. In addition, variables associated with a successful outcome have also been identified and, in the same way, laid out in check-list form. Some of the predictive factors of eventual and successful return are not likely to cause surprise, such as the significance of close family links while the child is away and the importance of an accepting warm relationship between mother and absent child, but others are less obvious and could only be established by careful research.

The use of such predictive factors in assessing the outcomes of care interventions is less common in child-care than in medicine or delinquency studies. Unfortunately, such predictions cannot be fool-proof and we have illustrated several exceptions to the rule. The check-lists are intended to aid professionals making decisions about return, not to replace the need for careful evaluation of each case as it arises. Neither are these indices intended to be the only fruits of research in this area and further validation and development work is underway.

However, whatever the limitations of the study, several messages helpful to social workers faced with return decisions have emerged. Initially, and perhaps most importantly, is the need to recognise that most children looked after by local authorities return home. If we keep this one fact firmly in mind at the point of separation then key decisions about the child's future may change.

We are also encouraged to foster a positive ethos with regard to the child's family and to allow such an ethos to seep into all decision-making, particularly those concerned with adolescents. But, we do not have to wait for decisions on children to be reviewed. The check-lists will highlight youngsters drifting in care for whom return plans could be accelerated. As we are so often reminded in child-care, even the darkest prospects can brighten.

The discovery that so many short-term outcomes are positive should bring comfort to social workers. We might also stress that the situation in the long-term is often more satisfactory than we like to imagine, especially for abused and neglected children. Indeed, these acute cases arouse much less anxiety several years on than the quiescent, skill-less, drifting adolescents, boys as well as girls, who become bereft of support and seem unable to seek succour.

For them, and for all children in need, improved services will be likely. The study coincides with the implementation of the 1989 *Children Act* which stresses partnership between social services and families. However, 'shared care' should not be interpreted as a crude division, for instance allowing the child to spend four days in a foster home and the remainder of the week with parents. We have found that such a rigid plan would seldom work. Repeated returns are not easy for participants to manage and, when the pattern does endure, it can encourage the child in later years to choose flight as a strategy to cope with stress.

Consequently, we would emphasise much more the value of keeping parents on the scene, making separation and return part of a package and the fostering of parental responsibility as described in the 1989 legislation. The attitude and involvement of all participants is more important to the child's future than administrative arrangements such as who lives where.

Indeed, we have found a mismatch between the management of the care experience and the perceptions of family members. For the parents and children we have studied, life's course is marked by a series of episodes, hence our approach to the intensive data. If we are to take on board the messages of the *Children Act* we will have to work to the timescales of parents and children and remember that in a care career the situation at one moment in time is very much fashioned by preceding events.

Are more resources needed to ease children's returns? If we are faced with limited resources, then one way forward is to work most intensively with those families requiring greatest help. Increasingly, research is highlighting a variety of indices which identify vulnerable children and the check-lists described in this study can also be used to pinpoint the most worrying cases. We now have plentiful information on not only who is long looked after and faces difficulties in getting home but also who will need extra support after reunion.

This study has also highlighted children's and families' needs for a sense of continuity and meaning in the face of disruption, separation and random difficulty. Return is a process and by looking at key moments as the drama enfolds, it becomes clear how reunion is coloured by what has gone before. The recognition that return means a re-negotiation of cherished roles and the sharing or surrendering of territory and possessions is also very important. These fraught negotiations particularly affect step-parents and newcomers, cohabitees and their children. Above all, unease, friction and argument do not signify a breakdown of return but seem to be a common feature of all families experiencing reunion, not only those haunted by poverty, illness and re-constitution. Thus, stress does not always lead to a poor outcome, indeed we might almost suggest the reverse.

As such, the solution for the child and family of these inevitable disputes lies not in flight or withdrawal but in negotiating, with social work support, a *modus vivendi.* Particularly important is for the social worker and other supports to be available in the days that follow the restoration. Many respondents felt that the resolution of disputes during these early days provided a valuable opportunity for children and parents to understand better the reasons behind the separation.

Working with the family after return will be eased if, during separation, social workers have nurtured continuities, however tenuous these may be. Moreover, while temporal continuities may wither naturally, they should not be severed abruptly. So, just as one strives to keep the family involved during the child's absence in care, one should similarly try after return to keep the care experience alive. Maintaining links with foster parents or a residential centre and the surrounding environment can have a considerable pay-off, especially for those youngsters who oscillate between social services and parents.

Above all, this study amply illustrates what previous social work has often implied, preoccupied as it has been with other child-care concerns: *viz,* reunion is quite as stressful as separation for both children and parents. Reconciliation involves facing up to one's personal responsibilities and failures because the fantasies which maintain every-day life have to be examined in the cold light of day and because inexorable change reminds all that the past cannot be undone. It thus needs all of the preparation of a foster or adoptive placement.

But it greatly helps to know that reunion does not mean taking up, once more, abruptly and without support, the duties so precipitately thrown down on separation. It also helps to realise that preparation, counselling and support are not wasted efforts as return takes place. Just as a shoulder to cry on is important in managing separation so a go-between to yell at on return, someone who can catch the flying plates and interpret what is happening, is particularly important. Thus, as the social worker hurries back down the garden path, clasping a check-list and brimming with sensitivity to the pains of reunion, even the errant chip van as it rounds the corner might offer wondrous insights and opportunities!

References

Aldgate, J., Heath, A. and Colton, M. (1991), *The Educational Progress of Children in Care*, Report to ESRC, Oxford University.

++++

Ball, S. (1981), *Beachside Comprehensive*, London: Cambridge University Press.

Becker, H.S. (1958), 'Problems of inference and proof in participant observation', *American Sociological Review*, 23, (Dec.), pp. 652-659.

Becker, H.S. and Geer, B. (1960), 'Participant observation: the analysis of qualitative field data' in Adams, R.N. and Preiss, J.J. (Eds.), *Human Organisation Research, Field Relations and Techniques*, Illinois: Davsey Press.

Berridge, D. (1985), *Children's Homes*, Oxford: Blackwell.

Berridge, D. and Cleaver, H. (1987), *Foster Home Breakdown*, Oxford: Blackwell.

Biehal, N. and Stein, M. (1992), *Prepared for Living: A Study of Young People Leaving the Care of Three Local Authorities*, London: National Children's Bureau.

Block, N. and Libowitz, A. (1983), *Recidivism in Foster Care*, New York: Child Welfare League of America.

Bonnerjea, L. (1990), *Leaving Care in London,* London Boroughs' Children's Regional Planning Committee.

Bowlby, J. (1952), *Maternal Care and Mental Health*, Geneva: WHO.

Brearley, P., Black, J., Gutridge, P., Roberts, G. and Tarran, E. (1982), *Leaving Residential Care*, London: Tavistock.

Bullock, R., Hosie, K., Little, M. and Millham, S. (1990), 'Secure accommodation for very difficult adolescents: some recent research findings', *Journal of Adolescence*, XIII, pp.205-216.

Bullock, R., Little, M. and Millham, S. (1991), *A Re-analysis of Children's Care Experiences to Discover Factors Associated with Return Outcomes*, Dartington Social Research Unit.

Bullock, R., Little, M. and Millham, S. (1992), 'The relationships between quantitative and qualitative approaches in social policy research' in Brannen, J. (ed.), *Mixing Methods: Qualitative and Quantitative Research*, Aldershot: Avebury, pp. 81-100.

Burford, G. and Casson, S. (1989), 'Including families in residential work: educational and agency tasks', *British Journal of Social Work*, XIX, pp. 17-37.

Burgess, C. (1981), *In Care and Into Work*, London: Tavistock.

++++

Cawson, P. (1988), 'Children in exile', *Insight*, Sept., pp. 12-15.

Chandler, J., Bryant, L. and Dunkerley, D. (1987), *Naval Families Research Project*, Plymouth: Polytechnic South West.

Coleman, J.S. (1961), *The Adolescent Society*, Glencoe: Free Press.

Corrigan, P. (1979), *Schooling the Smash Street Kids*, London: Macmillan.

++++

Denzin, N.K. (1970), *Sociological Methods: A Sourcebook*, London: Butterworths.

Department of Health (1991), *Assessing Outcomes in Child Care*, London: HMSO.

Department of Health (1991), *Patterns and Outcomes in Child Placement*, London: HMSO.

Department of Health and Social Security (1987), *The Law on Child Care and Family Services*, CM. 62, London, HMSO.

++++

Fanshel, D. and Shinn, E. (1978), *Children in Foster Care*, New York: Columbia University Press.

Farmer, E. and Parker, R.A. (1991), *Trials and Tribulations*, London: HMSO.

Farrington, D.P. (1990), 'Implications of criminal career research for the prevention of offending', *Journal of Adolescence*, XIII, pp. 93-114.

Festinger, T. (1983), *No-one Ever Asked Us*, New York: Columbia University Press.

Filstead, W.J. (1970), *Qualitative Methodology; First Hand Involvement with the Social World*, Chicago, Markham.

Fleeman, A.M.F. (1984), 'From special to secondary school for children with learning difficulties', *Special Education: Forward Trends*, Vol. 11, No.3, Research Supplement.

Fletcher-Campbell, F. and Hall, C. (1991), *Changing Schools? Changing People? The Education of Children in Care*, Slough: National Foundation for Educational Research.

++++

Garnett, L. (1992), *Leaving Care and After,* London: National Children's Bureau.

Giddens, A. (1982), *New Rules of Sociological Method*, London: Hutchinson.

Goerge, R. (1990), 'The re-unification process in substitute care', *Social Services Review*, LXIV, pp. 422-457.

++++

Haimes, E. and Timms, N. (1985), *Adoption, Identity and Social Policy*, Aldershot: Gower.

Hall, P. and Stacey, M. (1979), *Beyond Separation: Further Studies of Children in Hospital,* London: Routledge and Kegan Paul.

Hammersley, M. and Atkinson, P. (1983), *Ethnography: Principles in Practice*, London: Routledge and Kegan Paul .

Hargreaves, D.H. (1967), *Social Relations in a Secondary School*, London: Routledge and Kegan Paul.

Hazel, N. (1981), *A Bridge to Independence*, Oxford: Blackwell.

Heath, A., Colton, M. and Aldgate, J. (1989), 'The education of children in care', *British Journal of Social Work*, XIX, pp. 447-460.

Hess, P. and Proch, K. (1988), *Family Visiting in Out-of-Home Care: A Guide to Good Practice*, Washington DC: Child Welfare League of America.

Hess, P and Proch, K.O. (1992), 'Visiting: The heart of family re-unification' in Pine, B.A., Warsh, R. and Mallucio, A. (Eds.), *Together Again: Re-unification in Foster Care*, Washington DC: Child Welfare League of America.

HMSO (1945), *Report by Sir William Monckton on the Circumstances which led to the Boarding Out of Denis and Terence O'Neill at Bank Farm, Minsterley*, Cmnd. 6636.

HMSO (1946), *Report of the Care of Children Committee* (The Curtis Committee) Cmnd. 6922.

HMSO (1984), *The Second Report from the House of Commons Social Services Committee,*session 1983-4; HC360-1.

Hobson, R.P. (1985), 'On the ways of knowing childhood' in Rutter, M. and Hersov, L. (Eds.), *Child and Adolescent Psychiatry*, Oxford: Blackwell.

Home Office (1927), *Report of the Departmental Committee on the Treatment of Young Offenders*, Cmnd. 2831, London: HMSO.

Hundleby, M. (1988), 'Returning children home' in Family Rights Group, *Planning for Children*, London: FRG.

++++

Jackson, S. (1987), *The Education of Children in Care*, Bristol Papers in Applied Social Studies, 1, Bristol University.

Johnson, B.S. (1968) (ed.), *The Evacuees,* London: Gollancz.

Jolly, R. (1987), *Military Man, Family Man, Crown Property?* London: Brassey's Defence Publishers.

++++

Kahan, B. (1979), *Growing Up In Care*, Oxford: Blackwell.

Keegan, J. (1976), *The Face of Battle*, London: Pimlico.

Kellmer Pringle, M. (1975), *The Needs of Children,* London: Hutchinson.

Kreiger, R., Maluccio, A.N. and Pine, B.A. (1991), *Teaching Re-Unification: A Sourcebook,* Centre for the Study of Child Welfare, University of Connecticut.

++++

Lambert, R. and Millham, S. (1968), *The Hothouse Society*, London: Wiedenfeld and Nicolson.

Lodge, D. (1962), *Ginger, You're Barmy*, London: MacGibbon and Key.

Lambert, R., Bullock, R. and Millham, S. (1975), *The Chance of a Lifetime? A Study of Boarding Education,* London: Wiedenfeld and Nicolson.

Little, M. (1990), *Young Men in Prison*, Aldershot: Dartmouth.

Lofland, J. and Lofland, L.M. (1970), *Analyzing Social Settings: A Guide to Qualitative Observation and Analysis*, Belmont, Calif.: Wadsworth.

London Borough of Brent (1985), *A Child in Trust, The Report of the Panel of Inquiry into the Circumstances Surrounding the Death of Jasmine Beckford*, London: Kingswood Press.

++++

MacIntyre, A. (1981), *After Virtue*, London: Duckworth.

Maluccio, A.N. and Sinanoglu, P.A. (Eds.) (1981), *The Challenge of Partnership: Working with Parents of Children in Foster Care*, New York: Child Welfare League of America.

Maluccio, A.N., Fein, E. and Olmstead, K.A. (1986), *Permanency Planning for Children: Concepts and Methods*, London: Routledge, Chapman and Hall.

Millham, S., Bullock, R., Hosie, K. and Little, M. (1986), *Lost in Care*, Aldershot: Gower.

Millham, S., Bullock, R., Hosie, K. and Little, M. (1989), *Access Disputes in Child-Care*, Aldershot: Gower

Millham, S., Bullock, R., Hosie, K. and Little, M. (1989), *The Experiences and Careers of Young People Leaving the YTC's*, Dartington Social Research Unit.

Millham, S., Bullock, R. and Hosie, K. (1978), *Locking Up Children*, Farnborough: Saxon House.

Ministry of Health (1959), *The Welfare of Children in Hospital (The Platt Report)*, London: HMSO.

Morris, P. (1965), *Prisoners and their Families,* London: Allen and Unwin.

++++

Packman, J., Randall, J. and Jacques, N. (1986), *Who Needs Care?* Oxford: Blackwell.

Page, R. (1977), *Who Cares?* London: National Children's Bureau.

Parker, R.A. (1966), *Decisions in Child Care*, London: Allen and Unwin.

Parker, R.A. (1990), *Away from Home: A History of Child Care*, Barkingside: Barnardo's.

Piaget, J. (1954), *The Construction of Reality in the Child*, New York: Basic Books.

Pickup, M. (1987), *A Critical Analysis of a Research Study by A.M.F. Fleeman (1984)*, M.Ed Thesis, University of Exeter.

Pill, R. (1979), 'Status and career: a sociological approach to the study of child patients' in Hall, D. and Stacey, M., *Beyond Separation, q.v.*

Pine, B., Warsh, A. and Maluccio, A., (eds.) (1992), *Together Again: Family Re-unification in Foster Care,* Washington DC: Child Welfare League of America.

++++

Quinton, D. and Rutter, M. (1988), *Parenting Breakdown*, Aldershot: Avebury.

++++

Rapoport, R., Rapoport, R. and Skelitz, Z. (1977), *Fathers, Mothers and Others*, London: Routledge and Kegan Paul.

Robbins, D. (1990), *Child Care Policy: Putting it in Writing*, London: HMSO.

Robertson, J. (1970), *Young Children in Hospital*, London: Tavistock.

Rowe, J. (1976), *Adoption and Fostering in the 70's*, London: ABAA.

Rowe, J., Hundleby, M. and Garnett, L. (1989), *Child Care Now*, London: BAAF.

Rutter, M. (1972), *Maternal Deprivation Reassessed*, Harmondsworth: Penguin.

Rutter, M. (1975), *Helping Troubled Children*, Harmondsworth: Penguin.

++++

Shaw, R. (1987), *Children of Imprisoned Fathers*, London: Hodder and Stoughton.

Simard, M., Vachon, J. and Moisan, M. (1991), *La Réinsertion Familiale de L'Enfant Placé: Facteurs de Succes et d'Échec*, University of Laval, Centre de Recherche sur les Services Communautaires.

Smeaton, G. (1869), *Memoir of Alexander Thompson*, London: Edmonton and Douglas (as quoted in Ward (1990), qv.).

Sneath, P.H.A. and Langham, C.D. (1989), 'Outlier: a basic program for detecting outlying members of multi-variate clusters based on presence-absence data', *Computers and Geosciences*, 15, 6, pp 939-964.

Stein, M. and Carey, K. (1986), *Leaving Care*, Oxford: Blackwell.

++++

Thoburn, J. (1980), *Captive Clients*, London: Routledge and Kegan Paul.

Titmuss, R. (1976), *History of the Second World War*, London: HMSO.

Triseliotis, J. and Russell, J. (1984), *Hard to Place*, London: Heinemann.

Tunstall, J. (1962), *The Fishermen*, London: Routledge and Kegan Paul.

++++

Upton, G., Bundy, C. and Speed, B. (1986), 'Parental and family involvement in residential schools for the maladjusted', *Maladjustment and Therapeutic Education*, IV, pp. 3-11.

++++

Vernon, J. and Fruin, D. (1986), *In Care: A Study of Social Work Decision Making*, London: National Children's Bureau.

++++

Ward, H. (1990), *The Charitable Relationship: Parents, Children and the Waifs and Strays Society*, Ph.D. Thesis, Department of Social Policy and Social Planning, University of Bristol.

Wedge P. and Mantle, G. (1991), *Sibling Groups and Social Work*, Aldershot: Avebury.

Wendelken, C. (1983), *Children In and Out of Care*, London: Heinemann.

West, D. and Farrington, D.P. (1977), *The Delinquent Way of Life*, London: Heinemann.

Whitaker D., Cook J., Dunne C. and Lunn-Rockliffe S. (1986), *The Experience of Residential Care from the Perspectives of Children, Parents and Caregivers*. University of York, Report to the RSRC.

Whyte, W.F. (1982), 'Interviewing in field research' in Burgess, R.G. (Ed.), *Field Research: A Sourcebook and Field Manual*, London: Allen and Unwin.

Willis, P. (1977), *Learning to Labour*, Farnborough: Saxon House.

Winnicott, D.W. (1984), *Deprivation and Delinquency*, London: Tavistock.

Woods, P. (1986), *Inside Schools: Ethnography in Education Research*, London: Routledge and Kegan Paul.

Woodward, J. (1978), *Has Your Child Been in Hospital?*, London: NAWCH.

++++

Young, M. and Willmott, P. (1973), *The Symmetrical Family*, London: Routledge, Kegan Paul.

Appendix A: The statistical analysis used to predict children's return outcomes

In Chapters Six, Seven and Eight, we described the findings of an extensive study of 875 children in care. Part of the analysis led us to produce sets of criteria which predict the likelihood of a child returning within certain time periods and, if the reunion does take place, the chances of success of the restoration. How did we arrive at the final set of indicators?

We used a rigorous statistical procedure designed to select a small group of indicators from the many which correlate with the various outcomes under scrutiny. Thus, for example, while there were over 50 dependent variables significantly associated with a child's return within six months of entry to care, we were able to identify three of those which, in combination, best predicted this particular outcome.

The procedure has five steps. Firstly, by using a range of statistical tests, we selected the 15 most statistically and consequently significant variables for consideration. Secondly, we constructed a correlation matrix using Goodman and Kruskal's *gamma* to measure the association between the dependent variables. Thirdly, we checked the data for *outliers*, individual cases which defy predictions but whose idiosyncrasy is explicable in terms of particular events or situations and which, therefore, significantly affect the final statistical model. Here we benefited from an approach applied in the field of bacteriology by Sneath and Langham (1989).

As a fourth step, we used a special type of multi-variate analysis, a log-linear approach known as 'logit', to select two, three or, at most, four factors which, in combination, best predict the outcome under study. Using calculations based upon results of the logit procedure, we were then able to estimate the odds of a child returning within certain time periods or going home successfully, given specified conditions.

Finally, having established the best set of factors, we repeated the logit procedure but excluding the *outlier* cases. This gave a better indication of the true predictive power of the statistical model. We have discussed the strengths and weaknesses of this approach at length in Chapter Five. We feel that, given the data set used in the exercise, the approach described is the best available for selecting predictive criteria.

We undertook this procedure five times, once for each of the outcomes being predicted. The full analysis is described elsewhere (Bullock, Little and Millham, 1991) but here we summarise the findings, giving basic details of the levels of statistical association and the variables discarded on the way to our final sets. Let us look first at factors associated with early returns, that is within six months of entry to care.

Predicting who goes home

i) Return within six months after entry to care

As we saw in Chapter Six, we explored several dimensions of the early reunion of children absent in care, including their family situation, reasons for the child's entry to care, different types of social work intervention and the care experience itself. The 15 variables selected for inclusion in the correlation matrix are laid out in the following table.

Table A1: The relationship between variables associated with return home to relatives within six months of separation

	A	B	C	D	E	F	G	H	I	J	K	L	M	N
R.	-3	+4	+5	+3	+6	+5	+6	+5	+3	+3	+4	+3	+3	+6
A		+2	+1	+0	+4	+0	+2	+0	+4	+5	+0	+2	+0	+2
B			-1	+0	+0	-1	-2	+2	+2	-0	-2	-0	+2	+6
C				+9	+7	+5	-2	+4	+0	+1	+9	+4	-0	-0
D					+4	+3	-1	+1	+1	+2	+8	+4	+1	+1
E						+8	-6	+5	+3	+3	+4	+4	+3	+0
F							-6	+6	+2	+2	+3	+4	+4	+0
G								-8	-2	-1	-0	-0	-3	-1
H									-1	-2	+1	-0	+3	-3
I										+4	+0	+1	+1	+4
J											-0	+4	+3	+8
K												+5	-0	-0
L													+1	+1
M														+1

Key letters represent variables: R = return 0-6 months; A = age of child; B = child's legal status; C = level of contact with mother; D = who provides child's emotional support; E = child's feelings for mother; F = mother's feelings for child; G = does quality of relationship between child and parent affect access decisions; H = social workers' attitude to links between child and parents; I = type of placement first experienced by child; J = child admitted to care with siblings; K = primary female carer is child's natural mother; L = household on Supplementary Benefit; M = reason social worker chooses first placement; N = child has been convicted. Numbers represent power of relationship, i.e. +6 = *gamma* g+0.600001 to +0.699999 and -0 = -0.000001 to -0.099999.

From this analysis, we were able to exclude certain variables which, although highly correlated with the early return of children in care to relatives, had the same explanatory power as other criteria. For example, variable G, which deals with access decisions and the quality of family relationships, is highly associated with Variable H which is concerned with social workers' overall attitude to links between the child and his or her parents. There would be little benefit in including both variables in any statistical model.

Further log-linear analysis allowed us to narrow down the best indicators of an early return to three variables. These are: (1) the level of contact between the child and his or her mother during the period of separation in care; (2) the attitude of the social worker to links between the family and absent child and; (3) the legal status of the child. We were able to explore the explanatory power of these three variables further using 391 cases on which there was clear-cut evidence of the child's situation prior to restoration. Three-fifths (59%) or 230 of the 391 children returned within six months of entry to care, while 161 remained apart from relatives.

Of the 391 children studied, none who enjoyed irregular contact with mother *and* had family links discouraged by the social worker *and* were compulsorily committed to care returned to relatives within six months of entry. However, 14 children who had two of these adverse features were reunited with kin and another four were identified as *outliers* described above.

We then undertook the log-linear analysis summarised in the following table. This shows that a child who enjoys regular contact with parents during separation in care, has these links encouraged by the social worker and is received into care rather than being removed from home using compulsion has a much higher chance of returning home within six months than a child for whom the opposite conditions apply. The expected odds given this model of three variables is 3.5 to 1. By excluding the 14 *outliers*, the power of the predictive model rises to over 4 to 1.

Table A2: Log-linear multi-analysis of variables associated with early return

391 cases: 230 returned versus 161 who did not return.

	Co-efficient	Co-eff.*2	Antilog
Intercept	0.265	0.530	1.699
Regular contact with parents	-0.250	-0.500	0.607
Social worker encourages links	-0.328	-0.656	0.519
Child received voluntarily	-0.314	-0.628	0.537
Expected odds given this model			3.362 to 1
Likelihood ration chi square 6.86586 df=4 p=0.143 Pearson chi square 5.9925 df=4 p=0.200			

ii) Return between seven and 24 months

We have seen that a high proportion of children return to relatives soon after entering care. What of those who fail to get back home quickly? As we can see from the following table, a smaller number of variables were found to correlate with return during the period seven to 24 months after entry to care. Moreover, these variables have more to do with the child's situation and family characteristics than was the case with early leavers who are more influenced by aspects of social work intervention.

Once again, there is a high correlation between those factors associated with reunion and, as before, the most powerful single indicators are not necessarily the most useful in combination with others. The correlation matrix and preliminary log-linear analysis suggested three variables which best predicted return to relatives seven to 24 months after the child initially came into care. These were: (i) the absence of any evidence of abuse and neglect, (ii) not being placed in care with siblings, (iii) parents' participation in the care process.

We looked at 169 of the 189 children who might have returned between seven and 24 months after entry to care. We excluded 20 cases where there was some ambiguity relevant to a variable, for example, with regard to whether parents felt they were fully participating in the local authority's care of their child. We then compared the 74 children who returned during this period with the 94 who did not.

Table A3: The relationship between variables associated with return home to relatives seven to 24 months after separation

	A	B	C	D	E	F	G	H
R.	+2	-3	+3	+4	+4	+2	+4	-4
	A	+1	+0	+6	+5	+2	+6	-1
		B	-0	-2	-1	+2	-2	+9
			C	+5	+3	-1	+0	-1
				D	+9	-0	+5	-2
					E	+0	+5	-2
						F	+5	-0
							G	-1

Key letters represent variables: R = return 7-24 months; A = age of child; B = child's legal status; C = child previously in care; D = abuse or neglect features; E = parental care has broken down; F = social worker encourages access; G = Child placed with siblings; H = parents participate in social work decisions. Numbers represent power of relationship, i.e. +6 = *gamma* g+0.600001 to +0.699999 and -0 = -0.000001 to -0.099999.

The log-linear analysis suggested that those children who were not abused or neglected prior to coming into care, *and* who were not placed with siblings, *and* had parents who fully participated in the care process, had a much greater chance of reunion than others who displayed opposite characteristics. Indeed, only three children from two families defied all three predictors and returned to relatives during the seven to 24 month period. Two of these cases, Melanie and Michelle, were described in some detail in Chapters Eight and Sixteen.

The following table summarises the log-linear logit analysis of the combined effect of the three selected variables; 1) no abuse or neglect; 2) child not placed with siblings; 3) parents participate in the care process. A child exhibiting all three of these features is five times more likely to return to relatives between seven and 24 months after entry to care as a child displaying the opposite characteristics. Excluding the three outlying cases made only a marginal difference to the power of this prediction; leaving out increases the odds of return given the three criteria to 5.5 to 1. The relative size of the anti-log of the intercept and the likelihood ratio chi-square indicate that the combined effect of these three variables is more important than their individual value, although the absence of abuse and neglect certainly makes a powerful contribution to a positive outcome.

Table A4: Log-linear multi-variate analysis of variables associated with return between seven and 24 months after separation

169 cases: 75 returned versus 94 who did not return.

	Co-efficient	Co-eff*2	Antilog
Intercept	0.2776	0.5552	1.7423
No abuse or neglect	0.2491	0.4982	1.6458
Siblings separated	0.1875	0.3750	1.4550
Parents participate	-0.2235	-0.4470	0.6395
Expected odds given this model:			5.482 to 1
Likelihood ratio chi-square 0.32352 df=4 p=0.099 Pearson chi-square 0.32755 df=4 p=0.988			

iii) Return between 25 and 60 months

Let us now turn to children reunited with relatives two to five years after they first came into care. By this late stage in the children's care careers, an already heterogeneous group of children has become very varied indeed. As such, there are few reliable indicators of return. Nonetheless, we can see from the following table that five variables were considered for the log-linear analysis and the return of those children long in care is more influenced by the family situation with aspects of social work intervention making only a small contribution. This pattern of reduced social services' influence in the lives of the older child is equally pronounced in our re-examination of the careers of very difficult adolescents

Table A5: The relationship between variables associated with return home to relatives between 25 and 60 months after separation

	A	B	C	D	E
R.	-4	+3	-5	-4	-4
	A	-3	+1	+0	-1
		B	-0	+1	+4
			C	+9	+1
				D	+4

Key letters represent variables: R = return 25-60 months; A = gender; B = breakdown in parental care; C = natural mother is main provider of emotional support; D = primary female in child's life is natural mother; E = household on supplementary benefit. Numbers represent power of relationship, i.e. +6 = *gamma* g+0.600001 to +0.699999 and -0 = -0.000001 to -0.099999.

The multi-variate analysis suggested that three variables in combination made the best predictors of return during the two to five year period. These were; whether the child's natural mother was the main provider of emotional support; the child's gender and thirdly, whether the household was dependent upon supplementary benefit. Boys belonging to poor families which included the natural mother had a much greater chance of return than children displaying not all of these characteristics. Indeed, only two children with the reverse of these features went home in the last three years of our scrutiny.

Table A6: Log-linear multi-variate analysis of variables associated with return between 25 and 60 months after separation

113 cases: 50 returned versus 63 who did not return

	Co-efficient	Co-eff.*2	Antilog
Intercept	0.5256	1.0512	2.8611
Mother is main provider of emotional support	-0.2773	-0.5546	0.5743
Child is a boy	-0.2296	-0.4592	0.6317
Household on supplementary benefit	-0.2465	-0.4930	0.6108
Expected odds given this model			4.677to 1
Likelihood ration chi square 11.125 df=4 p=0.025 Pearson chi square 8.896 df=4 p=0.064			

Predicting the success of children's returns

So much for our attempts to forecast who goes home within specified time periods. How successful are children once back with the family? It will be recalled from Chapter Eight that we undertook the analysis of this outcome for two separate groups, firstly, *care and protection* children, who were usually younger, and, secondly, those who were *beyond control*, a group comprising mostly adolescents. Let us look at the variables associated with these return outcomes beginning first with the *care and protection* group of children, that is those entering care for neglect, abuse or other damaging family experiences.

i) Care and protection children

In order to assess the outcomes for these younger vulnerable children, we looked at whether, in the eyes of independent experts, there had been a positive outcome for the child. As we can see from the following table, nine variables were found to be highly correlated with a positive outcome and few of these dependent variables were associated with each other. Moreover, one variable, whether or not there had been evidence of highly competent social work, is clearly more powerful than the others.

Table A7: The relationship between variables associated with a positive outcome for protected children placed at home on trial

	A	B	C	D	E	F	G	H	I
R.	+5	+3	+4	+4	+4	+5	-4	-4	+7
	A	+1	+5	+3	-0	+2	-0	-4	+3
		B	+3	+1	+2	+2	-1	+1	-0
			C	+3	+1	+0	-0	+0	+5
				D	+2	+1	+2	-2	+2
					E	+1	-0	+0	+4
						F	+0	-4	+8
							G	+1	+2
								H	+0

Key letters represent variables: R = positive or other outcome; A = child previously returned home; B = other concerns at time of care order; C = only one substitute placement during separation; D = foster placement preceded return; E = child returns to same family members; F = child's progress regularly reviewed; G = no concern expressed by other agencies; H = discharge of care order considered; I = evidence of highly competent social work.

Numbers represent power of relationship, i.e. +6 = *gamma* g+0.600001 to +0.699999 and -0 = -0.000001 to -0.099999.

Thus, as we can see from the following table, which details the log-linear analysis, one indicator overwhelms the statistical model. This result leads us to two conclusions. Firstly, all three of the variables described in Table A8 are useful in predicting a positive outcome. Secondly, however, for the vulnerable abused or neglected child, special social work efforts can make considerable differences to the outcomes of returning children. Indeed, good social work can overcome all of the negative features of a case which would otherwise suggest a poor prognosis and a probable breakdown of the home placement.

Table A8: Log-linear multi-variate analysis of variables associated with a positive outcome for the care and protection children.

147 cases: 65 with a positive outcome versus 82 with other outcomes

	Co-efficient	Co-eff*2	Antilog
Intercept	-0.2142	-0.4284	0.6516
Evidence of highly competent social work	0.5896	1.1792	3.2518
Child never previously returned	0.3641	0.6922	1.9981
Social worker considers discharge of care order	-0.2794	-0.5588	0.5719
Expected odds given this model:			6.473to 1
Likelihood ratio chi-square 22.716 df=4 p=0.0006 Pearson chi-square 24.18425 df=4 p=0.0008			

There were 18 *outliers* in this exercise, that is children who because of unique reasons, either met all of the criteria and experienced problems at home or those that failed to meet any of the positive factors associated with successful outcome and, nevertheless, did well on reunion. If we repeat the above analysis without these *outliers* the power of the prediction rises to 7 to 1.

Children beyond control

Finally, let us look at the relationship between those variables associated with a positive outcome for the children beyond the control of their parents or other relatives returning home. The following table shows that, once again, several factors are highly correlated with the independent variable but that there is little correlation between the carriers.

However, three variables do combine to produce a model helpful in the prediction of a positive outcome for the difficult to control children who are returned home on trial. All three can only be gauged once the child has been reunited with relatives and they reflect the relative harmony in the family home after the reunion. If social workers are welcomed into the home, are able to consider a discharge of the care order and if the child is not an offender, then the prognosis for the case will be much improved. We can also report that there were no outlier cases which defied our prediction.

Table A9: The relationship between variables associated with a positive outcome for disaffected children placed home on trial

	A	B	C	D	E
R.	+5	+7	+5	+5	+4
	A	+1	+5	+2	+3
		B	+2	+1	+1
			C	+0	+1
				D	+1

Key letters represent variables: R = positive or other outcome; A = child previously returned home; B = difficulties in social workers' access to the family; C = discharge of care order considered; D = child offends; E = child's progress regularly reviewed. Numbers represent power of relationship, i.e. +6 = gamma g+0.600001 to +0.699999 and -0 = -0.000001 to -0.099999.

Table A10: Log-linear multi-variate analysis of variables associated with a positive outcome for disaffected children placed home on trial

138 cases: 58 with a positive outcome versus 80 with other outcomes

	Co-efficient	Co-eff*2	Antilog
Intercept	0.4785	0.9570	2.6039
Social worker experiences no difficulty in gaining access to family	-0.4827	-0.9654	0.3808
Discharge of care order considered	0.3126	0.6242	1.8668
Child does not offend	-0.3268	-0.6536	0.5201
Expected odds given this model:			5.3716 to 1
Likelihood ratio chi-square 1.71383 df=4 p=0.788 Pearson chi-square 1.34994 df=4 p=0.853			

Conclusion

This concludes our summary of the analysis used to reduce the large number of variables statistically associated with a particular outcome to the smaller groups of three or four variables which, in combination, best predict return within different time periods and its success. The method used is, we feel, the best available, given the data-set under scrutiny.

Appendix B: Making assessments of the quality of relationships between the members of the families of children in care

In the extensive study, we found that the quality of family relationships is important in understanding return outcomes. Like social workers, when we work intensively with families we can get a 'feel' for the quality of relationships between members, but on what are such assessments based?

Initially, we would stress that any assessment is relative to the particular experience of the families of children looked after by social services. They are often deprived and, in such contexts, there is little to be gained from making assessments used to gauge the situation of middle-class families. When visiting the families of children in care, who tend by nature to be more reticent, there are few obvious positive attributes which indicate a high quality of relationships and there is a tendency to note the absence of negative features, for example, relatively little conflict between siblings.

But even in middle-class contexts, there is a danger of judging children's positive experiences, for example 'doing well at violin class', as indicative of a happy family life. A clever use of verbal skills can be an effective strategy to conceal troubled family relationships. It is quite possible to be very unhappy in a conflict-torn or rejecting home and still be described by a subject teacher as 'doing well'.

Similarly, in deprived families, all may not be what it seems. There may be a united capacity to offer their children 'good enough parenting', in terms of meeting needs for warm and caring, affectionate support. It is this 'quality' of relationships we are seeking to assess. This is made more difficult since often, in consequence of past experience either in their own families or with other 'authority figures', family members are likely to be reticent, mistrustful and defensive.

There are other difficulties to overcome. There is always a danger of misinterpreting the signs given by family members. A dominant relationship in which a parent overwhelms a child or one sibling eclipses another is not necessarily a deep relationship. There is a need to look beyond superficial indicators and to accept that some aspects of the relationship between family members may be ritualistic, for instance visiting absent children to keep up appearances.

There are many dimensions to the assessment. Initially, we have to take into account the age of the child. The interaction appropriate to a mother and her four year old may be totally inappropriate when the child is older. The position of children in families is also important; children in the middle of a large group may get less attention than a new baby or the first born. We have also to ask, which relationship are we assessing? Different measures are required for scrutiny of mother-offspring dynamics than for inter-sibling relationships. The role of wider family members, such as grand-parents, aunts and uncles, also needs to be kept in mind as well as their impact, if any, on family relationships, both overt and covert.

We have found it useful to consider the quality of family relationships from a range of perspectives. Obviously important is the societal view, such as that applied by social workers when they consider a child's restoration. There are, however, sub-cultural norms. Does the local community accept or even value the way family members interact with each other? More important still are the perceptions of family members and of the child him or herself. Often, socially unacceptable practices are viewed as acceptable or even normal within a particular family group. Parker and colleagues (1991) have stressed that situations such as poor health or neglect are widely accepted as being negative features, while positive criteria for children's progress are often culturally specific, as, for example, with regard to obedience, success at school or observance of religious rules and practices.

But what aspects of the family relationship are we assessing? In our experience from several studies of children in care, we have found three dimensions to be important. Firstly, there is a spiritual, expressive component to family relationships. We have consistently stressed the importance of caring relationships and of asking the question 'Is there a sense of belonging between parents and children? Are they partisan? Do they love each other?'.

Secondly, as in any relationship, there is a functional dimension to family dynamics. Does the family meet the needs of the child, his or her care and protection or emotional, educational and health requirements? Just as important, does the child meet the needs of the family, for instance by enhancing parental identity or simple self-interest such as financial well-being?

Finally, we have to address the structural and material requirements of a family. Is it a viable unit? There may be a high quality of relationships between members but this does not mean that parents and children can live together. Particularly important is the family's ability to provide accommodation, especially a bed for the child, to have a membership which is compatible with the child's needs and wishes and to offer a reasonably stable environment for the child's upbringing.

From this basis, we can begin to make judgements about the quality of relationships between the family members of children in care. However, in many cases, this assessment will have to be made during the child's absence from home and any views about the way in which, for example, mother and child interacted when they were living together will be clouded by the problems which led to the separation.

How do we measure the quality of relationships between a family and an absent member? Morris's (1965) work on prisoners' families, Shaw's (1987) work on prisoners' wives, West and Farrington's (1977) research on the family life of delinquents, Quinton and Rutter's (1981) studies of adolescents' family lives, Parker and colleagues' (1991) work on child care outcomes and our previous work on the families of children looked after by social services have all been useful in seeking an answer to this question. Initially, we can begin by looking at *contact*, such as by asking how often do family members see each other?

Parental contact, however, can be misleading. Frequent visiting may reflect loyalty rather than love or be a collusion against authority. Nonetheless, looking at contact in its broadest sense, that is to include visits, telephone calls, letters and the exchange and cherishing of photographs can be helpful, especially if observations include the range of perspectives described above.

Assessing how dependent children are upon their families and *vice-versa* is also helpful. We find the reciprocity of relationships between relatives and absent child to be another important dimension to this problem. This means looking at the quality and continuity of communications between family members, the ability of the parent to provide emotional security for the child, the ability of parent and child to help solve each other's problems, the consistency of support provided and the stability of relationships in the face of adverse circumstances.

In this discussion, we have already described many of the questions we ask when assessing the quality of relationships between the members of the families of children in care. We have tried to capture the various dimensions of the problem in the following set of questions. As in the other parts of this study, we are not attempting to provide a definitive scale as this would be unduly optimistic given the complexity of situations under scrutiny. Rather, we are seeking to provide an instrument which, in combination with other information, helps social workers make effective decisions on the return of children from care. The aim of the exercise is to assess whether the cumulative relationships within the home are good. Thus, the general picture may be encouraging even when relationships between individual members are rocky and the answers to some of the following questions are negative.

A) Spiritual/Expressive

1. Does the social worker perceive a sense of belonging between family members? (n.b. exchange and cherishing of photographs, remarks defensive of each other)

2. Does the child share one-to-one tasks with other family members? (eg. shopping, sporting/leisure activity)

3. Do the family see themselves as one unit? (ie. is there a family identity?) Are there any emotional outlets for tensions within the family?

4. Does the child want to go home? Is the child wanted by sufficient family members to offset those who are ambivalent about the return? When asked, 'where would you most like to live?', does the child answer 'at home'? When you ask the child to list his/her favourite people, are family members mentioned?

B) Functional

1. From the social worker's perspective, does the family meet the child's needs? (n.b. emotional, educational, physical, health)

2. Will the neighbourhood in which the family live relieve or exacerbate family stresses? (n.b. are there strategies for strengthening local networks for this family?)

3. Does the family perceive the child to have special needs? Is the family strong enough to overcome the anxieties of return? (n.b. are

they prepared for this?) Is there anybody, including wider family members, who will spend time with the child and will focus on his/her specific needs? (n.b. importance of siblings)

4. Is the child able to get his/her view across about what s/he wants?

C) **Structural**

1. Is there a mutually accepted dependency between family members? Does the child have a home, a bed, toys and belongings at home? Is the parents' health of sufficient quality to sustain meaningful relationships over time?

2. Is the family structure and identity acceptable to the local community? (n.b. Is there anything we can do to improve neighbours' views of this family?)

3. Do family members have strategies for offsetting structural weaknesses within the family (eg. overcrowding, poverty)? Are tensions within the family acknowledged by members (eg. step-parents and children)?

4. How does the child feel about structural weaknesses within the family? (n.b. problems of moving from substitute care placement which is relatively well off)

Index